Breastfeeding in Combat Boots

A Survival Guide to Breastfeeding Successfully While Serving in the Military

By Robyn Roche-Paull, BSN, RN, BS, IBCLC, LLLL

Breastfeeding in Combat Boots
A Survival Guide to Breastfeeding Successfully While Serving in the Military

Robyn Roche-Paull, BSN, RN, BS, IBCLC, LLLL

© Copyright 2010 Robyn Roche-Paull, BSN, RN, BS, IBCLC, LLLL
Illustrations by Christian Bressler

Hale Publishing, L.P.
1712 N. Forest St.
Amarillo, TX 79106-7017
806-376-9900
800-378-1317
www.iBreastfeeding.com

Disclaimers:
The appearance of women in uniform in this book does not indicate express or implied endorsement of this book by any branch of military service, the Department of Defense, or the U.S. Federal Government.

The views expressed in this book are solely the author's and do not reflect any official position of any branch of military service, the Department of Defense, or the U.S. Federal Government.

Library of Congress Control Number: 2010929290
ISBN-13: 978-0-9845039-4-0

Printed in Canada.

This book is dedicated to my children:
Morgan, Siobhan, and Tiernan
Who taught me all I know about breastfeeding!

And

To all the women who have served our country while raising children:
My heartfelt appreciation for the sacrifices you make every day,
As a Sailor, a Mother, and an American
THANK YOU

Acknowledgements

This book has been a long time coming and is a true labor of love. This book would not have been possible without the help and support of so many of my clients, colleagues, friends, and family. I owe a huge debt of gratitude to Angela Love-Zaranka, Diana Cassar-Uhl, Karen Gromada, and Liz Flight, who were the first of many lactation professionals to encourage me to write this book because there was no military-specific breastfeeding resource for either mothers or healthcare professionals.

I want to express my appreciation to Dr. Hale and the Hale Publishing team for taking a chance on me, a first-time author. To my acquisitions editor, Kathleen Kendall-Tackett, who saw my vision and understood how much military mothers would need this book; my wonderful editor, Janet Rourke, for bearing with me and taking me by the hand to lead me through the process, all the while making this the best book that it can be; and to Christian Bressler for the fabulous illustrations, many of which required much attention to detail to be sure the military details were correct. Many thanks to Linda Smith for her fabulous foreword (and on such short notice, too) and her encouragement during the writing process. Special thanks also go to: Jarold 'Tom' Johnston for his contribution to the book and his support throughout the writing process; Amy Peterson and Mindy Harmer for generously sharing portions of their work on making bottle-feeding more like breastfeeding; Diane Wiessinger for the use of her handout; and Barbara Wilson-Clay and Kay Hoover for the use of their photographs.

I am grateful to all the women, named here and those who chose to remain anonymous, who graciously allowed me to use their stories and photographs in this book: Abby Keffer, Abigail Archabald, Amanda Ferguson, Amber Harris, Amber Wilson, Anna Gillette, Ashley Grosch, Beth Lane, Carissa Cucci-Bennett, Christine Luna, Christine Williams, Courtney Power, Dara Lowe, Diana Cassar-Uhl, Emily Nolan, Ginger Bohl, Gloria Miles, Heather Mace, Jenny Desaulniers, Julie Hansen, Katherine Seto, Kelly O'Connor, Krista Dent, Kendra Laird, Kristina Transue, Laine Gallup, Laura Bowin, Laura Marko, Leah Bailey, Linda Penning, Judy Federigan, Mabel Balduf, Mariah LeBlanc, Rachel Davis, Renee Mercier, Rose Ryon, Rosemary Hernandez-Oglesby, Sarah Kinzer, Stephanie Vogel, Sunshine Haupt, Tami Viskochil, Valencia Jackson, Xotichil Roberts, and Zahiea Martinez. You have made this book more than a collection of do's and don'ts, but rather a heartwarming and positive book filled with true stories. Thanks, too, to all the anonymous women who've posted questions on my website or the forums, and to the many women who have reached out to me for help over the years. You are my inspiration for this book, and I hope I have done right by you. Thank you for trusting me with your precious babies.

This wouldn't be complete without thanking La Leche League International and the many Leaders over the years who have supported me, both as a breastfeeding mother and later as a Leader. From the very first Leader who helped this first-time military mom latch her baby and then supported me when I went back to work at 6 weeks; to Ann Russell, LLL Leader and IBCLC, who believed in me and encouraged me to become a Leader and then an IBCLC. You are a treasured friend and mentor. And to the many Leaders I have had the pleasure of knowing and working with over the years, thank you for helping to make me the mother I am today.

I am so grateful to my family for putting up with me while I researched, wrote, and edited this book. Special thanks go to my children, Morgan, Siobhan, and Tiernan, who had the extra burden to bear of having their father gone on deployment, while my nose was buried in the computer. You three are the light of my life and I appreciate (more than you can know) the many nights you made dinner, did your chores without asking, and reminded me to eat and sleep! To my dear husband, Steve, who works extraordinarily long hours and yet is always supportive of my work with breastfeeding mothers, even when he is halfway around the world on deployment! You cook delicious meals and put up with me (and that's saying a lot!), and I love you so much for that and many other reasons. Finally, my love and thanks to my parents, Richard and JoAnn, and my brother, Robert. You have been my support team from day one, from telling me that there wasn't anything I couldn't do to lending an ear when I've had a bad day. Your support means more than words can say.

Foreword

Robyn Roche-Paull's book "Breastfeeding in Combat Boots" is far more than a "survival guide"–it is practical, well-referenced, and totally awe-inspiring! Military mothers–from pilots, mechanics, sailors, soldiers, and technicians to healthcare providers–face the most daunting of challenges to motherhood, in general, and breastfeeding, in particular, because of the unique and often "unusual" nature of their workplaces and the legal requirements of military service.

The personal stories of officers and enlisted women in the U.S. armed forces are sobering, stimulating, and fascinating. As a military spouse, I've worked closely with military families for my entire career in lactation support. Robyn's stories of courage, creativity, and determination weave a powerful thread through this realistic, no-nonsense book. Bravo!

Linda J. Smith, BSE, FACCE, IBCLC

Military spouse of a USAF Colonel with 26 years service

Table of Contents

Section Four. In The Field: Dealing With Workplace Issues

Section Five. Off Duty: Your Support Network

A Breastfeeding Mother in Combat Boots

I became pregnant with my son, Morgan, while on active duty in the U.S. Navy. Since he was my first, I had no idea how much life would change for me. I had been a gung-ho, take-charge airframes mechanic on the A-6 Intruder attack jet and had just come off my sea-duty rotation and a Mediterranean deployment on the USS Eisenhower. As an aircraft mechanic, my job entailed dirty, greasy work with long hours that coincided with the flight schedule (which is erratic and unpredictable at best). Little did I know that in a few short months, I would find myself trying to breastfeed, or pump, in an all-male environment that did not support my efforts. At times, it was extraordinarily difficult. But was it worth it? Absolutely!

My story begins when my husband (also on active duty) and I wanted to start a family. We believed that shore duty was the best time to do so. I had an uneventful pregnancy and a typical labor and delivery experience at Naval Medical Center Portsmouth. I had read a lot about breastfeeding while pregnant, but didn't know anyone who was breastfeeding in the area, and my co-workers were all male and of no help whatsoever. I did not know about La Leche League and I wasn't given time-off to attend breastfeeding classes. I also didn't have any family in the area; my mother was 3,000 miles away in California.

I had a very rocky start, with many problems to overcome, including sore and cracked nipples, latch difficulties, and mastitis. Needless to say, reading a book about breastfeeding is far different than actually putting a baby to your breast. It took a full six weeks of perseverance and the help of both a lactation consultant and a La Leche League Leader to resolve the problems my baby and I were dealing with. Maternity leave in the military is only six weeks. So just as I got all the breastfeeding problems resolved and began to enjoy breastfeeding my son, it was time to return to work.

I returned to full-time active-duty status full of mothering hormones and breastfeeding zeal. Unfortunately, my co-workers and supervisors did not share my enthusiasm. As the only female in a male-dominated work place, I found no support for my need to pump and was often the brunt of jokes about breastmilk, pumping, and cows. I had to demand the right to take two 15-minute breaks twice a day to pump, while my co-workers took 10 minute smoke breaks every hour.

It was uncomfortable for me to talk to my male supervisor about my breasts and the need to pump, but I felt that my baby's health was worth my embarrassment. Unfortunately, the only other female in my chain of command, my Chief, had formula-fed her children, did not believe in the benefits of breastfeeding, and was not at all supportive. Oftentimes, my break time to pump was not granted. I would become engorged and leak milk all over my uniform. I faced other constraints, such as long, irregular hours due to watch standing duties (ever try pumping while standing guard shack duty at 0200 and no relief in sight?) and the flight schedule (which changes constantly as the planes are fixed and brought to "up" status or break and made "down" status), training deployments away from home, running the PRT, and a lack of a proper place to pump.

I made breastfeeding work through utter determination, and I was determined not to take "no" for an answer. I found a corner in the women's locker-room with an outlet to pump, as I refused to pump in the restroom. Many times, other women would walk in on me pumping and make faces or derogatory remarks. Only once did I receive a compliment that I was doing something special for my baby. Some days, I was only granted time to pump once or twice for 5-10 minutes, other days I could manage three or four pumping sessions for 15-20 minutes. It all depended on the flight schedule, the workload, and my supervisor.

I was a good and fast producer, and I let-down easily and quickly to the pump. I kept a picture of my son in my locker and massaged my breasts while pumping to stimulate my let-down. I could usually pump six to eight ounces at a sitting, and I always took plenty of extra bottles to fill, just in case I was kept late to repair an airplane or to stand watch. Fortunately for me, my baby "reverse-cycled" his nursing, which meant he nursed a lot when I was home and at night, so I was able to build up a great freezer stash of my frozen milk. I found a wonderful day-care provider close to my home who had breastfed all of her children. She knew to hold my baby when feeding him, and that he would get hungry quicker than his formula-fed counterparts. She knew the ins and outs of preparing my breastmilk and not to feed him right before I was to pick him up.

I especially enjoyed coming home to him after work. Oftentimes, my milk would start letting down as I drove into the driveway at the daycare. My infant son's face would light up, and he would reach for my shirt as if to help me unbutton it faster so that he could nurse when I picked him up from the daycare provider. My biggest support in combining breastfeeding and being on active duty was my husband, who understood the difficulties I faced and cheered me on when I had a rough day. He helped to clean my breast pump parts and made sure I ate well and got enough sleep, and he did a lot of the baby care and household chores, so I could focus on breastfeeding when I was at home.

I breastfed and pumped my breastmilk for a total of 13 months while on active duty. I cherished every drop of my milk that my son received, and I am proud to say he never had an ounce of formula. He went on to nurse well past his second birthday, as did his younger sister and brother. I don't regret for a minute my choice to combine breastfeeding while serving my country in the military, despite the obstacles I faced.

Introduction

Over the years, both as an active-duty sailor breastfeeding her own baby, and later, as an IBCLC helping other active-duty moms to breastfeed their babies, I've heard the same questions and concerns over and over from mothers like yourself, "Can I breastfeed while on active duty?" and "How often do I need to pump during a 12-hour shift?" While other questions are very specific, such as "I work with JP-8 fueling aircraft every day, can I feed my baby my pumped milk?" or "I will be deploying to Iraq for four months. Can I pump and ship my milk home from overseas?"

Although the questions are all very different, what the mothers asking these questions want is the best for their babies. They know that breastfeeding is the "best" way to feed their babies, but they (and you) need answers that are not readily available in the civilian world.

As a former active-duty breastfeeding mom myself, these questions hit me particularly hard. I remembered the difficulties I faced pumping my milk for my son and wondering if it was really worth the extra sacrifice I was making. There were no policies in place at that time, and I was told repeatedly that if the Navy wanted me to have, let alone breastfeed my baby, they would've issued me one (in my seabag).

Fortunately, things *are* changing for the better for breastfeeding mothers in the armed forces. Due to the overwhelming evidence that breastfeeding is healthier for baby and mom, most of the services now have written policies in place supporting breastfeeding and directing commanders to provide a place and time for pumping breastmilk. (Unfortunately, however, operational commitments will ALWAYS trump your time off to pump).

In today's military, women make up nearly 20% of the total active-duty force. While women have served in the military, officially or not, since the Revolutionary War, it has only been relatively recently that women have become truly integrated into the military. Prior to World War II, women were not part of the regular active-duty forces, and up until 1971, any military woman found to be pregnant was automatically discharged from the service (Manning, 2005).

This is not the case today, where the majority of women on active duty are of childbearing age, and many do start families while pursuing a career in the military. Given that most women will at least give breastfeeding a try for the six weeks they are home on maternity leave, there are *literally thousands* of mothers who will be looking for information and support on combining breastfeeding and the military (Schumer & Maloney, 2007). Like your civilian counterparts, military mothers who are breastfeeding need information on the basics of breastfeeding and pumping, such as how the breast makes milk, proper positioning and latch, which breast pump to buy, and how often to pump.

Military mothers also face some additional challenges. How do I get breastfeeding off to a good start in only six short weeks? Can I pump while in the desert for training exercises? Is my pump allowed onboard ship? Do I need to pump and dump if I've been exposed to tear gas? These are just a few of the concerns that military mothers face on a daily basis.

I wrote *Breastfeeding in Combat Boots* to answer those, and many other questions. More importantly, I want to reassure and provide military moms with insight into the rewarding, and yes, wonderful aspects of breastfeeding on active duty, while also giving a realistic look at the challenges that lay ahead. And finally, I want to give military breastfeeding moms the tools they need to succeed. I want to show that, except for some very unusual circumstances, with a little preparation, a "can do" attitude, and some creativity, it is possible to breastfeed on active duty.

Of course, this doesn't mean it is going to be a walk in the park. There are going to be times and situations in your military career when breastfeeding is simply impossible. You may be deployed to a war zone, stationed onboard a ship at sea for six months, or working with hazardous chemicals that are known to cross into breastmilk. There are going to be times when you miss a pumping or two (or three), your breasts hurt, and you don't have enough milk for the next day. Or you have to listen to your co-workers complain about "all the time off you take," when in reality you only got one ounce because ten minutes, twice-a-day, isn't enough time to pump. But with the information, policies, and support that is available in today's military, combined with the very powerful and compact breast pumps on the market, it is far easier, healthier, and cheaper to continue breastfeeding--even part-time--than it used to be.

The bottom line is: you and your breastmilk are *irreplaceable.* There is no one and nothing else like it on earth, period. Being a breastfeeding mother in the military is going to be an adventure: an exhausting, love-filled, sometimes difficult, and yet very rewarding adventure. There will be spilled milk and tears (yours and your baby's), all sorts of challenges, and emotional ups and downs. But it can be done--and this book will help.

It *is* possible to work full time on active duty and still be there to nurture and nurse your baby. What it takes is dedication, organization, and knowledge on your part, along with the support, encouragement, and information offered in these pages. This book assumes that you are committed to breastfeeding while on active duty. If so, you will find that it is a practical guide to help you combine active-duty service in the military with breastfeeding your baby: two very important, very demanding, yet fulfilling jobs! While breastfeeding and employment are included in many mainstream books, none cover the unique circumstances and demands that accompany breastfeeding while on active duty. Hopefully, this book will fill that void.

Who Is This Book For?

Breastfeeding in Combat Boots is written primarily for pregnant and breastfeeding moms serving on active duty in any of the five branches of the U.S. military: Air Force, Army, Marines, Navy, and Coast Guard, as well as the Reserves and the National Guard. However, women in other militaries around the world may find the information (except for the policies) in this book applicable to their situations as well. Women in professions such as firefighting, police, EMT, long-haul trucking, or any other job with unusual hours, time away from home, and heavy physical exertion, or who work in a male-dominated environment may also find this book to be helpful.

What Is In This Book?

As with other breastfeeding how-to books, I want to make the information as accessible as possible. *Breastfeeding in Combat Boots* has been written to be read either straight through from beginning to end, or in sections as the need arises. I've structured this book around the military lifestyle and grouped the chapters into five major sections. Each section is prefaced with a true story written by a current or former active-duty mother who breastfed her child(ren) while serving in the military.

- **Section 1. Indoctrination** is devoted to explaining the importance of breastfeeding for you, your baby, and your command, using the latest research and evidence-based information available.

- **Section 2. Basic Training** gives an overview of the basics of breastfeeding and how to survive those all-important first six weeks.

- **Section 3. Duty Calls** discusses the breastfeeding policies of each branch of the military, pumps and pumping basics, and breastfeeding-friendly childcare tips.

- **Section 4. In the Field** examines the many different challenges that military duty presents for the breastfeeding mother, such as workplace environments, HAZMAT, deployments, PRT/PFT, uniforms, and co-worker issues.

- **Section 5. Off Duty** covers the many types of breastfeeding support that are available on and off-base for the military mother.

Within each section, there are several chapters covering the information concisely and in-depth. You will find boxes with tips and techniques, quotes, and statistics that reinforce the information found in the main portion of the chapter. The back of the book has numerous appendices with references, websites, books, and handouts that I have found helpful for active-duty breastfeeding mothers over the years.

The companion to this book is my website www.BreastfeedinginCombat Boots.com where you will find updated information, documents you can download, message boards to find community and support, and more. You can also find the *Breastfeeding in Combat Boots* Fan Page on Facebook for even more support. Be sure to drop by sometime and check it out. I want to hear your stories and find out from you what has and has not worked for you while breastfeeding in the military, so please visit the website or send me an e-mail. With your help, I can have more answers for future active-duty mothers and their babies.

A Note on Terminology

This book has been written to cover women serving in all branches of the armed forces and, therefore, must cover the many different terms, acronyms, and scenarios that are used throughout the military. Rather than alienate anyone or start a riot between the services, I have decided to call everyone in the military "service member." I have tried to use the most commonly used acronyms in the military, and will write them out with the first use. I have also tried to balance the stories and scenarios I've included between the various branches. If any one branch of the military seems underrepresented, it was not done intentionally. My apologies in advance!

Because this book is written for women in the military, I have used the "she" pronoun when referring to the mother and the "he" pronoun when referring to the baby. This is not meant to slight any girl babies (I have a girl myself), but instead to reduce confusion.

I use the term "partner" throughout the book to include the many different family arrangements that are out there. I know that not everyone has a "typical American family" with mom, dad, baby, and a dog—you may have a husband, close friend, sister, or your mom who provides most of the parenting help and that person is your partner! If you are a single active-duty mom, I salute you! I hope there is someone who can provide you with help, as you have the hardest job on the planet. (And yes, breastfeeding *will* make that job just a wee bit easier in the long run. Trust me!)

The term "care provider" is used throughout the book to talk about the person caring for your baby while you are at work, whether that is your mom or the CDC on base.

Finally, I use the terms "pump" and "pumping" when talking about expressing milk from your breasts. I know of a few women who can (and do) hand express with ease and exclusively provide milk for their babies while on active-duty. But the majority of women, especially in the military, will be using a pump and pumping their milk, so it just makes sense to use those terms. Keep in mind, though, hand expression is a wonderful tool to know when you are stuck on maneuvers overnight in the desert with no electricity!

Who Am I to Write this Book?

You may be wondering what makes me the expert on breastfeeding in the military. And where do I come up with all the information and recommendations I'm giving? Let me be straight with you from the get-go…I am not a doctor, lawyer, or military commander. All of the medical, legal, and military advice in this book has been reviewed by experts--and by real moms, just like you. Nevertheless, you should still check with your own healthcare professional, JAG, and/or Commanding Officer before trying it out on yourself and your baby. Nothing in this book should be construed as medical, legal, or military advice (OK, disclaimer over!).

I wrote this book as a veteran with experience breastfeeding on active duty and as an IBCLC with a desire and the knowledge to help military mothers be successful at breastfeeding while serving their country. I have over a decade of experience helping military mother's breastfeed their babies, and resources with evidence-based, up-to-date information to back-up my recommendations. Unfortunately, there just isn't that much written about *breastfeeding in the military*. So a lot of the information and recommendations in this book are what has worked for other employed women and has been modified for the military mother. Where there is solid evidence in the literature for what I am suggesting, I will put it in citations. Otherwise, I provide advice based on my own experience and the collective experiences of those active-duty breastfeeding mothers who have gone before you.

There are a number of common things that breastfeeding women struggle with, usually due to a lack of information and support. In writing this book, I have tried to offer you that information and support, so you'll be successful breastfeeding your baby while serving in the military. I want you to think of this book as your SOP (Standard Operating Procedure) manual, covering everything from the basic course on breastfeeding to very specific pumping scenarios. Some of what you read won't pertain to your situation. Use the book to get the information you do need, and then keep it handy for the unexpected problems that may arise. If it isn't in this book, I hope that I've given you enough resources to point you in the right direction to get the help you need.

Not everything in this book is going to work for everyone. Every mother and baby is unique, and every pumping or military experience is different.

What is important is that you take what works for you--and leave the rest. My goal for this book is that when you are finished reading it, you will know all your options and find that breastfeeding in the military is one of them. I want you to get off to a good start with breastfeeding, so you can pump at work and keep your milk supply up, which will allow you to breastfeed when you are at home and enjoy all that breastfeeding has to offer you and your baby.

In summary, is breastfeeding on active duty worth it? Yes, you bet it is! Breastfeeding is one of the most rewarding things you will ever do. You won't regret for a moment the time and energy or the love and commitment those bottles of pumped breastmilk represent. The inconveniences you may endure will be worth it a hundred times over when your baby gazes up at you with adoring eyes as he is snuggled up at your breast. With the number of military mothers I've spoken with over the years, I've never met one who didn't tell me it was the hardest thing they ever did…and who also said that it was the one thing they were most proud of. You can do it too!

The author on active duty with her then 3-month old son, Morgan.

*Photo courtesy Robyn Roche-Paull.
Used with permission.*

SECTION ONE

Indoctrination: Importance of Breastfeeding

Leah's Story

I am a breastfeeding mother, a member of La Leche League, and on active duty in the U.S. Air Force. Before my son, Eliot, was born, I was determined to breastfeed, regardless of my working situation, but I was not sure how exactly I could make it happen. I knew of only a couple of other active-duty mothers who had nursed their babies and pumped at work. They had breastfed their children for up to six months. My goal was similar: I would nurse my son for at least six months, and I hoped I could continue for a year. I purchased a double electric pump and found a place to use it at work. After I gave birth, the Air Force gave me six weeks of maternity leave, and I took two additional weeks on top of that. We needed that time to establish a good nursing relationship because breastfeeding got off to a rough start for us. I was committed to giving Eliot only my milk, but it wasn't as easy as I thought it would be. With my local La Leche League Leader's help, I was able to get past sore and cracked nipples, poor latch-on, and mastitis. By the time I went back to work, Eliot was breastfeeding like a champ!

Going back to work was a heartbreaking and emotional time. It was so tough to leave my son every day, but I had signed a contract, and I was obligated to fulfill it. One regulation in my favor was that after the delivery, the Air Force gives new mothers six months* recovery time and stabilization: so I knew that I could breastfeed and not worry about deployment for that six-month period. Unfortunately, that is all the time we get. So, even though the American Academy of Pediatrics recommends that a mother breastfeed for at least the child's first year, a mother in the military can't be guaranteed that time. Luckily, the Air Force and my immediate supervisors have been very supportive of my breastfeeding. My husband is a stay-at-home dad and is able to bring Eliot to me to nurse during my lunch. I have been provided with a room to breastfeed in, and both Eliot and my husband are always welcome. I have been able to pump on my breaks, and when our schedule permits, I attend La Leche League meetings on post. The meetings are very refreshing, and they encourage me to continue to provide my son with the best nutrition and nurturing possible.

I realize that my situation is somewhat unique, and for that, I am grateful. Breastfeeding has been everything I have hoped for and more. One of my favorite benefits of breastfeeding is that even after a 12-hour day, I can take my son into my arms, put him at the breast, and all that time just melts away. There is no better way to reconnect and stay attached. My son and I are fortunate that we have been able to maintain our nursing relationship for over 16 months now, with no temporary separations or deployments, and I hope that we can continue until he weans naturally.

*The Air Force now offers 12 months deferment.

Chapter 1

Breastfeeding:
The Biological Norm

Congratulations on the birth of your baby and your decision to breastfeed while serving your country on active duty. Breastfeeding is more than just food; it is also a relationship like no other between you and your baby. It is inexpensive, convenient, and comforting; it is love and nourishment in one package. There are so many reasons to choose to breastfeed after your return from maternity leave, from the health benefits for you both and the money you will save every month by not buying formula, to the wonderful intimacy you will share with your baby. However, with the decision to breastfeed your baby while serving in the military, you will also embark on one of the most exciting, demanding, and fulfilling times in your life. Unlike your civilian counterparts, you will have to learn to manage the impact that breastfeeding and military life have on each other. This isn't an easy combination, but it will be well worth it, for yourself and your baby.

Breastfeeding is important for you, your baby, your family, and even your command. The American Academy of Pediatrics (AAP) (Gartner et al., 2005) and the World Health Organization (WHO) (World Health Organization, 2009) both state that babies should be breastfed exclusively for the first six months, and then for at least a year with additional complementary foods, in order to realize the many significant and important outcomes associated with breastmilk and breastfeeding (Gartner et al., 2005). Of course, this may be impractical for some mothers. And it's important to realize that even one breastfeeding per day makes a difference, particularly if it is continued throughout the first year of life. Each mother needs to weigh her options and choices and find what will work best in her home and work situations. Breastfeeding is not a lifestyle choice; it is an important health choice.

You may be more interested in the how-to's of breastfeeding, but learning about the importance of human milk and breastfeeding might be just enough to strengthen your commitment and allow you to keep nursing during those times when you wonder if it is worth the effort. For many active-duty mothers, the answer is "yes," it is worth the effort!

Human Milk for Human Babies

So what makes human milk the first and only choice for human babies? One of the best arguments that your breastmilk is the ideal food for your baby is in the scientific literature that shows that our species-specific milk is adapted and uniquely designed to meet the very specific growth needs of our babies. There are many different mammals in the world, and each one makes milk unique to its own young. Just as a whale makes milk high in fat to help her calf build a layer of blubber to survive the cold seas, and a young calf or foal receives milk high in calcium and protein to build strong bones and muscles to follow mom around the pasture, humans make milk high in nutrients to help their infant's tremendous brain growth in the first three years. Human milk is also quite dilute, requiring that a newborn nurse very frequently. This ensures a plentiful milk supply and also lets you cuddle and hold your baby close, creating an intimate bond every time your baby is nourished at the breast.

Human milk has been perfected over thousands of years to have all the proper ingredients and needed immune properties to promote *normal* growth and development. Infant formula, on the other hand, has only been around and widely used for about the last 80 years or so. Infant formula can never fully replicate human milk, as it is based on cow's milk or soy. In fact, it is a distant fourth option for feeding human babies. According to the *Global Strategy for Infant and Young Child Feeding* (UNICEF, 2003), babies should be fed the following in order from healthiest to least healthy:

- Mother's own fresh milk

- Mother's thawed, previously frozen milk

- Pasteurized breastmilk from a milk bank or donor mother milk

- Artificial baby milk (formula)

Your breastmilk is a unique solution of proteins, sugars (carbohydrates), vitamins and minerals, and fats. Many of these ingredients have more than one function in the body or work together in ways that are not yet completely understood, and there are numerous ingredients in human milk that have yet to be identified. And certain components, such as antibodies, simply cannot be replicated at all. Infant formula manufacturers can produce formula that approximates the levels of proteins, fats, and carbohydrates found in human milk, but the quality is nowhere near the same, and the composition differs greatly. Because human babies are so totally dependent upon breastmilk or formula for proper growth and development, even a minor difference can have a big impact later in life. This is not to say your baby will not grow if you give formula, but your milk is uniquely suited to your baby and is the standard against which all breastmilk substitutes are measured. Your milk provides all the fluids and nutrients that your baby will need for the first six months of life. It is a constant source of important and essential nutrition well into the second year of life. Here then is a primer of the many amazing ingredients in your milk:

- **Enzymes, Immunoglobulins, and White Blood Cells.** Breastmilk is a living fluid; fresh from the breast, it contains over three million living cells per teaspoon. Colostrum, the first milk your baby receives, has about twenty-one million living cells per teaspoon. Breastmilk contains many different substances that boost your baby's immune system, including enzymes, secretory IgA, and white blood cells. From the very first feedings after birth, your milk contains white blood cells (leukocytes and macrophages) that seek out and destroy bacteria, such as *Salmonella, E. coli,* streptococci, and pneumococci. Enzymes, such as lysosome, dissolve the cell walls of pathogens and are found in quantities five thousand times higher than that of formula. Immunoglobulins (there are five types) are found in human milk, and the most abundant type is secretory IgA. It coats the stomach and intestines and prevents infections and allergens from crossing into the blood stream. Infants don't produce IgA on their own until about six to nine months, so your breastmilk is the only source of this protection. IgA also improves the effectiveness of the antibodies your body produces, which is then passed on to your baby through your milk. For the military mother, this is very important because it means your breasts will make antibodies specific to the pathogens in your environment and your baby's environment (such as at childcare). Within a few days, your baby will be protected by your breastmilk against those same pathogens (Nathavitharana, Catty, & McNeish, 1994).

- **Probiotics, Lactoferrin, Interferon, and Fatty Acids.** Human milk is full of naturally occurring probiotics, such as *Lactobacillus bifidus,* a good bacteria that crowds out the nasty pathogens that cause gastrointestinal illness (it is also why breastfed babies' stools don't stink). Lactoferrin limits the growth of bacteria (such as *Staphylococcus aureus*) by binding to the iron they need to live on. There are various antiviral agents in breastmilk, including interferon and fatty acids that work by damaging the cell membranes of viruses, including those for RSV, *Giardia lamblia,* group B strep, and chicken pox. Other immune factors prevent pathogens, such as *Haemophilus influenza* and rotavirus, from attaching and binding to your baby's respiratory and intestinal tracts. All of these components found in breastmilk, but not in formula, allow your baby's immune system to function and mature normally. When given vaccinations, your baby will produce antibodies quicker and in higher amounts than his formula-fed counterparts (Dòrea, 2009).

- **Proteins.** Different animals grow at different rates, and much of this is due to the amount of protein found in each animal's milk. Humans grow the slowest of all the mammal species, and hence human milk has the lowest amount of protein of any mammal; unlike calves who need to grow rapidly and drink milk that is high in protein. Formula that is derived from cow's milk is also high in protein. The main proteins in human and cow milk are casein and whey. Human milk protein is composed of 70% whey and 30% casein, whereas cow milk is composed of 18% whey and 82% casein. While human milk has less protein overall than formula, it is used more efficiently and is digested much easier (and faster) due to the higher whey content. The protein in formula, on the other hand, forms a tough, rubbery curd that requires a lot of energy (and time) to digest and is incompletely digested to boot. The protein in human milk is nearly 100% utilized, virtually none is excreted. A baby fed formula wastes about half the protein in his diet (and hence must drink about twice as much to get enough usable protein). The protein in human milk is the building block for human growth and also helps protect babies from infection. The whey in human milk contains the disease-fighting antibodies and immune properties that babies need to remain healthy. Cystine is another protein found naturally in human milk; it is important for skeletal growth. The amount of cystine in formula is very low compared to the amount in breastmilk.

- **Fats.** The fats in human milk provide 40%-50% of the calories your baby needs for the massive growth that occurs during the first year of life. Fats are also essential for the proper development of your baby's brain and nervous system. Human milk is chock-full of DHA (docosahexaenoic acid) and ARA (arachidonic acid), both of which are long-chain polyunsaturated fatty acids and are essential for normal brain and visual functioning. Infant formula manufacturers have begun to add synthetically created versions of DHA and ARA (derived from soil fungus and algae) to their formulas, but they cannot replicate the unique composition and amounts found naturally in human milk, nor do they know the optimum amounts needed for your baby. Recent studies have shown that DHA and ARA added to infant formula provides no benefit to infants (Simmer, Patole, & Rao, 2008). Cholesterol is present in human milk in much higher amounts than in formula; it is required for your baby's growing nervous system.

- **Carbohydrates.** The main carbohydrate found in human milk is lactose (also known as milk sugar). It is found in far greater quantities in human milk than in formula, which helps to explain why human milk is so much sweeter. Lactose provides energy (in the form of calories), and it improves the absorption of minerals, such as calcium, which are good for your baby's growing bones. Lactose also promotes the growth of "good" bacteria in your baby's gut, creating an acidic environment that keeps out the "bad" bacteria that leads to diarrhea. Infant formula manufacturers are beginning to add "probiotics" to formula to replicate this benefit of human milk. Finally, lactose breaks down to produce galactose, which is necessary for the development of brain tissue. In fact, it has been shown that in mammals, the more lactose in the milk, the bigger the brain.

- **Vitamins and Minerals.** Much like with protein levels, vitamin and mineral levels in milk seem to be related to the growth of the animal, with human milk having lower amounts. Human milk has a quarter as much calcium as that found in cow's milk. Breastfed babies simply do not need a lot of calcium for proper growth, and formula-fed babies are getting too much calcium, leading to larger and heavier skeletons (not necessarily a good thing). Likewise, the iron found in human milk, needed to make red blood cells, is present in low levels, but is 50% "bioavailable" or absorbed and used by your baby's body. Compare that to the iron in formula, where only 4% is utilized and the rest is digested and excreted. Babies receiving their mother's milk receive all the vitamins necessary for proper growth, with the exception of Vitamin D. (The AAP recommends a 400 IU daily supplement for ALL breastfed babies.) And your milk remains fairly stable, even with chilling, freezing, and reheating, unlike formula which degrades over time. There are many other micronutrients that are found in human milk, with many more yet to be discovered, that perform vital functions. Most of these are not found in formula or are added after they are discovered in human milk.

Reasons to Breastfeed: Baby

Even with all of the above information on the many irreplaceable properties found in milk, you may be wondering why you should go to the trouble to breastfeed. What's in it for you, for your baby? Aside from breastmilk being the most complete form of nutrition for infants, there are many other compelling reasons to give your baby your milk. And many of them have to do with the complex relationship that the ingredients listed above have with one another. The many health outcomes noted below differ greatly between those infants (and mothers) who breastfeed and those who don't. After reading this, it will be clear that breastmilk is the "norm" and that formula is by far the inferior choice. Refer back to these reasons when you need some motivation to keep pumping or when well-meaning friends and co-workers question your hard work.

Probably one of the most well-known and important reasons to breastfeed is protection against illnesses and infectious diseases. A recent study stated that:

> Compared with breastfed infants, formula-fed infants face higher risks of infectious morbidity in the first year of life. These differences in health outcomes can be explained, in part, by specific and innate immune factors present in human milk (Stuebe, 2009).

What this means is not breastfeeding for at least four to six months increases the frequency and severity of many illnesses, such as ear infections (formula-fed babies experience twice as many), respiratory infections, pneumonia and bronchitis, spinal meningitis, and urinary tract infections, to name just a few (Ip et al., 2007). And that the increase in illness and infections is due to the lack of immune properties found in formula. Formula-fed babies also have an increased risk of developing allergies, eczema (atopic dermatitis), and possibly asthma as well. This is due to both a lowered immune system and exposure to foreign antigens in the formula (Ip et al., 2007).

Not as well-known, but just as important, are the many chronic or adult-onset diseases that formula does not guard against. While it might seem a long ways off to be thinking about your baby as an adult, many diseases get their start in infancy, and it is never too early to defend your baby against them. Diabetes, inflammatory bowel diseases (including Crohn's and ulcerative colitis), childhood leukemia, high blood pressure, and obesity are just a few of the more common diseases that formula-fed infants are not protected against (Gartner et al., 2005; Horta, Bahl, Martines, & Victora, 2007). The protection that breastfeeding provides against these long-term diseases is dose-dependent; meaning the longer you can provide your milk, the more protection your baby receives.

Formula-fed infants have an increased number and more severe bouts of vomiting and diarrhea than breastfed infants; the protective effect of breastfeeding against gastrointestinal disease is greatest while the baby is exclusively breastfed (Kramer et al., 2008). Formula-fed babies also have more constipation, gas, colic, and spitting up as compared to breastfed babies because formula is harder to digest. For babies born too early, there are many health problems to overcome, but one of the most devastating is the serious and sometimes fatal bowel infection called NEC (necrotizing enterocolitis). Premature infants are especially at risk for contracting NEC; however, preemies fed human milk are much less likely to develop NEC (and if they do, it is much less severe) than those fed formula (Ip et al., 2007).

There are many, many more reasons to breastfeed, and chief among them is the lowered risk of Sudden Infant Death Syndrome. Researchers are not sure whether this effect is due to the breastmilk itself, the reduced illnesses that breastfed infants suffer from, the increased contact of mother and baby due to feeding at the breast, or a combination of factors (Vennemann et al., 2009). Another reason to breastfeed is the link between breastfeeding and intelligence. Breastmilk aids in the proper development of baby's brain and nervous system (due in part to DHA and ARA). Numerous studies (on both full-term and preterm infants) have found that children who were not breastfed as infants achieved significantly lower test scores than children who were breastfed, even after accounting for the parents education and socioeconomic status (Kramer et al., 2008).

Because breastfeeding uses the proper jaw muscles and positions the tongue correctly in the mouth, breastfed infants develop proper jaw alignment and facial structure, which helps with speech development and reduces the need for orthodontic braces later in life. Breastfeeding has been shown to reduce sleep apnea and is also protective against dental cavities (Palmer, 1998). Breastfed babies also receive bilateral visual stimulation because they feed from alternating breasts, as opposed to formula-fed babies who are often fed from the same side at all feedings. This helps with eye-hand coordination and is important for the visual centers in the developing infant brain. Breastfed babies are more inclined to try new foods as they have received breastmilk that is flavored by whatever you eat, rather than the same flat taste of formula at every feeding (Mennella, Jagnow, & Beauchamp, 2001).

Breastfeeding provides security, comfort, physical contact, social interaction, and food for your baby, in one package. The security, physical contact, and social interaction are as important to an infant's growth and development as the immune factors and nutrition in human milk. Your baby has a biological need for both physical closeness and your milk. And your breasts need to be regularly drained and stimulated to produce milk. Breastfeeding makes sure that both of these needs are met, and does so in a wonderful interaction that deepens the bond between you both that will last long after breastmilk ceases to be his only source of nutrition. Babies who breastfeed are, by default, held for their feedings (you can't prop a breast!) and enjoy frequent social interaction. The security and comfort that come from being held and talked to, also help with bonding and brain development. Finally, the physical contact of breastfeeding your baby during vaccinations, heel sticks, and blood draws is a wonderful way to reduce his pain. The act of breastfeeding is a natural pain reliever, much better than Tylenol or a pacifier, and works on teething and everyday bumps and bruises as well.

A final thought, children who are breastfed and see other children or siblings being breastfed, grow up understanding what breasts are for, and are, in turn, empowered to breastfeed their children. This is a wonderful cycle to begin again and is equally important for boys as well as girls.

Reasons to Breastfeed: Mom

Many women begin breastfeeding for their baby's sake, not realizing the many, but no-less-significant reasons that you, the mother, should breastfeed your infant. Of the many physical and emotional reasons to breastfeed, one of the most important is to complete the natural reproductive cycle that your body expects after pregnancy. This ensures that your body does not succumb to the myriad of diseases (short-and long-term) that befall women who short-circuit this process by formula-feeding. There are numerous health risks associated with not breastfeeding or with weaning prematurely. In addition, there are a number of emotional benefits for you when you breastfeed your baby.

One of the most noticeable, and early, side-effects of breastfeeding that most women experience is the abdominal cramping (AKA, afterpains) that occur when you nurse your newborn. This cramping sensation is the result of uterine contractions that are triggered by the hormone oxytocin that is released every time your baby nurses. Oxytocin plays a key role in releasing milk from your breasts (see Chapter 3). However, during the postpartum period, the contractions brought on by oxytocin also help the uterus return to its normal size after birth. These contractions lessen postpartum bleeding and blood loss as well.

Another effect of breastfeeding that some women experience is a delay in the return of your menstrual periods. This is due to the hormone prolactin, also released when your baby nurses, which suppresses ovulation. If you practice *exclusive breastfeeding* (no supplementation with formula, juice, or water), you may be able to delay your menstrual period anywhere from a few months to a year or more. This amenorrhea (lack of menstrual periods) helps to conserve and replenish the iron stores that were lost during pregnancy, childbirth, and postpartum. It can also provide temporary contraception (see LAM, Chapter 5) for mothers who are exclusively breastfeeding. However, the delay in the resumption of menstruation is not as strong for employed mothers, unless you practice unrestricted breastfeeding when at home and can pump often while at work.

Formula feeding has been shown to increase your risk of contracting pre-menopausal breast cancer in numerous studies (Ip et al., 2007). There are many risk factors for breast cancer that are out of your control, such as your age at first menstruation, genetics, family history, and age of menopause. However, one very big factor you can control is the age of your first pregnancy and your lifetime duration of breastfeeding. The shorter that period of time is, the higher your risk of contracting breast cancer. It is believed that this is due to the more numerous and repeated cycles of ovulation that occur in women who do not breastfeed. Women who do not breastfeed or do so for less than three months have an 11% increase in contracting breast cancer, whereas women who breastfeed for a combined total of 24 months see a 25%

reduction in breast cancer (Newcomb et al., 1994). Not breastfeeding your daughter also increases her risk of breast cancer as well.

Not breastfeeding leads to decreased protection against cervical, ovarian, and uterine cancers. Rheumatoid arthritis is increased in mothers who formula-feed, and hip fractures and osteoporosis after menopause are also increased in mothers who do not breastfeed (Ip et al., 2007). Women who use formula also suffer more urinary tract infections (and those are no fun while on a FTX).

What would you say to losing weight, up to two pounds a month in the first six months, by doing nothing more than nursing your baby? The production of breastmilk requires 500-600 calories a day and ramps up your metabolism as well. Most of those calories are burned from your stores of body fat that you put on during pregnancy (all that weight on your hips). Studies have shown that breastfeeding helps you return to your pre-pregnancy weight faster, at around three months postpartum, than women who formula-feed only. This is important for maintaining weight standards and passing the PRT (see Chapter 15), as well getting back into your regular uniforms. In addition, it has been shown that women who do not breastfeed are more likely to develop metabolic syndrome, a cluster of health risks, such as high blood pressure, high triglyceride levels, insulin resistance, and obesity, that can lead to heart disease, stroke, and diabetes (Type 2) (Stuebe, Rich-Edwards, Willett, Manson, & Michels, 2005). These differences in metabolism between mothers who breastfeed and those who do not persist well into later life.

How would you like to have a built-in, natural, and free way to reduce your fatigue, stress, and chances of depression, while boosting your own immune system? Let's face it, women in the military face a lot of stress and fatigue on an everyday basis. It's part of the job description. Now add in the increased stressors of a baby, postpartum fatigue, and managing a household to the mix and you have a recipe for depression and increased illness. Women who formula-feed are shown to have higher levels of fatigue and stress hormones, as well as increased illness rates and postpartum depression (Groer & Davis, 2006). Not so for breastfeeding mothers, who are more rested, better able to cope with stress, and don't suffer from illnesses or depression nearly as much (Dennis & McQueen, 2009). It has been shown that formula-feeding mothers wake more often and get less overall sleep than their breastfeeding counterparts. A lack of sleep has been shown to be a factor in both postpartum depression (PPD) and in lowering the immune system. Breastfeeding mothers are helped in two ways: they get more sleep (which affects mood and the immune system), and they have a hormonal cascade that mitigates the effects of PPD and chemical changes that help bolster the immune system (see more about PPD in Chapter 5).

Let's not overlook what may be considered minor, but no less important, reasons to breastfeed, such as convenience and portability. Breastfeeding is both convenient and portable; you can give your baby immediate satisfaction by breastfeeding whenever and wherever you are. You can go to the store or across the world on a PCS move with ease. No matter where you and your baby are, so is your milk: ready and at the right temperature! There is no need to carry and mix formula or warm bottles, with a screaming, hungry baby. During natural disasters, breastfeeding is, quite literally, life- and sanity-saving. The absence of clean drinking water for mixing formula (and cleaning bottles) can be deadly for an infant, even here in the United States (remember Hurricane Katrina?).

Breastfeeding is comforting and calming to both you and your baby. It requires you to sit down and take some quiet time, something that is very much needed in the day-to-day craziness that is the life of a military mother. Breastfeeding releases the hormones, prolactin and oxytocin, otherwise known as the "mothering hormones," which produce a relaxing and calming sensation. Both you and your baby feel the effects of these hormones and come away from the nursing session physically relaxed and emotionally calm. These same hormones, along with the need to physically hold your baby while nursing, promote feelings of closeness and bonding with your baby. As a military mother who may be gone for long hours each day, this is very important to maintaining your sense of connection with your baby.

Finally, many breastfeeding mothers have an increased sense of self-confidence and pride in themselves and their bodies when they see how their babies grow and thrive on the milk they produce. It is a wonderful feeling to see your baby develop, grow, and reach milestones; knowing it is all due to the milk you are making and providing to your baby!

Reasons to Breastfeed: Family and Partner

While breastfeeding isn't free, it does save you and your family money. Let's face it, most military families are not rich. We serve our country out of a sense of duty. It is certainly not for the paycheck! Because breastfeeding requires about 500 extra calories a day (the equivalent of a peanut butter sandwich), you won't need to add very much to your food budget. In addition, the new WIC guidelines provide breastfeeding mothers with more food than their formula-feeding counterparts. In contrast, formula-feeding costs approximately $1000 - $2300 a year, depending on the brand and type of formula you buy (powdered or ready-to-feed). The Women, Infants, and Children's Food Program (WIC) does not provide the full amount of formula a full-term infant needs to grow properly. So formula-feeding mothers will still have to buy formula, and they do not get a full food package for themselves, either. However, WIC does provide a full food package for breastfeeding mothers that includes: juice, milk, breakfast cereal, fruits and vegetables, canned fish, whole wheat bread, cheese, eggs, beans, and peanut butter. Even with the purchase of a breast pump and bottles for return to work (approximately $200-350) and a consult with an IBCLC for breastfeeding guidance or problems ($150-200), it is still far less than the cost of a year's supply of formula. That is money well spent for a lifetime of health for you and your baby.

Let's not overlook the very real benefit of easier middle-of-the-night feedings for the whole family. When a baby is breastfed and sleeping near you, there is no need to shuffle to the kitchen with a screaming baby (who wakes up everyone) to make bottles, or ask whose turn it is to feed the baby. While breastfed babies do wake more often to eat, usually every two to three hours, even at night, those sharing sleep in a co-sleeper or the parent's bed (see Chapter 4 for more information on Safe Sleep), can be fed quickly and quietly, with a minimum of fuss, ensuring that everyone gets a good night's sleep. Mothers and babies who are breastfeeding and share sleep synchronize their sleep patterns and have more overall restful sleep during the night than formula-feeding mom and baby pairs (McKenna & McDade, 2005).

Sometimes partners of breastfeeding mothers feel left out. However, there are many ways they can be supportive (see Chapter 19). Partners who support the breastfeeding mother can feel proud knowing that they have contributed to the health and well-being of both mother and child. And while it may be surprising to think of your breasts in this way, breastfeeding can be a new way for your partner (and you) to appreciate your body. Your breasts may have previously provided pleasure to you and your partner, and now they are providing nourishment and nurturing to the baby you both created.

★ Sex and Breastfeeding ★

Let's talk about sex while breastfeeding. You may be afraid to ask, so I'll tell you. Breastfeeding (and for that matter, parenting) will impact your sex lives. Both of you need to know that some mothers have an increased libido (thanks to repetitive oxytocin surges). While others have a decreased libido (thanks to prolactin and a decrease in estrogen). Fathers may face problems with the "Madonna Complex" (She's a mother now). But perhaps most important for fathers to understand is that breastfeeding, and all aspects of parenting, are demanding, physical work, with only short bursts of sleep, interrupted by a newborn that demands attention at inconvenient times. Mom will need constant support and help from her lover. The more help she can get from her husband, the more energy she will have for other activities. In other words "You've got to give a little, to get a little." **With thanks to Major Jarold "Tom" Johnston, CNM, IBCLC. Used with permission.**

If you have older children you will find that nursing your new baby gives you one hand free, allowing you to give more time and attention to the older siblings. You can more easily read a book or play Lego's® with the older child, which helps with that oft-dreaded and feared sibling jealousy.

Reasons to Breastfeed: Command

You may be stationed at a command that doesn't have a breastfeeding policy in place, or you might be the first woman in your command to ask for a place and time to pump and need some reasons to give to your chain of command about why it is in their best interests to do so. Here are a few reasons that have been shown to be helpful in the civilian world and might be useful to mothers in the military as well.

Commands need to support breastfeeding because it helps retain qualified and trained personnel. It costs the military hundreds of thousands of dollars to recruit and train qualified enlisted and officer personnel to fill the many billets worldwide. By permitting women the place and time to pump their breasts, commands will find that morale is increased among breastfeeding women, their productivity will not suffer, and in the long-term, many more women will reenlist or continue to serve because they feel supported (Uriell, Perry, Kee, & Burress, 2009). As this mother in the Navy says, "*I am ecstatic about the changes (in policy) and it is one of the reasons I am reenlisting.*"

In addition, not having to recruit and train new personnel due to women leaving the service because of breastfeeding-related issues, lessens manning shortages (Bell & Ritchie, 2003b). Furthermore, in order to sustain military readiness, the Department of Defense (DOD) has made it a requirement to achieve the goals of the *Healthy People 2010 Blueprint*, which requires implementing health promotion practices, such as breastfeeding (Department of Defense, 2003). By allowing service members the time and place to breastfeed or pump, commands are improving the health of their personnel, which is a win-win situation for everyone.

Another equally important reason to support breastfeeding mothers is reduced absenteeism from work. Military mothers who breastfeed their infants don't miss as much work due to illnesses, in themselves or their babies, even those attending childcare. It also reduces costs for the military healthcare system, TRICARE (Bell & Ritchie, 2003a; Bell & Ritchie, 2003b). Studies have shown that mothers who formula-feed have increased absences (Cohen, Mrtek, & Mrtek, 1995). It is a fact of life that children get sick and that means working parents have to take time off to care for the ill child. And oftentimes, the parent ends up sick, too. Let's face it, the military doesn't look too favorably upon granting SIQ chits or repeated requests for time off to care for a sick baby (see Chapter 20 for more information on how commands can support breastfeeding mothers).

Reasons to Breastfeed: Society

Some final reasons why breastfeeding is beneficial involve the planet and society as a whole. The decision to breastfeed affects more than just yourself and your baby. It also impacts the economy, our society, and the environment as well. It has been stated repeatedly that not breastfeeding makes for sicker mothers and babies, and that increases healthcare costs for everyone. While military medicine may be free to you as a service member, it does cost the government money, which is passed on to taxpayers (you and me). Formula-fed infants typically need more sick care visits, prescriptions, and hospitalizations, which potentially costs thousands of dollars over the lifetime of the child (Ball & Bennett, 2001). A recent study showed that if 90% of new mothers exclusively breastfed their infants to the recommended six months, the United States would save $13 billion per year and over 900 lives would be saved (Bartick & Reinhold, 2010). These figures do NOT include the healthcare costs for mothers who do not breastfeed and have increased rates of heart disease, diabetes, and cancer. If you were to add together the potential savings in healthcare costs of both breastfeeding mothers *and* babies in this country, you would see that billions of dollars and many lives could be saved per year.

Babies who are breastfed today grow up to be our leaders of tomorrow. It is a comforting thought to know that the nutrition and nurturing they receive at the breast will allow them to reach their full potential; whether that is as a CEO of a large corporation, a schoolteacher, or a service member. Conversely, babies who face health disadvantages early in life, including not being breastfed, may not reach their full potential--and that affects us all, too.

Finally, breastfeeding is the ultimate in going green, as it has a "zero carbon" footprint. Not so for formula, which has a huge impact on our environment and natural resources. The production of formula requires massive amounts of energy, water, plastic, paper, and metal. The feeding of cows (cow's milk being the main ingredient in formula) or the raising of soybean crops uses valuable land, water, and food, and it pollutes the water and air with fertilizer and waste run-off. The milk and soy crops must be transported to the factories to be processed, and then to the stores to be sold, increasing pollution levels.

Formula-feeding contributes to the solid waste stream, due to the disposal of used formula containers, worn-out bottles and nipples (which can take between 200-450 years to degrade), as well as the increased garbage produced by formula-feeding women who are menstruating and must dispose of their tampons and pads, and the increased dirty diapers of formula-fed babies (Palmer, 2009). For example, an estimated 550 million formula cans, with 86,000 tons of metal and 800,000 pounds of paper packaging, is added to U.S. landfills every year (United States Breastfeeding Committee, 2002). When you stop and think about all the resources that formula requires for its manufacture, shipping, consumption, and waste, and the huge environmental impact it creates, it is both frightening and mind-boggling. Even with the added costs of breast pumps, bottles, and nipples for working mothers, the costs and environmental impact is nowhere near that generated by feeding formula for a year.

This is just a summary of the many important reasons why you should breastfeed your baby. You may or may not be able to breastfeed full-time given your circumstances. But be assured that even breastfeeding for only a few weeks is better than not breastfeeding at all. Any breastmilk your baby receives is better than none. You can continue to breastfeed, even if it is only once a day, for as long as you wish after your return to active duty. Every mother needs to find the balance that will work in her life; whether that means exclusively breastfeeding and pumping your milk while at work or formula-feeding during the day at work and breastfeeding only at home. Remember, that breastfeeding is a gift only you can give your baby!

Risks Associated with Formula and Guilt

We all know people, including many of us, who were fed formula and are smart, healthy individuals with great teeth. That's not the point. Statistically speaking, babies fed formula have higher risks of short- and long-term health problems. It doesn't mean that every baby fed formula is going to get an ear infection. Just that the risk and severity of contracting an ear infection is much higher. What it does mean is that your breastfed baby is less likely to have an ear infection, and if he does get one, it is more likely to be much less severe. You are *reducing the risk*, not eliminating it. What is important to understand is that while breastfeeding is not a magic bullet that eliminates all disease, it is also not some kind of "extra" or "fringe" benefit.

Remember, human babies are meant to have human breastmilk, and mothers are meant to breastfeed. Our bodies are designed to give and receive breastmilk. So the health outcomes we see in babies fed mothers own milk and in women who breastfeed are what is *normal*. On the other hand, the health of babies fed formula (either cow's milk or soy), or women who formula-feed, is *abnormal* since formula is a food not meant for our biology (we are not calves or soybean plants). Here is one example: breastfed babies are *not* smarter. Their brains are growing and developing to their natural potential. It is that formula-fed babies have IQs that are 8-10 points lower, perhaps due to the lack of proper fatty acids for brain growth. And many of the "health benefits" of breastmilk are *dose-dependent*: the longer you can breastfeed or provide breastmilk, the greater the effects. The strongest effects are for babies who are exclusively breastfed for six months.

Now, this does NOT mean you are a horrible mother who will have a child that grows up to be sickly and stupid because you had to feed him formula. And this isn't about making you feel guilty for doing the best you can within the circumstances you are given. I would be remiss in not telling you that breastfeeding, and exclusive breastfeeding at that, is critical to your and your baby's health and well-being. The research and scientific evidence is overwhelming and leaves no doubt that it is the best choice. However, working in general, and serving in the military, in particular, *is* a significant barrier to breastfeeding. Virtually all women can produce enough milk for their baby when breastfeeding directly. But adding erratic pumping schedules, long hours, TDY (temporary duty) or field exercises, and a lack of command support to the mix can create problems for even the most die-hard breastfeeding mother. And that's when I will argue until I am red, white, *and* blue-in-the-face that whatever amount of breastmilk you can provide, whether that is "mostly breastfeeding" or "as much breastfeeding as possible" is perfectly viable. If it means you have to give some formula during the day or for a TDY assignment, that's OK. You are still a good mom.

This brings us to the topic of guilt--a very loaded and touchy subject. Mothers, the world over, feel guilty about everything from going back to work to what they feed their teenagers for breakfast. Guilt is what you feel when you know better and have the option to do the better thing, but choose not to anyway. When it comes to feeding your baby, you need to ask yourself whether you fit those criteria. Do you know that breastfeeding is better than formula? Do you have the option at your command to pump? Can you pump enough for your baby given your circumstances? Do you choose to pump (even if it isn't enough) and supplement if necessary? Or do you just say "the heck-with-it" and choose to formula-feed without trying to provide some breastmilk? Many military mothers may not have a choice about pumping or may not be able to maintain a full milk supply. Yet, if you try and pump as much breastmilk as possible and breastfeed when home, but still have to give formula during the workday, then you have no reason to feel guilty. It's that simple.

Barriers to Breastfeeding

While there is plenty of evidence showing many significant reasons to breastfeed, unfortunately, there are just as many personal and social barriers that keep women from beginning or continuing to breastfeed their babies. Knowing what these barriers are, and that you are not the first or only woman to face them, is the first step to overcoming them.

Probably the most common barrier is the apparent lack of information and support available to new mothers. While it may seem that you are bombarded everywhere you turn with the message that "Breast is Best," it is rare that it is followed up with actual help, both in the hospital and out. Factual and unbiased information can be hard to come by from friends and healthcare professionals alike. Oftentimes, when new mothers do run into trouble, there is no one to turn to for help. Or the very people you expect to help you cannot due to a lack of training. While it would seem obvious that your healthcare professional should be the first person to turn to for breastfeeding help, that is usually not the case. There are a few military doctors and nurses that have taken the extra time and expense to learn about breastfeeding by attending conferences or taking courses. However, for the majority, the extent of their knowledge is one day of breastfeeding instruction in medical or nursing school, or their wives (or their own) breastfeeding experience. A recent study found that only 8% of physicians feel that their advice on breastfeeding is important, while over one-third of their patients feel that it is very important (Taveras et al., 2004). Furthermore, many physicians still hand out formula marketing materials, which have been shown to reduce breastfeeding rates in new mothers. Combine that with the prevalent attitude that breastmilk and formula are equal and interchangeable and you have a recipe for failure.

For many mothers, the hospital experience undermines their efforts to breastfeed. While all military hospitals practice "family-centered maternity care," and two have reached "Baby-Friendly" status (BFUSA, 2009), there are still numerous hospital practices that undermine breastfeeding success, such as birth practices that do not encourage breastfeeding (cesareans and epidurals), lack of rooming-in, discharge in less than 48 hours, and handing out formula company discharge packs (DiGirolamo et al., 2008). And while most, if not all, military hospitals employ lactation consultants on staff, it is a reality that hospital-based lactation consultants have little time to see each patient (especially in the bigger military teaching hospitals) and even less time, if any, to offer follow-up services after new mothers are discharged. Even more troubling is the lack of insurance reimbursement via TRICARE for visits to a private practice lactation consultant. Lack of services and a lack of insurance reimbursement continue to be huge barriers to continued breastfeeding for civilian and military mothers alike.

You may also find that the experiences of your family members with breastfeeding, both good and bad, can influence the advice they give you. Did your mother breastfeed? How about your aunt or sister? Mother-in-law? In this country, we have a generation or two of mothers and grandmothers that did NOT breastfeed and who simply don't know how to help their daughters, sisters, and nieces when problems arise. Breastfeeding is an art that is supposed to be handed down from generation to generation. However, most grandmothers are not able to offer practical advice or assistance due to their own lack of experience. A lack of support due to ingrained beliefs in the inferiority of breastfeeding and breastmilk, or thoughts that breastfeeding is "old fashioned," "gross/disgusting," or similar sentiments can be detrimental to a new mother, especially when those thoughts come from your own mother or mother-in-law (see Chapter 19 for more information).

Do you know anyone, a shipmate or co-worker, who has breastfed a baby (successfully or not)? Is your partner supportive of your desire to breastfeed your baby? Have you had a previous unsuccessful breastfeeding experience and are reluctant to try again? Perhaps you have been the victim of sexual abuse or assault or have a negative body image, and direct breastfeeding just doesn't seem doable. All of these personal barriers to breastfeeding are valid, and most are able to be overcome with the proper information and support (which you will find in the pages of this book).

> *I didn't really get any good vibes from my fellow co-workers or mothers who had tried, but didn't succeed in breastfeeding. Mainly I heard, "Oh, just wait until you get back to work. If you do end up breastfeeding after he's born, you'll stop when you get back."* Petty Officer 3rd Class, USN

Probably the most pressing barrier to breastfeeding for the readers of this book is the return to active duty. It is a well-known fact that returning to work before 12 weeks, combined with regular and continued separation, poses a major obstacle to successful breastfeeding (Guendelman et al., 2009; Madlon-Kay & Carr, 1988). As an active-duty service member, you have two strikes against you from the get-go: you must return to work at six weeks and you will have regular and continued separation from your baby. While many women in the military are able to express milk at work, just as many work in positions where there is a lack of command support, inadequate facilities for pumping, upcoming deployments, or unsupportive co-workers. In addition, there are numerous other barriers within the military that can make maintaining a milk supply or providing enough expressed milk insurmountable as well (Bostock, 2001; Bristow, 1999; Hochhausen, 2001; Krueger, 2002; Stevens & Janke, 2003; Sykora, 1995; Vanderlaan, 1990).

Senior Airman Christine Luna, USAF, breastfeeding her daughter.

Photo courtesy of Christine Luna. Used with permission.

Breastfeeding in the Military: Is it worth it?

So why, you ask, should I even try to combine breastfeeding my baby with serving on active duty? You are reading this book, so you must have an idea that it is a worthwhile endeavor. And it is. Here are a few reasons why it IS worth your time and effort to breastfeed in the military. The first and most-often cited reason is to provide the health-related benefits and nutrition of breastmilk to your baby. As described above your baby will not get sick as often, something that is very important since he'll be in daycare and exposed to more infections. But he will also grow and thrive to his full potential on your milk. Equally important are the health and work-related benefits of breastfeeding for you. By breastfeeding (and pumping) for your baby, you will miss less work. This is good for you, and it'll make your co-workers and commander happier, too. No one likes a co-worker who is absent a lot, and you don't want to be calling in sick on behalf of your child. Of course, you will be healthier as well (remember all the info on cancer, heart disease, diabetes?) and will bounce back to your pre-pregnant weight quicker. You'll have less trouble passing the PFA (physical fitness assessment), and you'll get back into your pre-pregnancy uniforms quicker, all of which reflects well on you and maintains military readiness.

But those reasons are small potatoes compared to the following: many women feel some ambivalence about leaving their baby to go to work, and this is magnified in the military, where you have no choice about leaving and are sometimes gone for days or weeks at a time. Pumping your milk while you are separated can help you feel connected and closer to your baby. Breastfeeding your baby confirms that you are irreplaceable to your baby and him to you. Your care provider may see his first smile or steps, but only you two share the intimate bond of breastfeeding. Feeling your breasts filling with milk is a powerful reminder of the close physical bond you have with your baby, while expressing your milk helps to tie the two very different halves of your life together. While you are on duty, it can become easy to forget that you are a mother and not just a soldier or sailor. Each time you take a break to pump your breasts, it is a chance to focus on the larger picture and remember that you ARE a mother first and foremost.

Arguably, the most compelling and important reason to go to the trouble of pumping and breastfeeding while in the military is to keep your milk supply up, so you CAN enjoy the closeness and bonding that occurs when you are at home breastfeeding your baby. I won't lie to you. It IS a pain to pump and store breastmilk during the workday. But it is worth every minute of your time when you can come home after a TDY or a 12-hour shift and reconnect with your baby by nursing him. This Air Force Major sums up the rigors and the joys of breastfeeding in the military quite nicely:

> *Even though it may seem hard or stressful, and you think you can't do this because you're working, it's precisely because you're working that you need to do this. It's your special time to connect with your baby.*

For many women, breastfeeding in the military is about more than just the breastmilk. Sure, that is a very valid and important reason to go to the trouble of pumping and storing your milk. But it is about so much more than just the milk. You can't bottle the sense of connection that breastfeeding provides when you are apart, or the comfort and closeness when you are together. And neither can you bottle the confidence that comes from providing all of your baby's nutrition or watching him grow and thrive on your milk. Breastfeeding is a way to nourish your baby (and yourself) both body and soul, and that cannot be replicated or put in a bottle. By going to the trouble of pumping your breastmilk during the workday or while away on a TDY, you are ensuring that you will be able to enjoy the relationship that comes from breastfeeding, as well as the health benefits, when you are at home.

Your Attitude and Commitment

Is pumping and breastfeeding while in the military going to be hard? Yes, it is. But your attitude and commitment are the most important factors in making breastfeeding while on active duty a reality and are the keys to your success. It can be very easy to read this book, see all the obstacles in your way, and think to yourself, "Oh I can't breastfeed in the military; it'll be too hard, so why even try?" Don't *try* to breastfeed. DO IT! (Did you *try* to complete boot camp or OCS? Or did you believe you were going to be successful no matter what?) It is the same with breastfeeding while on active duty. Your attitude has to be confident and positive about making breastfeeding while on active duty a reality for you and your baby.

You know the reasons why you should breastfeed or you wouldn't be reading this book. Maybe you're pregnant and wondering if it is possible and worth the effort to breastfeed after your convalescent leave, and you're thinking you'll just do it for six weeks and stop. You might be a few weeks into this breastfeeding thing at this point and don't want to quit, but don't see how to make it work when you go back. Breastfeeding doesn't have to end. You and your baby can continue while you are on active duty, and it will offer tremendous joy and satisfaction as well as the above mentioned benefits to you and your baby.

> *I think my biggest advice to anyone wondering if they'll actually succeed at breastfeeding is: DO NOT TRY. Just do. You WILL breastfeed. Do not allow yourself an alternative. That's not to say that it'll be easy or that you will never give your son or daughter formula. You can always adjust your goal. However, make it a goal you WILL keep. I WILL breastfeed for three months or six months or a year or whatever. If you start out saying, "Oh, I will try..." you are already seeing yourself fail.* Petty Officer 2nd Class, USN

> *It was never a matter of whether breastfeeding would cause problems; I was going to do it!* Senior Airman, USAF

I never thought there was going to be a problem, so I think that was part of the reason there wasn't. If the books I read said I could breastfeed and work, I thought I must be able to do it. Lt. Col., USAF

It is important to remember that breastfeeding is something that only YOU can do for your baby. Anyone—your partner, childcare provider, or friend—can change a diaper, give a bath, or rock your baby to sleep. However, breastfeeding is different. It is something special, a part of yourself that you leave in a bottle for your baby while you are gone to work every day. Breastfeeding is more than food. It is a relationship and a connection that binds you and your baby together when you are apart. You are providing gifts to your baby with every bottle of pumped breastmilk: immunities from illness, perfect nourishment, lessened risk of some chronic diseases, and an irreplaceable bond only you two share.

It's one way I have of giving my special love and attention to my daughter. It's my way of communicating to her and to myself that I am still her mother, even though I have to work full-time. I treasure the time I have with her while we're nursing. Major, USAF

SECTION TWO

Basic Training: The Basics of Breastfeeding

Mariah's Story

I am a Staff Sergeant in the Air Force and I work as an X-Ray technician. I never thought I would BF my children...heck, I never even planned on having my own children — always just thought I would adopt. But after getting married, I decided that I did want to have children with my husband. So, off we started as a newly married couple and after a few years, we found ourselves pregnant with our first child. I really did not think about breastfeeding, just because I am really small up top. I took a breastfeeding class offered by Family Advocacy on base and really learned a lot. I decided right then and there that having a little information in my corner was a good thing since I really did not know all the benefits about breastfeeding. I did not realize that there were so many good things for both baby and mom. I was very excited about learning to breastfeed my soon-to-be baby, and I read everything I could about breastfeeding. There was no one that I really felt comfortable talking to about it, and I really did not have anyone to look to for the support that would have made things so much easier. I was active duty and did not have any family around, and I also worked in a male-dominated environment and did not have any other females around in which to bounce ideas off of. My husband and I were pretty much on our own...

In November of 2002, our son was born, and I was very excited about getting started. I knew that I would need to learn how to pump for when I went back to work, but decided that the first few weeks I would focus on just learning how to nurse my new baby. Things were not easy. I was frustrated with how long it was taking for us to figure it out. My son, nonetheless, was growing, and the doctor had no worries that he was nursing just fine. I, on the other hand, was in terrible pain. I went back to the hospital and found a LC there that was willing to sit down with us and help us figure out what the problem was. She found that my son was doing everything right and I was doing everything right. It's just that we were not syncing correctly. It took a good three months before I was able to nurse him without any pain, but after that, it was smooth sailing.

I practiced pumping at home before I had to go back to work. It was hard, but only because I felt like I was not going to be able to get enough to feed him. My husband quit his job to become a full time, stay-at-home-dad, and I knew that I would be able to go home at lunch in order to nurse my son, so I figured that I would only need to pump twice a day, once in the morning and once in the afternoon to make up for the feedings that I was not at home for. My husband would give my son a bottle of expressed milk at those times, and I knew that I needed to do my best in order to make enough, so we would not have to resort to formula. I drank water like I lived in the middle of a desert in order to stay hydrated. I ate oatmeal, even though I could not stand the taste of it, because I read that it would help with milk production. I did whatever I had to do in order to be able to make enough milk. I was successful to the point that I had built up a small freezer stash. I went on a three day TDY at one point and even had enough to cover all of my son's feedings. I felt guilty for having to pump and dump, but I had no practical way of getting the milk back to my son. Let me tell you, there's nothing like having to pump in the bathroom of a C-5 aircraft on a cross-country trip in the middle of turbulence!!

So as I was nursing my son, I would make small goals. The first one was six weeks, then three months, then six months, nine months, and then a year. At one point, after about one month, things got really bad and I just felt that I could not do it any longer. I was in a lot of pain and my son would just cry. My husband pulled a can of formula out of the pantry and said that it came in the mail as a sample sent from one of the big formula companies. He scooped the required amount in a bottle and put it on my nightstand with a bottle of water and told me that I had tried my best, and he would support me either way. I really wanted to make this work, and knew then that if I caved in and gave my son that bottle of formula, it would be too easy to just give up and quit nursing. I knew that I wanted the best for my son and I would continue to keep trying. Well, I never needed that bottle of formula and ended up giving away the container of formula. I made it to six months exclusively breastfeeding my son. I was so proud and knew that since I had made it that far, that one year would be no problem. At the one-year mark, the thought of stopping just did not cross my mind. He was a happy and healthy baby. He started taking a little bit of cow's milk, and eventually dropped his night feeding. Around 15 months, my son started preferring the cow's milk. He was easily distracted and nursing was hard because he could not keep his attention on eating. I was getting frustrated, so shortly before he turned 16 months, we stopped nursing. I was sad, but knew that I had done well.

Chapter 2
Preparing to Breastfeed

Now that you know all the reasons WHY it is so important for you to breastfeed, you need to know HOW to breastfeed successfully. Unfortunately, your time to do that is limited, with only six weeks to figure it all out. But you can do it. The most important thing for you to do while on your very short convalescent leave is learn about your baby and get breastfeeding well established. Just because you are a woman and have breasts does NOT mean you will automatically know what to do once the baby arrives. Breastfeeding is a natural act for both you and your baby. But lots of things, such as how your birth was handled, can interfere with both of your ability to do it. But even with a difficult start, you and your baby can learn how to breastfeed. Breastfeeding is OJT (on-the-job training) in the truest sense of the word! This chapter discusses preparing for breastfeeding. If you already have a nursing baby in arms, then feel free to skip ahead to the appropriate chapters.

Educate Yourself

Hopefully, you bought this book while still pregnant and have some time ahead of you to read and learn about breastfeeding before your baby arrives. If your baby is already here, don't worry as the information in this chapter will still be useful to you. If not for this baby, then maybe it will be useful for the next one. Basically all the preparation that is necessary for successful breastfeeding is to learn as much about it as possible before the baby is born.

Attending a breastfeeding class given by the military hospital or another community resource is not only very informative, but you may meet fellow active-duty mothers who are planning to breastfeed as well. Most people take a childbirth class in order to prepare for the birth, and most births last one to two days. Breastfeeding your baby can, and should, last much longer than that--and quite frankly, has much more of an impact on your baby's health than the birth. It only makes sense to take a breastfeeding class or two to help you prepare. Most hospitals and community resources offer a Basics of Breastfeeding and a Return to Work class, and often many Family Advocacy or New Parent Support programs on base will have a breastfeeding class as well (see Chapter 22).

As a new mother, lots of people will give you breastfeeding advice: professionals, friends, your mom, your partner, and maybe even your supervisor. Some of this will be good advice. Some will be bad. I'll help you try to differentiate between the two. You'll learn the basics of a good latch, feeding cues, what to look for if things are wrong, and basic pumping information. A class will give you the building blocks you need to get started, as well as contact information on lactation consultants, pump rentals, and other resources in your area. As this Air Force mother says,

> Before giving birth, the AFB Family Advocacy nurse (a certified LC) taught a class on breastfeeding. That knowledge really helped me go into breastfeeding confident that I could do it.

Of course, reading books and watching videos or browsing websites are another way of educating yourself, either in addition to attending a class or in place of one due to there not being any classes near to you. While educating yourself doesn't guarantee that you'll have a smooth breastfeeding experience, it does reduce the chances of breastfeeding problems and lets you be aware of what to look for ahead of time.

Support, Support, Support

Finding support for breastfeeding is probably one of the best things you can do to prepare for breastfeeding. It is never too early in your pregnancy to attend a support group meeting or talk with a co-worker who is currently nursing. Support group meetings, such as those run by La Leche League or the Mom-2-Mom breastfeeding groups, are invaluable not only for the information and support they offer, but also because you can talk to currently breastfeeding mothers (see Chapter 19). Attending meetings while you are pregnant gives you the chance to ask questions and actually "see" women breastfeeding babies of various ages (when was the last time you actually watched a mother nurse her baby?). Many of us grew up not seeing anyone in our families or circle of friend's breastfeed a baby, and unfortunately we don't see many babies being breastfed in public either. We don't know what to expect except by what is often portrayed inaccurately on TV or in the movies. And visualizing a good

Support is essential when you are just starting out.

Photo courtesy Kendra Laird. Used with permission.

latch from a description in a book is darn near impossible! There is nothing like seeing a baby nurse in real life or listening to mothers discuss how they overcame a bout of mastitis and lived to tell the tale to make you understand the realities and joys of breastfeeding.

Support also means finding other mothers, especially active-duty mothers, who have *successfully* breastfed and talking with them about what worked and what didn't, so you'll be prepared. This Air Force mom has this to say about finding a friend who was successful at breastfeeding in the military:

> *I had another active-duty friend and mother who had breastfed her son for seven months and pumped for her daughter for six weeks while she was away at training. Just knowing that there were other moms that did it, made it easier.*

It also means talking with your partner about breastfeeding, so you are both on the same page about your desires and needs (see Chapter 19). Rally supportive family members and friends around you, and make sure you have someone to run interference with family members that might undermine your efforts. You don't need to hear, "Are you sure he is getting enough to eat?" or "He's eating again? Are you sure you have enough milk?" every few hours, it's a sure-fire way to lose all confidence in yourself. You should also mention your desire to breastfeed to your OB/GYN or midwife, and if possible, see an IBCLC if you know you might have problems breastfeeding (a history of breast surgery, hormonal problems, flat or inverted nipples). Having the name and number of a good friend or co-worker, a LLL Leader, and an IBCLC to call when things are rough at 0300 can be a lifeline! See Section Five in this book for a more detailed explanation of the various types of support available to you, both inside and outside the main gates.

Supplies

What do you need to successfully breastfeed your baby? A pair of breasts and your arms, that's it really. All the other stuff is nice, but not really necessary. Obviously, you'll be going to back to work and will need a pump and bottles (see Chapter 7). But for now, while getting breastfeeding started, all you really need is your breasts. However, there are a few items that most mothers find helpful in the early days and weeks, such as nursing bras, nursing pads, and a sling or carrier.

- **Nursing Bras**. Do yourself a favor and spend the money on good, well-made nursing bras (see Appendix B). It is important to have a well-made and supportive bra while breastfeeding to support the extra weight of your milk-filled breasts (pregnancy causes the most sagging), and it is a uniform regulation to wear a bra. Furthermore, it is much easier to feed or pump with nursing bras that have flaps that move aside. As with any bra, it should fit properly, both in the cup and rib cage. Many IBCLCs are certified to fit nursing bras correctly, and it is worth your time to get fitted properly. Also be aware that you may need to buy different sizes of nursing bras throughout your nursing career as your breast size changes. You will need a couple at the end of your pregnancy and first week or so postpartum that are bigger to accommodate any engorgement. Then you will need a few (it's nice to have at least one to two to wear and one to two in the wash) in a smaller size for the duration of your nursing relationship. There are also specially made bras for pumping that hold the flanges in place that some mothers find very useful (see Chapter 10 and Appendix B).

- **Nursing Pads**. Some women leak milk a little, others a lot. Some women leak at the start of breastfeeding and by six weeks are over and done with it, while others leak until they dry up with weaning. In any case, breast pads are your best friends. They are worn inside your bra and soak up the excess milk, so it doesn't show through your clothing. Most women will agree that there is nothing more embarrassing than having two round wet marks on your uniform while talking to your male supervisor! Breast pads come in assorted styles: convenient disposable paper, reusable and washable cotton or wool, and non-absorbent, self-adhering silicone Lily Padz © (see Appendix B).

- **Sling**. A soft, cloth carrier or sling is an integral part of successful breastfeeding. Babies thrive on being close to mom, and you can better read your baby's hunger cues when he is worn on your body. With your return to work, you will find that carrying your baby in a sling while at home helps you reconnect with him and allows you to do the necessary chores (like cooking dinner!) with your arms free. Slings also allow for discreet nursing while out in public (see Chapter 4 for more information).

Items that are nice to have, but not necessary include nursing pillows, rockers, footstools, nipple ointments, and special nursing clothes. Nursing pillows tend to be a one-size-does-not-fit-all item. What works for one mom/ baby pair is too high or low or too big or small for another. Bed pillows work the best if you really need the support. They can be squished to just the right place and thickness to suit your needs. Furthermore, pillows should only be used to support *your* arms and not the baby and really only need to be used the first few weeks anyway. The best pillow available for your baby is your postpartum belly! Rocking chairs and footstools are another nicety, and again something that really needs to be sized for the individual. Any chair will do for nursing your baby. You do **NOT** need to have lanolin (Lansinoh® PurLan®) on hand during the early days. It simply is not necessary if your baby is latched correctly. If you do develop sore nipples, lanolin can help soothe and lessen the pain. However, it is **NOT** a cure for sore nipples. If you are suffering from soreness or damaged nipples, you need to be seen by a professional to identify and fix the problem that is causing the sore nipples (see Chapter 5). Finally, special nursing clothes can be very expensive, and aside from dresses for special occasions, you can nurse discreetly by layering t-shirts and button-down shirts or jackets when you are in civilian clothes. There is more about uniform issues while breastfeeding in Chapter 15.

★ TIP ★

Budget some money for breastfeeding! Breastfeeding is far cheaper than formula, but it is NOT free. Along with buying the layette and nursery items, set aside some money for a breast pump, breastfeeding supplies, and a lactation consultation. It will be money well-spent!

Breastfeeding Myths

There are many myths and bits of advice and lore regarding breastfeeding that get handed down from generation to generation and from friend to friend. Much of this advice is harmless. But some can be downright dangerous or painful. Some of what you might hear or be told to do in preparation for breastfeeding may include rolling, tugging, or rubbing your nipples with a rough towel. Your nipples do not need toughening-up; nipple tissue is an exquisitely sensitive, erectile tissue that is full of nerve endings for a reason. If nursing hurts, it means something is wrong!

You might also be told to use soap or alcohol to clean your nipples. Do NOT do this as it will only dry them out and strip away the natural oils and anti-bacterial substance the areola secretes. Neither should you try to express any of the colostrum that is present from the fifth month of your pregnancy. It is not necessary and may cause you to have premature contractions. Finally, do not use a heat lamp or "sunburn" your nipples to heal them if they become sore or cracked. This, too, will only serve to cause further pain and delay healing. Once you are successfully breastfeeding, there is no special care needed for your breasts. Wash them whenever you bathe or shower and be sure to rinse well with clear water. Do not apply creams, lotions, or oils to your breasts. It masks the natural smell that your baby relies on to locate you and your breasts, and it can interfere with the production of that natural, protective, oily substance that your breasts secrete to help keep the breast clean, lubricated, and germ-free.

Ditch the "Free" Formula

Have you received your "free" gift pack of formula yet? If you haven't, just wait. You'll get one about two weeks before your baby is due and again within a day or so of the birth. These "just-in-case" packs of ready-to-feed formula are sent to you as a courtesy from the formula companies (who get your name from the sign-in sheets at the clinic or maternity apparel stores) in the hopes that when going gets rough, you'll reach for a bottle of formula. Here's how it usually plays out:

- *What you are feeling: It's your first night home from the hospital and you have only a brief recollection of what the nurse told you about breastfeeding and a handout to look at.*

  ○ **What's really happening:** You didn't get enough breastfeeding help at the hospital and the "lactation specialist" nurse you saw didn't have any breastfeeding training. You really do have a poor latch resulting in sore nipples and your baby isn't transferring enough milk.

- *What you are feeling: Your baby is crying, you're all alone (Dad is deployed), you've tried nursing him and he just won't latch. Your breasts hurt, your hormones are all over the place, and you are sure your baby is starving.*

  ○ **What's really happening:** Your baby boy is crying because he is in a cold, loud world and his tummy hurts (he is hungry and is used to being fed 24/7). He is exhausted from the hard work of being born. Crying is his way of releasing tension and telling you he really just wants to be held.

- *What you are feeling: You give up and give your baby that bottle of "just in case" formula and miraculously he sucks it down in nothing flat and promptly falls asleep for four blessed hours. You think to yourself he MUST have been starving and that just proves that you didn't have any milk in your breasts after all.*

  ○ **What's really happening:** You just gave him a huge load of formula that his tummy can't digest, and it has basically drugged him into a stupor. So he gives up and falls asleep. In the morning, he is ready to breastfeed, but you have no confidence in your ability to make milk or be a good mother and find it easier to give another bottle, which will reduce your milk supply even further.

So what to do? Toss those formula samples, give them away to a shelter or return them to the sender. Your baby will NOT starve in 12 hours, and you can call your LLL Leader or IBCLC in the morning to get the help you need. Giving bottles of formula in the early days can reduce your milk supply, which, in turn, leads to more formula being given, which further reduces your milk supply. Before you know it, one bottle of formula has lead to a completely formula-fed baby. It can also lead to nipple confusion in the early days and weeks. All new mothers (and babies) go through a rough patch in the first week. It is NORMAL. This is when you need your support network to talk you through it and reassure you that your baby will not starve, you do have milk, and you can get the help you need.

Have a Good Birth

One of the best ways to prepare for successful breastfeeding is to have a good birth. While the time spent in labor is relatively short compared to the time you'll spend nursing your baby, it can have a huge impact on how well breastfeeding goes for you. Some of the common birth practices that can affect breastfeeding are inductions (especially those done too early based on inaccurate due dates), pitocin use, epidurals, cesarean sections, and other hospital routines, such as not allowing rooming-in or early discharge (Smith, 2010). As an active-duty service member, you do not have a choice as to where you can birth your baby, unlike even the spouses of your co-workers, you are required to deliver at the nearest MTF. Therefore, you will have to be an advocate for yourself to have the best possible birth.

Prepare for your birth by reading evidence-based books on childbirth that cover all your options. Take a childbirth class, so you know what to expect and have the tools to avoid medications if at all possible. Research has shown that babies are more alert for breastfeeding after an unmedicated birth (Ransjo-Arvidson et al., 2001). To help you reach the goal of an unmedicated birth, keep in mind these six principles that Lamaze International © has found to be the most important for a healthy full-term birth:

1. Let labor begin normally and without interventions.

2. Keep moving during labor.

3. Have a support person with you (partner, friend, doula).

4. Keep interventions to a minimum.

5. Avoid birthing on your back.

6. Room-in with your newborn.

You can find more information on these six principles by going to the website www.injoyvideos.com/mothersadvocate and downloading the booklet, *Healthy Birth Your Way*, and watching the accompanying videos. Another important item is to write a birth plan outlining what you want done during and after the birth using the principles above. Birth plans can be very useful towards ensuring that you DO have the birth you want and that your baby will be ready to breastfeed.

Hire a labor doula to be with you at the birth. A doula is a trained professional who will provide you with one-to-one continuous support and can offer comfort measures, such as massage, throughout your labor and birth. Having a doula at your birth has been shown to reduce the need for pain medications and Cesarean sections (McGrath & Kennell, 2008; Simkin & O'Hara, 2002). A doula can be a lifesaver, especially if you do not have anyone nearby to be your support person during the birth (see Appendices A and B).

You can also check and see if your MTF is Baby-Friendly, or working towards Baby-Friendly status as part of the Family Centered Care that TRICARE provides. On the next page is the Coalition on Improving Maternity Services (CIMS) Ten Steps of the Mother-Friendly Childbirth Initiative which has been integrated into the Baby-Friendly Hospital Initiative. While you cannot give birth outside the MTF as an active-duty service member, you can use these guidelines to ask questions and request changes at your birthing facility.

Ten Steps of the Mother-Friendly Childbirth Initiative
For Mother-Friendly Hospitals, Birth Centers, and Home Birth Services*

To receive CIMS designation as "mother-friendly," a hospital, birth center, or home birth service must carry out the philosophical principles by fulfilling the Ten Steps of Mother-Friendly Care outlined below.

A mother-friendly hospital, birth center, or home birth service:
1. Offers all birthing mothers:
   - Unrestricted access to the birth companions of her choice, including fathers, partners, children, family members, and friends.
   - Unrestricted access to continuous emotional and physical support from a skilled woman— for example, a doula* or labor-support professional.
   - Access to professional midwifery care.
2. Provides accurate descriptive and statistical information to the public about its practices and procedures for birth care, including measures of interventions and outcomes.
3. Provides culturally competent care—that is, care that is sensitive and responsive to the specific beliefs, values, and customs of the mother's ethnicity and religion.
4. Provides the birthing woman with the freedom to walk, move about, and assume the positions of her choice during labor and birth (unless restriction is specifically required to correct a complication), and discourages the use of the lithotomy (flat on back with legs elevated) position.
5. Has clearly defined policies and procedures for:
   - Collaborating and consulting throughout the perinatal period with other maternity services, including communicating with the original caregiver when transfer from one birth site to another is necessary.
   - Linking the mother and baby to appropriate community resources, including prenatal and post-discharge follow-up and breastfeeding support.
6. Does not routinely employ practices and procedures that are unsupported by scientific evidence, including but not limited to the following:
   - Shaving
   - Enemas
   - IVs (intravenous drip)
   - Withholding nourishment or water
   - Early rupture of membranes*
   - Electronic fetal monitoring
   - Other interventions are limited as follows:
   - Has an induction* rate of 10% or less.†
   - Has an episiotomy* rate of 20% or less, with a goal of 5% or less.
   - Has a total cesarean rate of 10% or less in community hospitals, and 15% or less in tertiary care (high-risk) hospitals.
   - Has a VBAC (vaginal birth after cesarean) rate of 60% or more with a goal of 75% or more.
7. Educates staff in non-drug methods of pain relief, and does not promote the use of analgesic or anesthetic drugs not specifically required to correct a complication.
8. Encourages all mothers and families, including those with sick or premature newborns or infants with congenital problems, to touch, hold, breastfeed, and care for their babies to the extent compatible with their conditions.
9. Discourages non-religious circumcision of the newborn.
10. Strives to achieve the WHO-UNICEF "Ten Steps of the Baby-Friendly Hospital Initiative" to promote successful breastfeeding:
    - Have a written breastfeeding policy that is routinely communicated to all healthcare staff.
    - Train all healthcare staff in skills necessary to implement this policy.
    - Inform all pregnant women about the benefits and management of breastfeeding.
    - Help mothers initiate breastfeeding within a half-hour of birth.
    - Show mothers how to breastfeed and how to maintain lactation even if they should be separated from their infants.
    - Give newborn infants no food or drink other than breastmilk unless medically indicated.
    - Practice rooming in: allow mothers and infants to remain together 24 hours a day.
    - Encourage breastfeeding on demand.
    - Give no artificial teat or pacifiers (also called dummies or soothers) to breastfeeding infants.
    - Foster the establishment of breastfeeding support groups and refer mothers to them on discharge from hospitals or clinics.

From Coalition for Improving Maternity Services (CIMS). www.motherfriendly.org.

While there are only two military hospitals at this time that are Baby-Friendly, Robert E. Bush Naval Hospital and Weed Army Community Hospital (The Baby-Friendly USA, 2010), many are practicing Family-Centered maternity care and should be following some of the above guidelines. You can ask at your facility if they are aware of and follow the CIMS Ten Steps. If not, try to follow the guidelines as best you can and incorporate them into your birth plan. Taking steps to ensure that you have the best possible birth experience can make a huge difference in whether or not you have the best possible breastfeeding experience.

Chapter 3
How the Breast Works

It may seem like you're sitting in class again reading this chapter, but it is important to have a basic understanding of how the breast works and what the different parts of your breast are. If you do have trouble breastfeeding, you can better troubleshoot what is wrong and more accurately tell your doctor or lactation consultant what is going on. Besides, you might find it pretty amazing what the female breast is capable of doing. So read on for a down-and-dirty explanation of the anatomy and physiology of the female lactating breast (complete with illustrations).

Inside the Breast

Your breasts are marvelous milk-making factories housed in flesh. They can nourish a baby completely and exclusively for at least six months given the proper stimulation. When you breastfeed your baby correctly, he stimulates the nerves in the **areola** (the dark part of the breast) and **nipple,** which tell the brain to release the hormone **prolactin.** Prolactin tells the **milk glands** in the breast to make milk, and another hormone, **oxytocin,** tells the **alveoli** to squeeze and release the milk. The milk travels down the milk glands into the **ducts** and out the **nipple pores** (openings). Your breast has a number of **lobes,** full of milk ducts, glands, and alveoli (they look like clusters of grapes), spaced around the breast much like the spokes on a bicycle wheel.

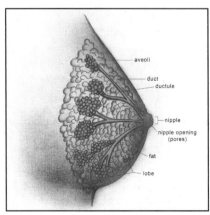

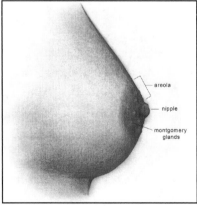

The bumps on your areola are called **Montgomery glands,** and they secrete an oily, anti-bacterial substance that keeps your nipples clean, soft, and pliable. They also release a scent that helps your newborn find the nipple. The milk glands and aveoli within your breasts are what produce the milk, and almost all women have enough glandular tissue to produce sufficent milk. **Fat tissue** in your breasts determines their size, and the size of your breasts has nothing to do with how much or how little milk you will make, only how much storage capacity you have. A mother with a small storage capacity will make the same amount of milk over a 24-hour period as a mother with a large storage capacity. Her baby just needs to remove the milk more often than the mother with a larger storage capacity.

The shape of the breast and nipple at rest are very different than when your baby is actively breastfeeding. When your baby is properly latched (see next chapter), your nipple will stretch two to three times its normal length to reach near the junction between the hard and soft palates. Do not be surprised if your baby pulls off the breast and your nipple looks really long. This is normal. It should not, however, be a totally different shape. While every mother's areola size is different, large or small, your baby should be latched on well behind the nipple to prevent soreness and allow the milk to flow, but also to stimulate the breast to make more milk.

Let-Down or Milk-Ejection Reflex

When oxytocin is released by the brain, it causes a "let-down" or milk ejection reflex (MER) to occur and the milk producing cells to release the milk they have made. Oxytocin is released by your baby's suckling, but it can also be released when you hear your baby cry, see a picture of him, smell his clothing, or even just think about him (which can be good or bad, depending on the situation). It is also released during sex in both men and women. Most mothers begin to feel their let-down around the fourth day after birth, when their milk begins to "come-in," and the milk supply becomes more plentiful. The MER is often described as a tingling sensation or a warm, heavy feeling in the breast. (Don't worry if you do not feel anything. Some mothers never do). You may notice the other breast leaking or feel very thirsty, and a very few women feel nauseous during let-downs.

One way to tell if you are having a MER is to watch your baby while he nurses. Babies will start breastfeeding with short, rapid sucks (non-nutritive sucking), also known as "flutter sucking," to get the milk flow started. It is during this flutter sucking that the nipple is being shaped and stimulated, causing the MER to occur. This is very different from the long, slow sucks (nutritive sucking) that occur after a few minutes when the milk is flowing. You should also hear swallowing once the milk is flowing, one to two sucks for every swallow is a good ratio. It is common for there to be more than one

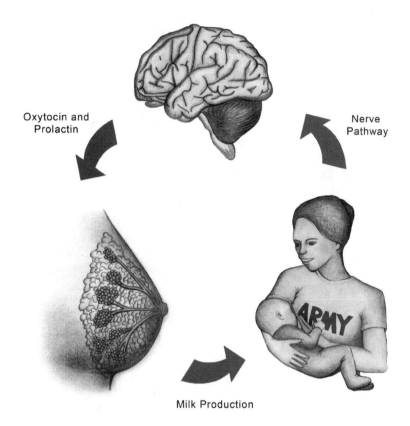

Oxytocin and Prolactin

Nerve Pathway

Milk Production

MER at each feeding (Geddes, 2009), and oftentimes mothers will have two to four. Your baby will suck-swallow through a let-down, pause and rest, and then suck-swallow again through another let-down.

Milk Composition

Human milk is a dynamic fluid that varies in composition, depending on stage of lactation, what you've eaten, what time of day it is, and how long the feeding lasts. **Colostrum** is the first milk your breasts produce. It is generally a clear to yellowish color, thick (almost a honey-like consistency), and easily digested by your baby. It is made in very small quantities and is perfect for mastering the art of suck, swallow, and breathe. It is high in proteins and rich in antibodies, making it your baby's first immunization. Colostrum also has a laxative effect, which is very good at ridding your baby's body of meconium and helping to prevent jaundice. Your **transitional milk** comes in around day two to three and rapidly increases over the next few days. As its name implies, it is neither colostrum nor mature milk, but an in-between milk that is thinner and becoming more plentiful. Finally, your **mature milk** will appear, usually around days five to seven. It is thinner, but the volume has greatly increased. Mature milk is higher in lactose and fat and lower in protein than colostrum, and it is all your baby needs until he starts solids.

You have probably heard about foremilk and hindmilk. This is referring to the fat content of your milk from the beginning to the end of a feeding at *one breast*. At the beginning of each feeding, the fat content of your milk is low. This milk has a high water content and basically quenches your baby's thirst. It also flows faster to give him a reward for his hard work. During the feeding, the milk gradually increases in fat as the breast is drained. The longer your baby is at one breast, the higher the fat content. This milk at the end of a feeding makes him feel full, puts weight on him, and makes him poop. You can judge whether your baby is getting enough hindmilk by the color of his poop: yellow, seedy-looking poop equals plenty of hindmilk. Green poop indicates too much foremilk, whether by switching breasts too soon or not nursing long enough.

Supply and Demand

If you let your baby breastfeed as often as he wants to in the first weeks, it will help to ensure a plentiful milk supply. You need to empty your breasts at least eight times a day, with either your baby or a breast pump. Making milk is a very simple process: the more milk you or your baby removes from your breasts, the more milk your breasts make. This is why it is called supply and demand. Think of it this way. Your breasts work like a factory making pens. If the factory makes a lot of pens (milk), but the consumer (your baby) doesn't buy them, the pens back up and soon the factory owner (your brain) tells the factory to stop making pens. However, if the factory makes the pens and the consumer keeps buying them, the factory will make even more pens to meet the demand.

It takes about six weeks to build up your full supply, and that is why it is so important that you breastfeed your baby frequently in the first weeks. You need to set the factory up to keep making a high rate of pens (milk) for the long haul. However, the addition of bottles before three to four weeks can sabotage your milk supply. If you don't remove the milk from your breasts by pumping every time you feed your baby from a bottle, that tells your breasts not to make milk at that feeding. Over time, you will lose your milk supply. Remember, *to make milk you need to remove milk at least eight times a day*.

Chapter 4
Getting Started:
The First Days and Weeks

While breastfeeding may seem to be the natural and easy way to feed a baby, it does not always come naturally (or easily) to mothers. That is why there are numerous books, classes, and websites available to help new mothers. I encourage you to buy or borrow a comprehensive breastfeeding book, attend classes, and browse websites for more information on the basics of breastfeeding (see Appendices A and B), in addition to what I've written here. I wrote this book to focus on and provide information about maintaining a breastfeeding relationship while serving in the military. However, I feel it is important to include the most relevant information on getting started and the basics of breastfeeding. Without a good start to breastfeeding and establishing a good milk supply, all the information on returning to work in this book will be useless. This chapter will cover the importance of skin-to-skin, hunger cues, proper latch and positioning, how to know your baby is getting enough, safe sleep, and other important topics to know in the first few weeks of breastfeeding.

Childbirth

In the previous chapter, I mentioned the need to prepare for your birth, as the type of birth you have *can* impact your ability to get breastfeeding off to a good start. But no matter how much you prepare, things can and will get FUBAR'ed, and you may end up with an induction, epidural, or cesarean section. All is not lost! Many babies do just fine breastfeeding after less-than-ideal births, and there are a few things you can do to help overcome any possible difficulties. First, remember that you did the best you could and beating yourself up over it won't help anyone. Second, you and your baby CAN learn to breastfeed! Finally, rooming-in and reminding the staff that your baby is not to have any pacifiers or bottles can go a long ways towards supporting breastfeeding.

Unfortunately, according to the U.S. National Center for Health Statistics, the rate of cesarean section (c-section) births has sky-rocketed, increasing 53% since 1996, with the U.S. national average now around 32% (Martin et al., 2009). That means many of you will end up having major abdominal surgery, even if you plan and do everything to avoid a c-section.

If that does happen, do not be misled into thinking that you cannot breastfeed after a c-section. Recognize that it does pose some challenges. But it is most certainly possible, and many mothers feel that breastfeeding helps them feel better about not having had the birth they wanted. Having a c-section means you will need extra help while you recover from surgery, so have a support person with you for the first days and weeks after the birth. You can breastfeed immediately if you were given an epidural or spinal, and as soon as you feel ready after a general anesthetic. Medications given for a c-section, such as antibiotics and pain relievers, are safe to take (see Chapter 6 for more information on medications). The best positions for breastfeeding after a c-section are any that do not put weight on your incision, such as the football or side-lying (see later in this chapter for more information). Finally, practicing skin-to-skin with your baby is one of the best things you can do to ensure that breastfeeding gets off to a good start, whether you've had a c-section or not.

Skin-to-Skin

Skin-to-skin is the practice of holding your naked (or diapered only) baby against your bare chest--and isn't just for premature babies. Full-term babies benefit from it as well. It is within the first hour after birth that a newborn is most alert and ready to interact, and the sucking reflex is at its strongest. That sucking reflex won't be as strong again until nearly forty hours later. The initial time spent at the breast, skin-to-skin, allows you both to bond and teaches your baby the first lessons in breastfeeding. Many times, when being held between his mother's breasts, a baby will bob and weave and search out the nipple on his own. If you can't practice skin-to-skin within the first hour, don't worry; skin-to-skin can be used at home to awaken your baby's feeding behaviors and allow you to learn your baby's feeding cues. Fathers, too, can practice skin-to-skin. Babies love the deep rumble of a male voice and the feel of chest hair.

Feeding Cues

While practicing skin-to-skin, you are given the perfect opportunity to learn about the feeding cues your baby is giving you. Babies do best at feeding when they are calm. A baby will show you feeding cues long before he begins to cry. Some cues to look for include rapid eye movement, rousing from sleep, smacking or licking his lips, sticking his tongue out, bringing his fists to his face, turning his head, and rooting on anything nearby. These cues or signs can be very subtle. But they let you know he is hungry.

Don't wait for him to cry. Crying is a late sign of hunger, and your baby will act frantic (he is!) and be very disorganized, making latching difficult. You will need to calm him down (via skin-to-skin) before trying to feed him. He will also become exhausted from crying and will likely fall right to sleep once you do finally get him latched. Feed your baby at the first signs of hunger.

It is important that you pay attention to your baby and not the clock. Feed your baby when he shows signs of hunger and trust that his body knows what is best. Listen to your instincts about what is best for baby, not what your friend or mother-in-law may tell you. Breastfeeding is wonderful in that it allows you to learn to read your baby's unspoken language. It teaches you and your baby to trust one another and deepens your attachment, both of which are very important to the military mother.

Latch and Positioning

Knowing how to hold your baby and what a good latch looks (and feels) like can make the difference between an easy or rough start to breastfeeding. Proper latch and positioning can prevent or reduce sore nipples, stimulate your milk production, and ensure a plentiful milk supply weeks from now. A bad latch and incorrect positioning, on the other hand, often lead to sore and cracked nipples, a decrease in milk supply, and weaning. There are two "styles" of positioning: baby-led, where the baby is allowed to follow his instinctive feeding behaviors; and mother-led, where you support the breast and guide, position, and help your baby to latch. The biggest difference between them is that baby-led feeding is based on trusting your baby and allowing him to figure it out on his own versus mother-led feeding that is based on controlling your baby's movements and following certain steps. You should practice both styles and see which one works better for you and your baby.

Baby-led feeding. Healthy, full-term babies are born knowing "how" to breastfeed (Smillie, 2008). It is up to us, as mothers, to learn how to recognize, accept, and support their reflexes, behaviors, and movements when they are attempting to latch. There is a set of predictable behaviors that all babies go through to find, latch, and feed from the breast. Allowing your baby to go through these at his own pace will lead to successful breastfeeding. Baby-led feeding can be used right from the start. But as Dr. Christina Smillie found in her practice, skin-to-skin works wonders with even older babies. She had babies in her practice who had never breastfed at six, eight, and even 12 weeks. Once they had skin-to-skin contact with their mothers, this contact triggered their inborn feeding behaviors.

In baby-led positioning, you need to support yourself with pillows so that you are leaning back slightly, and you should be bare-chested (as is your baby), with your bodies remaining in contact with one another at all times. Do not swaddle your baby as this limits his movements and disrupts his natural instincts. The skin-to-skin contact will help awaken his natural feeding behaviors. Your baby will begin to bob his head and cycle his arms and legs;

he may brush your nipple and try sucking on his own hands. Have patience; he needs to go through these movements to organize himself for feeding. Let his feet rest on your body or a pillow for support. Once you have both found a comfortable position, you may put a hand on his back to provide stability. Your baby will touch your breast with his face, usually chin first, his mouth will open, and his head will tip back as he latches. It is very important that your baby has breast to chin contact for the best latch. This style of feeding takes a lot of patience and trust on your part, but is worth it in the long run.

Mother-led feeding. These are the positions that most mothers are familiar with from books, DVDs, and breastfeeding classes. They are the cradle, cross-cradle, football (clutch), and lying down positions. In all mother-led feeding positions, you are controlling where and how your baby is positioned. This style of feeding is best used for babies that are having trouble with baby-led feeding (due to a medical issue or medications during labor) or if you feel more comfortable with structure and defined steps to follow. You can still apply some of the baby-led feeding steps here by trusting what your baby is doing and giving him time to master each step.

With any style of positioning, you need to be comfortable. Have pillows (bed pillows are best, but try a variety to see what "fits" you best) available for yourself and your baby. Pillows allow you to recline and lift your baby to the level of your breasts, and give support to your arms so that he can be well supported throughout the feeding. Bring your baby to the breast, NOT the breast to the baby! Most women find it helpful to support their breast, especially in the early days and weeks or if they have heavy or large breasts (you can use a rolled up towel or burp cloth). Be sure that you cup your breast with four fingers below and your thumb on top, parallel to your baby's lips. Your fingers need to be well behind the areola and away from the nipple to prevent your fingers from getting in the way when your baby latches.

Cross cradle. *This is an excellent learning position; it is also very useful if you have a small baby or one who is having trouble latching, as it gives you a good view of his mouth on your breast.* Support your baby with the opposite forearm and hand of the breast being used (right hand and arm, left breast). Support your breast with the same hand (left hand, left breast). Make sure your baby is chest-to-chest and tummy-to-tummy with you and that his shoulders, hips, and feet are all in a line. The hand that is supporting your baby should be placed with the palm between his shoulder blades and your thumb and forefinger behind his ears. The arm supporting him can be used to quickly guide him on when he latches. Your nipple should be pointed at his nose for a deep latch.

Cradle. *A popular position better suited for the older, experienced baby after the learning period.* Support your baby with his head on your forearm and your hand cupping his bottom or thigh. His whole body should be faced towards you, tummy-to-tummy, and his lower arm should be tucked under your breast or around your waist. You can use your opposite hand to support your breast. His nose needs to be pointed at your nipple for a deep, asymmetrical latch.

Football. *Another popular position for small babies, those having trouble latching on, or mothers with c-sections, flat nipples, or large breasts. This position allows you to see your baby's mouth and move his head easily.* In this position, you place your baby to nurse on the same side as your supporting arm (right breast, right arm). Support your breast with the opposite hand (right breast, left hand). Hold your baby like a football, with his head at your breast (remember nose to nipple) and his feet towards your back. If you are in a chair, you can bend his body at the hips, so his bottom is on the back of the chair and his feet point up (a pillow behind your back is helpful). Your forearm supports his back and your hand supports his shoulders, neck, and base of his head (another pillow under your arm is useful here). To prevent the reflex that will cause him to arch his back and head away from the breast, keep direct pressure off the back his head.

Lying down. *Excellent position for resting after a cesarean section or at night (see the section on Safe Sleep in this chapter).* To start, roll onto one side and put several pillows against your back, one under your head, and

another between your knees. Keep your back and hips in a straight line and place your lower arm around your baby, his head will be in the crook of your elbow. Pull him in close and turn him on his side so that you are both facing tummy-to-tummy. His nose should be pointed towards your nipple, and you can use your opposite (upper) hand to support your breast.

Asymmetrical Latch technique. It used to be that mothers were taught to center the nipple in their baby's mouth. But now we know that babies can remove milk better and more efficiently if they have more breast tissue against the tongue and lower jaw. To latch your baby asymmetrically:

1. Stroke your baby's lip with your nipple to get him to open his mouth.

2. Repeat until he opens his mouth wide, like a yawn, with his tongue down.

3. Bring his chin and lower jaw to the breast first, aiming his lower lip as far away from the nipple as possible.

4. Jaw should be wide open, lips flanged, chin pressed against breast.

Some tips to keep in mind for a proper latch include: In all of the positions (cradle, cross cradle, football, and lying down), your baby's nose should be lined up with your nipple and his chin should make contact with your breast first. Latching this way makes him latch with more of the areola below the nipple, which allows the breast to go deeper into his mouth. A deep latch means more effective milk removal (sucking is triggered by the **nipple** at the hard and soft **palate** junction on the roof of the mouth).

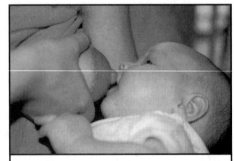

Proper latching-on

Used with permission, B. Wilson-Clay, K. Hoover, Normal Breastfeeding Photo Set, www.BreastfeedingMaterials.com, 2009.

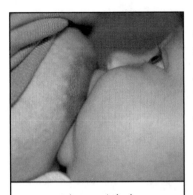

Asymmetric latch

Used with permission, B. Wilson-Clay, K. Hoover, The Breastfeeding Atlas. 4th ed. 2008.

With a proper latch, you should see more areola above the top lip (keeping in mind that areola sizes differ among women, a small areola may disappear entirely with a wide, deep latch). Your baby's tongue will be visible between the breast and lower gum, and his lips should be flanged out. If they are not, you can gently flip them out with your finger. If his nose is buried in the breast, bring his lower body closer to yours to help tilt his head back and bring his chin into the breast (go to www. breastfeedingmadesimple.com and click on the tab to view an animated latch).

Don't shove or push your nipple in his mouth, and remember to keep the base of your hand at his shoulders and upper back, and not on his head. Your baby should be compressing the milk ducts, NOT the nipple. You will feel tugging on your nipple, but it should not be uncomfortable. If it is, unlatch him by sliding your pinky into the corner of his mouth to break suction, and try again. Your nipple should come out looking like it did going in, rounded… not flattened or like a tube of lipstick. If you hear clicking, see his cheeks pulling inwards, or feel pain, take him off and try again. If the nipple pain continues or gets worse (remember, it should NOT hurt!), then see the section on Sore Nipples later in this chapter.

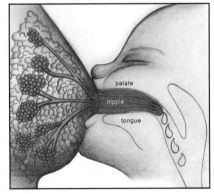

Engorgement

You've probably heard from friends or co-workers about engorgement, and how painful and uncomfortable it can be. Engorgement is the swelling and filling with milk of your breasts that occurs when your milk "comes-in." Your breasts will become larger, firmer, heavier, warmer, and oftentimes tender. This generally occurs about two to three days after the birth of your baby for a normal, vaginal, full-term birth. Engorgement can be delayed if you have had a cesarean or medications during labor. It is usually worse in first-time mothers or mothers who do not breastfeed often in the first few days.

Engorgement occurs when your milk becomes more abundant, and it can be prevented by nursing on demand or at least every two hours from birth. But engorgement is not due just to milk, it is also caused by increased fluids and blood flow to the breast. Your breasts may be engorged because of IV fluids you received during labor. Should your breasts become rock hard, swollen, or tender despite frequent nursing, there are a few things you can do keep the milk flowing and reduce the swelling:

- Use a pump or hand expression to soften the breast enough for your baby to latch.

- Apply warm, moist heat to your breasts, stand in the shower with warm water flowing over your breasts, or lean over and soak your breasts in a sink of warm water right before nursing.

- Use cold packs between nursing sessions, 20 minutes on, 20 minutes off.

- Apply cabbage leaves (washed) inside your bra, wear them until they wilt, and then replace.

- If pain is severe, you can take a mild pain reliever.

- If engorgement is severe or lasts beyond 24-48 hours, you need to see an IBCLC.

If your breasts remain engorged, it can affect your milk supply. But more importantly, engorgement makes it hard for your baby to latch correctly because your nipple is flattened out. If he cannot latch correctly, he can't remove milk, and this can lead to sore nipples. There is a technique you can use called Reverse Pressure Softening (RPS) to help reduce the swelling around your nipples, so your baby can latch properly (Cotterman, 2004). RPS works by moving the extra fluid away from the areola, relieves overfull ducts, and often triggers a let-down. It is done by practicing the following steps (http://www. kellymom/bf/concerns/mom/rev_pressure_soft_cotterman.html):

- Using your fingertips (if your nails are short), place six fingers on your breast, three on each side at the base of your nipple.

- Press inward towards your ribs, firmly but gently (this should be painless).

- Hold the pressure from one to five minutes or until you see "dimples" or can feel the areola softening.

- Do RPS sitting up or lying down (lying down will speed the process).

- Quickly latch your baby after removing your fingers.

Remember that nursing frequently after birth should prevent engorgement from occurring. But if it does happen, you can still breastfeed. Engorgement is usually temporary, so don't give up. And get help if it is not getting better within 24-48 hours.

Frequency of Feeds

What is normal when it comes to how often a newborn should nurse? You've probably heard everything from "whenever he demands" to "no more than every four hours." So which is it? Here is the short version: **newborns need to eat frequently**. Most newborns will nurse *at least* 8-12 times in 24 hours, or about every one and a half to three hours during the day and up to four hours during the night. Most babies get their days and nights mixed up for the first few days, and many babies like to *cluster feed* (several feedings close together, about every 30-60 minutes, usually in the evenings). This is all normal! However, some babies do NOT ask to nurse a whole lot in the first two to three days because they are sleepy or uninterested. But if they are in contact with their mothers, they breastfeed more frequently than if separated—even while they are sleepy.

Childbirth medications can make breastfeeding very difficult by causing babies to be sleepy or not able to nurse effectively. If you've had medications during labor, it will be up to you to wake your baby every two to three hours. If your baby is sleeping longer than three hours and you do not wake him to nurse, you could put your milk supply jeopardy. You can and should wake him by doing the following: loosen or remove his clothing, do skin-to-skin, burp him, try massage, or wipe him with a cool washcloth. It is important to wake him and keep him awake for feedings until he can manage it on his own. Most babies will "wake-up" or snap out of it around the time your milk "comes-in."

One of the best things you can do is "watch the baby, not the clock," meaning pay attention to your baby and the cues and clues he is giving you. He'll let you know when he is hungry (lip smacking, rooting) and when he is full (coming off the breast, limp and drowsy). All YOU have to do is pay attention! Remember, he has been fed 24/7 while you were carrying him. And his body is growing at a remarkable pace right now. So he needs and wants to be fed often.

Something to keep in mind is the size of your baby's stomach. All too often we forget, or are just not aware, how tiny a newborn's stomach really is! The average full-term newborn's tummy on day one is the size of a shooter marble and can only hold one teaspoon of breastmilk. By day three, his tummy is about the size of a ping pong ball and can hold about five teaspoons. And by day ten, his tummy can hold about one-third of a cup of breastmilk. Because his stomach is so small and can hold only small amounts and because breastmilk digests so quickly, it's no wonder that he asks to nurse so frequently in the first days.

You should let him finish breastfeeding at his own pace (remember, pay attention to your baby and the cues he gives you). At some nursing sessions, he may finish one side and root around looking for the other breast. While other times, he will conk out after only one side. Babies will normally fall asleep or pull off the breast if they have full tummies, even after only nursing from one side. You can take this time to burp him, change his diaper, and offer the other side. But don't be alarmed if he doesn't nurse. Just remember to start with that breast at the next feeding. If for some reason you need to take him off the breast before he is done, do NOT pull him off, as that will only cause pain and trauma to your nipples. Instead put your pinky finger in the corner of his mouth, between the gums, and break the suction. Then you can remove your breast.

Is My Baby Getting Enough?

You've read the books, watched the DVDs, and followed all the directions. But you still aren't sure your baby is "really" getting anything to eat. Just how are you supposed to know for sure? While we don't have graduated marks on our breasts with an "E" and an "F" to help us know, there are a number of signs to look for. Keep in mind that these signs are not set in stone, and they vary from baby to baby. These are averages, and some of them need to be looked at together.

Watch your baby while he nurses. There are some definite signs that you can see and hear that will let you know that he is nursing correctly and receiving milk. You should hear him swallowing, a soft "cuh" sound when your baby exhales, about every suck or two. You might also see his ears wiggle, and if you watch closely, he will nurse with rhythmic, wide, slow motions of his jaw. He will have a brief pause at the widest open point, that is when the milk is filling his mouth before he swallows.

Your baby will be alert, content, and gaining weight at a steady rate. He should be waking up to nurse on his own about every two to three hours (at least 8-12 times) in 24 hours. His eyes should remain open while nursing, he will come off the breast by himself, and you might see milk pooling in his mouth or dribbling down his chin. He will become drowsy and full, and your breasts will feel softer and lighter at the end of each feeding. His little fists will unclench and hang loosely at his sides, and he will act satisfied between feedings. While it is normal for breastfed babies to lose a few ounces in the first few days (no more than 10%), they should be back up to birth weight by 10 days, and continue gaining weight (about four to seven ounces a week) after that.

The most reliable sign that he is getting enough to eat are his diapers… what goes in must come out! During the first few days, before your milk comes in, he should have one dirty diaper for each day of life (Day One = one poop,

Day Two = two poops, etc.). By the fourth or fifth day, your baby should have six to eight wet diapers every 24 hours, and the urine should be a pale or clear color. *(You may want to put a strip of toilet paper or a liner inside a disposable diaper to tell if it is wet)*. Your baby's stools should have changed from black and tarry to green to a seedy, yellow color. He should have two to five stools every 24 hours after your milk has increased. Some babies poop and pee every time they eat. Others save it up for a few large deposits.

★ How to Tell if Your Baby is Getting Enough Breastmilk ★

- Your baby is emptying your breast 8-12 times in 24 hours.

- Your baby is alert, content, and gaining weight at a steady rate.

- When your baby nurses, you can see his ears wiggle and hear (or see) swallowing after every one to two sucks.

- Your baby comes off the breast by himself and seems satisfied.

- Your breasts feel softer and lighter at the end of each feeding.

- Your baby has six to eight wet diapers and two to five stools every 24 hours.

Some mothers do not make enough milk. Usually, it is due to not breastfeeding often enough or because of a poor latch. Rarely, a mother actually does not have enough glandular tissue or has a hormonal imbalance, which causes her to not make a sufficient amount of milk. Often, she will notice that her breasts didn't grow at all during the pregnancy or her milk doesn't come in during the first week after birth. If you feel that this is a possibility, you should see an IBCLC as soon as possible. If you are really worried that your baby is not getting enough breastmilk, there are signs of dehydration to look for:

- **He is listless or acts sick.**

- **His urine is dark yellow.**

- **His mouth and lips are dry.**

- **His fontanel (soft spot) is sunken in.**

All of these signs are serious, and you need to take your baby to the hospital as soon as possible.

During the first few days and weeks, some babies will fall asleep at the breast if the flow of milk isn't fast enough for them, which leads to them actually NOT getting enough to eat. **Breast compressions** are one way of getting your baby to stay interested in the breast and to help him get enough milk while he's there. They work by mimicking a let-down and often will actually stimulate a let-down as well. Breast compressions keep the flow of milk going, and your baby will get more hindmilk, too. You can use breast compressions for a baby that is not gaining well, for one that is fussy at the breast, and while pumping to get extra milk. Here is how to do breast compressions:

- Hold your baby in whichever position is most comfortable.

- Use your free hand to hold the breast with your thumb on one side and fingers on the other, well away from the nipple.

- Watch your baby, when he slows down and is nibbling, compress your breast firmly, but gently. Do not hurt yourself.

- Hold the compression once he starts drinking again and release when he stops sucking. Some mothers prefer to hold the compressions, others like to do compressions in a rhythmic fashion. Either way works, find what works best for you.

- Once he is no longer sucking at all, even with compressions, switch to the other side and repeat.

Growth Spurts

Everything has been going smoothly for a few weeks. You've both settled into a comfortable rhythm. And you're enjoying this whole breastfeeding thing when suddenly your baby is asking to nurse ALL THE TIME. He'll act fussy and famished all day long. You may think that you aren't making enough milk, but that is NOT the case. This is a growth spurt! Babies go through periods of nursing more often (sometimes MUCH more often) at about ten days, four to six weeks, three months, and again around six months. They nurse more often in an attempt to build up your milk production. And this insatiable appetite only lasts a day or two before subsiding back into that normal pattern again.

The best thing that you can do is trust that your baby knows what he is doing and allow him to nurse as much as he wants over these growth-spurt days. You may feel as though you aren't getting anything else done when you are nursing 12-18 times in 24 hours. But it doesn't last forever! Quickly enough (usually within 24-48 hours), your breasts will ramp up their production of milk--remember "supply and demand"--and your baby will go back to his usual routine. (See Chapter 10 for information on dealing with growth spurts when you are back at work.) Another item to keep in mind—it is very normal for your breasts to feel softer and not as full right around the 10-14 day period, just when your baby is also having a growth spurt. You may worry that you don't have any milk. You have plenty of milk. The softness of your breasts is due to the initial swelling having gone down. Remember, this is normal. Keep nursing frequently, and you will make plenty of milk for your baby during his growth spurts.

Many times, mothers are told to supplement during a normal growth spurt under the mistaken notion that because your baby is asking to nurse "all the time," he must not be getting anything. Giving a supplement during a growth spurt, or at any time really, is the worst possible thing to do--unless it is medically indicated. Supplements, especially in the early days and weeks or during a growth spurt, tell your breasts NOT to make milk at the exact time they need the extra stimulation to make MORE milk. Supplementation interferes with your baby learning how to breastfeed properly and disrupts the establishment of your milk supply. It changes your baby's appetite, too. He'll be full when your breasts need emptying (which then means you need to pump). And since formula takes longer to digest, he'll still be full for the next feeding, too.

Here's what usually happens when supplements are given:

- You think your baby needs or are told to give a bottle of formula.

- Your baby sleeps for three to four hours and misses a breastfeeding session.

- Your breasts make less milk because they didn't get the signal (emptying the breast) to make more milk.

- Your baby is fussy at the next breastfeeding because your breasts now are making less milk.

- You give another bottle because you think he really is hungry. So your breasts make even less milk (due to another missed feeding and lack of stimulation).

- The cycle repeats with an ever lower supply of breastmilk and more supplementation.

- Eventually, your baby is completely on formula.

Most supplements are given in a bottle, and artificial nipples can alter the way your baby latches to the breast. This can cause you pain if he tries to latch onto you like he does the bottle. Or he may become accustomed to the faster flow of the artificial nipple and prefer it over your breast where he has to "work" for his food. This has nothing to do with introducing the bottle for your return to work. Instead, it is about giving unneeded supplements in the early days and weeks while breastfeeding is getting started. Once breastfeeding is firmly established and going well, then you can introduce the bottle, usually around the four-week mark (see Chapter 10 for more information on Introducing a Bottle). Supplementation for a newborn is hardly ever needed, except in unusual cases, and then should be done under the supervision of an IBCLC.

Pacifiers

Pacifiers are often given as baby shower gifts and are seen as a totally harmless baby item. Many parents find them indispensable for helping to care for and soothe a new baby. Unfortunately, there are some very real risks of pacifier use, especially in the first days and weeks. Pacifiers interfere with the establishment of your milk supply, and they require that your baby use a different suck (which can lead to both nipple confusion and sore nipples). Pacifiers are known to lead to increased illnesses, as well as early weaning from the breast, and if used long-term can interfere with proper tooth development. Of course, there are some very valid reasons to use a pacifier, such as for a baby with a high sucking need or when you are separated during the day at work. But for the most part, they are not needed and cause more trouble than they are worth.

If you choose to use a pacifier, there are certain guidelines you can follow that help to minimize the risks. Breastfed babies do best with a pacifier that has a cylindrical shape and wide base to more closely mimic the latch at the breast. It is important that you also choose one that is the correct size for the age of your baby (see the book, *Balancing Breast and Bottle: Reaching Your Breastfeeding Goals*, for more information). It is best to wait at least three to four weeks after birth to introduce a pacifier, once your milk supply is fully established. Whenever your baby uses a pacifier, be sure to check that his lips flange out and that his suck is same as when he is breastfeeding. Here are some further guidelines to follow that will help protect breastfeeding:

- Do not use except during separation or car rides.

- Avoid offering the pacifier 30-60 minutes before feeding (so you can see feeding cues).

- Don't use the pacifier to space feedings (you risk your milk supply).

- Don't use during a growth spurt.

- Don't offer when baby is content.

- Don't offer a pacifier to satisfy boredom, instead change his position or environment (or wear him in a sling, see next page).

There are a few more do's and don'ts and things to watch out for when it comes to using a pacifier. If you notice that your baby is having trouble latching or staying on the breast, not gaining weight, fussy at the breast, nursing less often, or getting sick more often, or if you are suffering from nipple pain, then you may want to stop using the pacifier. These are all signs that the pacifier is interfering with your breastfeeding relationship. Be sure that you sterilize the pacifier every day to prevent illnesses, and wean your baby off the pacifier by four months. Beyond four months, your baby can become emotionally attached to the pacifier, and it will be much harder to wean him from it. Continued pacifier use can interfere with beginning speech. Don't be alarmed if your baby refuses to use a pacifier. There are some babies that are very smart and will refuse to use a pacifier, realizing that it is a poor substitute for the real thing!

Pacifiers are great for entertaining babies and keeping them busy and quiet, especially when you must get dinner on the table or need to drive somewhere. Very often though, parents use pacifiers to stop them from fussing instead of finding out what is wrong. A pacifier should never be a replacement for your attention, but instead should be a tool that is used at certain times when it is really needed, such as when your breast is unavailable. When you are available, there is nothing wrong with using your breast to pacify your baby; and in fact, when you are at home that is the best thing to offer, instead of the pacifier. Offering your breast to your baby when he fusses has benefits for you both: it teaches him that his needs can be met by you, and it will help boost your milk supply as well. Used in moderation and for the right reasons, pacifiers can be a life-saver. Just don't use pacifiers as a way of life, especially if you value your breastfeeding relationship with your baby.

"Spoiling" Your Baby and Babywearing

It is a fact of life that babies cry and fuss for all sorts of reasons, as it is their only way to communicate with you and let you know that something is wrong. Crying is your baby's way of telling you he has a need to be held, rocked, changed, fed, burped, or soothed (although crying is a late sign of hunger, don't let it get that far!). It really doesn't matter what the reason is. When a baby cries, it is a very real need that needs to be responded to. When you meet his needs by picking him up, and he hears your voice and feels your arms and stops crying, then that is what he needs. You will not spoil your baby by picking him up and responding to his cries. By responding to his cries, you are teaching him trust and that his needs will get met. However, if these needs are not met, and he is allowed to cry hard and for long periods of time, the prolonged crying can cause an increase in his stress hormones, which increases his heart rate and can possibly eventually impact his brain development. Your baby also learns that crying does no good and that there is no one to trust to take care of his needs, which could lead to possible later emotional problems.

Some babies cry more than others, and some are "high-needs" babies who require *much* more holding and cuddling. So you may be wondering how you are supposed to manage with a newborn and get anything done. One option for meeting your baby's needs is to carry him in a sling or front-carrier. Studies have shown that babies who are carried cry 43% less (Hunziker & Barr, 1986) than babies who are not. Carrying your baby satisfies his need for being held, soothed, fed (you can nurse in a sling), and it allows you to manage household duties since your hands are free. Biologically speaking, we are meant to carry our infants on our bodies. Our milk is low in fat and requires that we nurse our babies often. And our babies are born with a grasping reflex to hold onto the hair that no longer covers our bodies. Carrying your baby replicates the time in the womb, where he was rocked and heard your heartbeat 24/7. It is kind of like a fourth trimester, a transition period where he can hear your voice and heartbeat, smell you, and be near you.

Most importantly for you as a working mother, after your return to duty, wearing your baby when you are at home will greatly increase the daily contact between you and your baby. The frequent interaction and physical contact of wearing your baby has been shown to increase prolactin, one of the mothering hormones, which is so important for maintaining your milk supply. Many military mothers have found that wearing their babies in a sling when at home or running errands is a great way to spend quality time and offsets the effects of the daily separations.

There are many different types of front carriers, slings, and backpacks available for carrying your baby. Front carriers and slings (either adjustable ring-type or pouch style) are best for younger babies, while backpacks are better for older babies/toddlers. Front carriers can be cumbersome to use as they have a number of buckles and straps. They are good only to about 15-20 pounds, and it is virtually impossible to breastfeed in them. Slings, on the other hand, slip easily over one shoulder and across the body, can be used in a variety of positions, and are good from birth to about three years old (35-40 pounds). You can easily and discreetly breastfeed your baby in the sling, and if your baby falls asleep in the sling, you can slip out

Wearing your baby in a sling
Photo courtesy Robyn Roche-Paull.
Used with permission.

of it, leaving your baby sleeping peacefully. It is important that you practice using the sling often with your baby, and don't give up if you or your baby don't like it at first. Like anything new, using a sling (and carrying your baby) takes some getting used to. Slings can be found at some maternity stores, LLL groups often sell them, or you can order one online.

Be sure you do NOT buy a so-called "bag" sling, such as those that were recently recalled by the CPSC, as they do not allow for proper and safe wearing positions. Any sling or front carrier you choose should keep your baby in an upright position, snug to your chest, and close to your face (unless you are actively breastfeeding). Make sure your baby is not curled up in a chin-to-chest position and that his back is straight and supported. Monitor your baby while he is in the sling and be sure nothing obstructs his face. Wearing your infant in a well-constructed sling and using proper babywearing techniques makes babywearing a beneficial and safe parenting tool.

Here are some very basic directions for using a sling. You can also look online for videos demonstrating how to properly and safely wear a sling (see Appendix B):

- Lift sling over head, place padded section on shoulder and rings where a corsage would go.

- Fluff fabric so it is not twisted.

- Balance baby on your shoulder (one without the sling) and guide his feet into the sling. For newborns, you may fold a small receiving blanket or towel under him for added support.

- Pull up three to five inches of sling between you and baby.

- With one hand under baby, lift him, and with other hand, pull on tab of sling to cinch it tighter, sling and baby should be right under your breasts.

- Walk or rock or jiggle to help him settle in sling.

As with most things parenting related, you need to find what works for you and your baby. Carrying your baby and using a sling isn't for everyone. If you find that you or your baby simply aren't enjoying it, then don't continue. A sling is just another tool to use to help you stay close to your baby. You don't need to hold and carry your baby every second of the day that you are at home to form a strong bond with your baby. But don't be scared to pick him up or carry him for fear of spoiling him. It just isn't possible. Babies have always needed to be picked up and carried when they fuss, and you are meeting his needs by doing so.

Safe Sleep

New parents are often asked, "Is your baby sleeping through the night yet"? It seems to be a rite of passage, at least here in the United States, to have your baby sleeping through the night as soon as possible after birth. And as a new parent and a working mother, you want and need your sleep. But babies don't sleep through the night, especially not breastfed babies--and for good reason. The milk-making hormone, prolactin, is highest between 0100 and 0500 hours, and your milk is also higher in fat at those hours. If you choose not to nurse at night, you are depriving your baby of needed calories for growth *and* sending the message to your breasts that they don't need to make milk. Breastfed babies wake to breastfeed about every two hours, even during the night, especially in the first few months. Formula-fed babies sleep longer (about four hours), due to the curd in the formula that is harder to digest. But very few babies sleep through the night, period. In fact, it is a myth that babies "sleep through the night," since the medical definition of sleeping through the night is considered one unbroken stretch of sleep of five hours.

So how do military mothers manage to feed their babies and get some much needed rest? Many choose to share sleep (co-sleep or bed-share) with their babies, and this makes particularly good sense for breastfed babies. Sharing sleep with a breastfed baby makes life easy for everyone involved. Because your sleep cycles are in sync, you are in a light sleep period as your baby begins rooting around for the nipple, you wake just enough to latch him on, and drift back to sleep. Your baby nurses without ever fully awakening and pops off when he is done, falling back into a deep sleep. You both get a full night's sleep, even if your baby wakens to nurse three to four times, as neither of you wakes up fully. Contrast this with the baby who spends the night alone in a crib in another room. He must wake up fully and cry loud enough and long enough to be heard by you down the hall. You too must wake up fully to get out of bed and pick him up, sit in a chair, and nurse him, and then carefully lay him back down in his crib. Repeat this three or four times through the night, and you can see why so many parents bring their babies into bed. In fact, researchers have found that mothers who breastfeed and share sleep get *more* sleep at night than formula-feeding mothers (Kendall-Tackett & Hale, 2009; Quillin & Glenn, 2004).

Many active-duty mothers feel that the benefits of sharing sleep go beyond the obvious easier breastfeeding and more sleep to include being together for an additional eight to nine hours of physical contact. It may not seem like much since you will both be asleep, but it is comforting for you both. Sharing sleep and allowing your baby to nurse at night also helps to maintain your milk supply. Some breastfed babies will make the decision for you by sleeping at daycare and not eating, but then will breastfeed frequently throughout the night, virtually requiring that he share sleep with you. This is called reverse-cycle feeding and is very normal, and not at all harmful. In fact, many mothers find that reverse-cycle feeding and bringing baby to bed is a wonderful thing, as it allows you to feel close to your baby and feed him, while decreasing the amount of pumped breastmilk needed at daycare.

Much like picking your baby up when he cries or wearing him, friends and family may tell you that allowing your baby to sleep with you will cause him to become spoiled, have emotional problems, or that he will never leave your bed. Just as with crying and carrying, when your baby is ready and his needs have been met, he will move to his own bed. Babies and children who sleep with their parents are very well-adjusted and require less psychiatric help than those who don't sleep with their parents (Forbes, Weiss, & Folen, 1992). Sleeping with your baby is the cultural norm in many places in the world, including other industrialized nations like Japan. And interestingly enough, SIDS cases are much lower in those countries where co-sleeping is the norm than here in the United States. Some of the reasons that sharing sleep may be protective against SIDS are due to the following: close proximity to mother and shared sleep cycles, lighter sleep and more arousals, sucking, and fewer illnesses in breastfed infants.

There are numerous ways to share sleep, none of which are any better or worse than another, but all share the same safety measures. Some parents find that dropping the rail of the crib and putting it right up along-side the adult bed works. While other parents buy a ready-made "Co-Sleeper" unit that attaches to the adult bed. Many parents start the baby out in their own crib, and then bring baby to bed with them at the first nursing session, while others choose to have baby in bed with them all night. If you choose to bed-share, follow these guidelines:

- Do not sleep with your baby if you or your partner is under the influence of alcohol or prescription drugs that make you sleepy.

- Do not sleep with your baby if you or your partner smokes.

- Do not sleep with your baby if you or your partner is obese.

- Do not co-sleep on a couch, sofa, recliner, or waterbed. Lay your baby down on a firm, flat, regular mattress.

- Make sure there is no space between the mattress and headboard or wall that would allow your baby's head to become entrapped.

- Do not have pillows, duvets, comforters, or stuffed animals near your baby.

- Do not leave your baby alone on an adult bed.

- Do not place your baby on a bed with other children or pets.

- Place your baby on his back (supine) to sleep.

Like most things to do with parenting and babies, you need to find what works for you and your situation. Your sleep is vitally important to your well-being and health. You may find that sharing sleep doesn't work for you and that sleep is a needed priority. No one can function properly at work while sleep deprived, and that can be dangerous, especially if you work with heavy machinery, weapons, or any other job that requires razor-sharp and lightning-fast reflexes. In that case, pumping a bottle of milk the last thing at night for your partner to give to your baby might be best for all concerned. However, if you find that sharing sleep is what works for your family, then rest assured that it is a healthy and wonderful way to remain close to your baby. It allows for breastfeeding through the night and can be done safely if you follow the guidelines given above. There is a lot more information available about co-sleeping (this book has only covered the main points). See the Resources section for the titles of some books that are highly recommended.

Chapter 5
Common Concerns

From premature babies to tattoos, this chapter gives a quick overview and explanation of some of the more common concerns and problems that can occur anytime during your breastfeeding career. This chapter cannot begin to cover the many concerns and questions that all mothers have about breastfeeding. So I urge you to have a comprehensive breastfeeding book handy and the name and number of a lactation consultant or La Leche League Leader should you need further assistance for anything not covered in this chapter.

Premature Baby

Premature babies are those babies born before 37 weeks of age. Some research points to higher rates of premature births in active-duty mothers, possibly due to the increased work hours, prolonged shift work, and standing (Evans & Rosen, 2000; McNeary & Lomenick, 2000). If you had a premature baby, you can most certainly breastfeed, and in fact, he will do better, as your breastmilk is perfectly suited to his needs. The breastmilk of a mother who has delivered a premature baby is different from the milk of a mother of a full-term baby. It is higher in protein, growth factors, antibodies, and other valuable nutrients, as well as being easier to digest. More importantly, it protects him from necrotizing enterocolitis, a potentially fatal infection.

While you probably will not be able to breastfeed directly at first, especially if he is extremely small, you can begin pumping while in the hospital and build up a good milk supply for when he is ready. Once he is ready to begin breastfeeding, do not be discouraged if he doesn't seem to know how or just licks and nuzzles the breast. It will take time and effort to teach him how to nurse, but will be very much worth it when you see how healthy your baby is. Breastfeeding and providing your breastmilk is something that only you can do, and it has short and long-term benefits for you both. It is very important that you see an IBCLC as soon as possible for help breastfeeding your preemie while in the hospital and later when you go home. An excellent resource for further information on breastfeeding and caring for a premature baby is *The Premature Baby Book: Everything You Need to Know About Your Premature Baby from Birth to Age One* by Dr. Sears.

Twins

If you are so blessed as to have twins, congratulations! You will be in for twice the work--but also twice the joy. And breastfeeding is not only possible (you have two breasts after all), but is actually easier than bottle-feeding. Breastfeeding offers you a way to bond with both babies and provides them with extra immunities and nutrition, something that is especially important since most twins are born early. Many mothers of twins worry (or are told) that they won't make enough milk. But just like nursing a singleton: **the more milk you remove, the more milk you make!** It is tricky learning how to position two babies at the breast, so you will definitely want an extra set of hands in those first few weeks while you learn. Some mothers find that the football hold works best. Others like the cradle hold, with both babies' legs crisscrossing in the middle. You'll need to experiment to find what works best for you. Sometimes you may want to just nurse one baby at a time for some extra one-on-one bonding and a chance for him to get a full feeding from both breasts.

Supplementation should not be needed if you are nursing on demand, and here again, you'll want to experiment to see what works best for you and your babies. Some mothers keep each baby on one breast and switch at the next feeding. Others nurse the babies individually. It is a good idea to keep a log in the first weeks, so you can be sure they are both gaining appropriately. It can be hard to nurse twins, but then it will be hard to parent twins, period...it is twice the work, so you will definitely want to call on your support network of friends and family to help. This section isn't meant to cover all the aspects of breastfeeding twins. You'll want to make an appointment with an IBCLC or a LLL Leader for more in-depth breastfeeding help. I would also recommend that you read a more comprehensive book on breastfeeding twins, such as *Mothering Multiples: Breastfeeding and Caring for Twins or More* by Karen Gromada, for a breastfeeding-friendly approach to raising twins.

Army Major Heather Mace, with her twin boys, breastfed 3.5 years

Photo courtesy Heather Mace. Used with permission.

And lest you think that you'll only be able to nurse your twins during your convalescent leave and then have to quit when you return to work, think again. Here is a quote from Army Major Heather Mace, who breastfed her twin boys until age three and a half years, while serving on active duty, with her thoughts on breastfeeding twins in the military.

Nursing the twins was a personal challenge, as well as a professional one. I was very determined to make nursing work with the twins. But, wow, it was the hardest thing I'd ever done. And the best! I took the six weeks of convalescent leave and an additional 30 days. I had my own office, and I pumped three to four times a day. TDY was a challenge, pumping was difficult because the tasks were concentrated inside of a few short days, and there was not much down time. At about 13 months, I got a nasty case of mastitis, and it was suggested that I wean. I knew that was unnecessary, so I did not. I continued to pump at lunch, and by the time the twins were two, I had dropped pumping and was nursing in the mornings, before and after day care, evenings, and at bedtime. They weaned at three and a half years old.

Sore Nipples

Sore nipples are by far the most common complaint made by new mothers, and usually the first thing you hear about is horror stories from your friends and co-workers. Unfortunately, many women think that having sore nipples is part and parcel of breastfeeding--and that simply is not true. If your nipples ARE sore, then something is wrong and needs to be corrected. Breastfeeding should not hurt! Far too many mothers give up on breastfeeding their babies due to sore nipples. The soreness can range from mild tenderness to toe-curling pain and is usually caused by incorrect latch and positioning. In most cases, sore nipples can be fixed quickly and easily, with the pain resolving within a day or so, *if* you see a La Leche League Leader or IBCLC at the first sign of a problem. It has been said before and it bears repeating: breastfeeding should NOT hurt! If it does, something is wrong.

Prevention of sore nipples is the best medicine, so be sure that your baby is latching properly, and that in all positions, he is being brought TO the breast, rather than bringing the breast to the baby. He should be snuggled in tight to your body, not dangling or hanging away from you, nor should he have his head turned or tilted at an odd angle to the breast. You shouldn't hear any clicking or smacking sounds, and your nipple should not be misshapen when it comes out his mouth. Some mothers will have an initial, very mild tenderness that goes away within seconds during the first few days of nursing that can be considered normal. But anything more than that warrants a closer look at what might be the matter. If you are already suffering from sore nipples, here are some remedies to try *while* you wait to get professional help.

- Nurse on the least sore side first when your baby's suck is the strongest, save the more sore side for when his hunger is subsided.

- Alternate positions at every feeding, this puts pressure on a different spot.

- Nurse more frequently, but for shorter lengths of time, so that he does not become ravenous and suck even harder.

- Take an over-the-counter pain reliever about 20 minutes before nursing.

- Use moist healing to prevent scabs (Lansinoh© or PurLan©) or hydrogel pads.

For very severe sore nipples, where there is bleeding, blistering, or cracking, you may need to rest your nipples for 24 hours and allow them time to heal by pumping and feeding your baby in another manner (cup, medicine dropper, spoon). You will probably need to see your HCP (healthcare provider) for antibiotics, as open wounds can lead to infection. However, if you get help at the first sign of pain, they should not progress to this point. Remember that sore nipples usually mean incorrect latch or positioning. But there could be something inside the baby's mouth that is causing the problem, such as a tongue-tie. If your baby is incorrectly latched, he will not stimulate your breasts correctly and your milk supply will suffer.

There are other reasons for sore nipples, such as thrush, a fungal infection caused by *Candida albicans,* that thrives on the milk on your nipples and in your baby's mouth. Thrush usually starts after the first week of breastfeeding and causes intense pain, itching, and flaking on the nipples, along with a shiny, red rash. It also shows up as white patches in your baby's mouth, along with a bright red diaper rash. Thrush often occurs after a round of antibiotics, when the good and bad bacteria are both wiped out and the normal fungi we all have on our bodies takes over.

If you feel that you might have thrush, you'll need to see your doctor and get a prescription for medication to treat BOTH of you. Keep taking the treatment for two weeks, even if you feel better after only a few days because thrush can be hard to kill. You can also try an over-the-counter anti-fungal, such as Lotrimin©. Just be sure to wipe it off before feeding your baby. Wash all bras and cloth breast pads in hot, soapy water, and be sure to wash your hands to prevent re-infection. If you get a thrush infection once you are back at work, you'll need to boil all your nipples, pacifiers, and bottles, as well as pump parts every day until the infection is clear. You can and should continue to breastfeed throughout a bout with thrush. However, thrush can live in frozen breastmilk and will re-infect your baby if given to him at a later date. You can either toss the frozen, contaminated milk, or you can boil it before using it (although some of the nutrients will be lost).

With any of the above situations, please get help as soon as possible. I cannot stress enough that breastfeeding is NOT supposed to hurt! If it does, something is the matter and it needs to be fixed. This may be true even if someone tells you that your latch "looks fine." There are other problems that can cause sore nipples, such as tongue-tie or Raynaud's, that are beyond the scope of this book. If you have tried all of the suggestions given here and are still in pain, call a LLL Leader or an IBCLC so that she can "see" what is going on and get you on the road to pain-free and enjoyable nursing. If even after a consult you are still in pain, get a second opinion. It's not always obvious what's going on inside the baby's mouth.

Plugged Ducts and Mastitis

Just as the name implies a plugged duct is a milk duct that is plugged and not draining. The milk backs up in the duct, which then becomes hardened and inflamed and often results in a tender spot or lump. The area can become infected if the plug is not loosened and drained. Plugged ducts are not as common as sore nipples, but every bit as bothersome. Most of the time they are your body's way of saying you are doing too much!

Unfortunately, working mothers tend to suffer from plugged ducts more often than their stay-at-home counterparts for a few reasons. Plugged ducts occur when feedings or pumpings are missed or the breast is not drained completely, due to increased activity, fatigue, stress, incorrect positioning and latch, and pressure or anything that restricts the flow of milk (underwire bras, backpack straps, or heavy gear on the chest). Some mothers find that they get plugged ducts when their baby sleeps through the night for the first time. Low fluid intake and eating food high in saturated fat and salt (fast-food, anyone?) can also cause them. Other mothers suffer plugged ducts repeatedly no matter what they do. Plugged ducts are easy to treat if they are caught in time. You will need to break up and move the hardened milk out of the duct by doing the following:

- Go to bed and rest.

- Nurse frequently.

- Start on the affected side and vary position, so all ducts are emptied.

- Apply warm, moist heat, and massage towards nipple. (You may see the plug come out, it will look like strings or beads of dried milk).

- Keep nursing or pumping to fully clear the plug (the milk will not hurt your baby).

If not caught early, a plugged duct can lead to mastitis, a breast infection. Mastitis starts with a red, hard, warm, very painful spot on breast and includes fatigue, fever, and aches (feels like you have the flu). If your fever is high or lasts more than 12 hours, you need to see a doctor and may be prescribed antibiotics. You do NOT need to wean. In fact, you should continue to nurse frequently to keep the milk moving so that you don't become engorged or develop an abscess.

Mastitis tends to cause a drop in milk supply, so your baby will probably ask to nurse constantly anyway. Your milk is safe for your baby: your breast is infected, not your milk. And any antibiotics you are given will not harm your baby. Be sure to finish all your medication, even if you begin to feel better, or the infection might come back. The treatment for mastitis is very similar to plugged ducts: rest and frequent breastfeeding on the affected side, massage, and warm, moist heat. If it is too painful to nurse on the affected side, you can pump (but the best pump is your baby). Mastitis is serious, but if caught early, it usually resolves with 24-48 hours. If left untreated, a breast infection can turn into an abscess, which requires surgical draining.

Jaundice

Jaundice is the yellowing of the eyes and skin due to excess bilirubin (red blood cells that built up in the womb) in the baby's bloodstream that doesn't getting broken down and flushed out quickly enough. There are two types of jaundice: physiological and pathological. Physiological jaundice is normal and often appears after the first 24 hours. It gradually increases, with a peak around three to four days, and then gradually disappears over the next week. Almost all babies suffer from this condition. In fact, some in the medical community believe it has a protective anti-oxidant effect.

Your baby's pediatrician will monitor it, and as long as the bilirubin count doesn't go over 20 mg/dl, it is probably not serious. The higher the bilirubin count, the more yellow your baby will look. Physiological jaundice is normally self-limiting and resolves on its own. But you can help by breastfeeding your baby frequently. Bilirubin is excreted via bowel movements, and breastfeeding is the best medicine, due to colostrum's natural laxative effect. The more you nurse your baby, the more breastmilk he will receive, and the faster he will rid his body of the excess bilirubin.

The second type of jaundice is pathological jaundice. This type of jaundice is serious, but also much rarer. It is usually due to an underlying medical condition, disease, drugs, or blood incompatibility and shows up within the first 24 hours after birth. There is a test that can be administered to determine which type of jaundice your baby has. Pathological jaundice must be treated because if left untreated, it can cause brain damage. Jaundice (of either type) can be treated using phototherapy, special lights that break down the bilirubin, and in neither case should breastfeeding be stopped. If your baby is receiving phototherapy, it can be interrupted for the length of a feeding, or you can request that a phototherapy blanket be used, which will allow you to breastfeed your baby while he continues to receive his treatment. Formula or sugar water should not be given to your baby, as it will not help clear the bilirubin. In fact, formula can make your baby constipated, which will make the problem worse. And sugar water does nothing because jaundice is cleared via bowel movements, not urine.

What about Alcohol, Caffeine, and Smoking?

While you were pregnant, you probably made some lifestyle changes, such as not smoking, not drinking alcohol, and cutting down on your coffee habit. You may be wondering if you'll have to continue to do so now that you are breastfeeding. There is good news and bad news. It is still important to limit your consumption of alcohol, caffeine, and nicotine, but in moderation these substances are OK.

Alcohol passes into breastmilk. Period. And we don't know how much is too much for a developing baby's brain. Some studies have shown motor delays when mothers have as little as one drink a day while breastfeeding, and the American Academy of Pediatrics recommends that mothers do not drink while breastfeeding. While an occasional drink may be acceptable, to be cautious, you will want to delay breastfeeding or pump and dump for two hours after a drink. You are pumping to relieve fullness and maintain your milk supply. Contrary to popular belief, pumping will NOT eliminate the alcohol from your breastmilk any faster. Alcohol leaves your breastmilk at the same rate it leaves your blood. So for every drink you have, you'll need to wait two hours before nursing. If you do decide to drink, do so immediately after nursing and on a full stomach. A breastfeeding mother should not consume more than two drinks a week. Another myth: alcohol does NOT increase your milk supply. In fact, it has been shown to delay and inhibit the let-down reflex and decrease the amount of milk your baby receives.

Caffeine is transferred into breastmilk, but only about one percent of what you drink. Drinking caffeine in moderation, no more than two to three caffeinated drinks a day, is generally OK for most breastfeeding babies. Any more than five drinks a day and you may notice that your baby is overstimulated and unable to sleep. Caffeine is found in coffee, tea, soda, and chocolate, with coffee generally having the highest caffeine content.

While you can breastfeed and continue to smoke, it is best if you quit or at least reduce your habit. Not only are you exposing your baby to the effects of secondhand smoke, but the nicotine and toxins pass through your milk to your baby. If you cannot quit smoking, breastfeeding is still preferable to formula-feeding for moderate smokers. The beneficial effects of breastfeeding against ear infections, wheezing, pneumonia, upper respiratory infections, and SIDS reduce the effects of secondhand smoke. If you must smoke, do NOT smoke around your baby, change your clothes before holding your baby, and smoke immediately after nursing to minimize the nicotine in your milk at the next feeding. Breastfeeding mothers can use the nicotine patch or gum. Be sure to remove the patch at night to reduce the level of nicotine in your milk. Speak with your PCP about the dosage and levels of nicotine in your milk while using the patch or gum.

Illness

If you become ill while breastfeeding, keep breastfeeding! There are very, very few illnesses that require weaning. In fact, for most illnesses, by the time you are showing symptoms (and feeling lousy), your baby has already been exposed. Weaning at this point will just make you feel worse (do you really want mastitis on top of whatever else you are suffering from?) and will stop the flow of antibodies to the illness in your milk from getting to your baby. Continue to nurse while you are sick and follow the usual precautions when ill: wash your hands, drink plenty of fluids (especially if you are vomiting, have diarrhea, or are feverish), and rest as much as possible. Your milk supply might decline a little while you are ill, but nothing that a few days of round the clock nursing won't fix. If you find that your supply is really dipping, you can always supplement with some stored expressed breastmilk. If you are prescribed medications for your illness, be assured that many are safe to take while breastfeeding (see the next paragraph) for most common illnesses.

Medications and Mother's Milk

A big question that many new mothers have is whether it is safe to take medications while breastfeeding. For the most part, yes, it is. But there are a lot of factors that go into any decision regarding taking medications, and this is one area that you will want to discuss with both your HCP and an IBCLC. Unfortunately, many doctors do NOT have updated references on the transfer of medications into breastmilk and instead rely on the information given to them by the drug manufacturer. The drug company information says that it will transfer into milk as they do not want to risk their company reputation. For many doctors then, the easy answer is to tell you to wean or use formula while taking the medication. Talk with an IBCLC who has a copy of the book, *Medications and Mothers' Milk*, to determine if the drug you need to take will be safe. You can also log-on to LACTMED, a drugs and lactation database hosted by the National Library of Medicine, at http://toxnet.nlm.nih.gov/cgi-bin/sis/htmlgen?LACT.

Medications transfer into milk as a result of the chemistry and molecular structure of that individual drug. Some transfer at higher or lower quantities than others, and just because a drug was unsafe while pregnant does not mean it will be unsafe while breastfeeding (and vice versa). Generally only one percent or less of a medication transfers to your baby through breastmilk, but it is dependent on many factors, including how the drug is administered (orally, injected, topically), how well it is absorbed, the size of the molecule, its pH, and so on.

The age of the baby plays a very important role, as well, because your baby's ability to absorb, metabolize, and excrete the medication is crucial to determine how much of the medication will stay in his system. Premature babies are at higher risk of medication problems, as their bodies are just not fully developed, and newborns are less able to clear drugs than an older baby. Furthermore, in the first few weeks after birth, the cells in the breast are loose and open, allowing drugs to pass from the bloodstream into the milk much easier than in later weeks when those cells close up tight. Whether a medication is safe isn't always about it transferring to the baby. Sometimes the concern is the effect of the drug on lactation itself, as a few medications affect milk production.

A final item to consider is how long the medication will need to be taken. Some medications are OK in the short-term, but can build up to unsafe levels if taken long-term. There are, of course, many other factors to consider when discussing medications taken while breastfeeding. This is only a brief overview. Like most things with breastfeeding, you'll need to weigh the risk of the medication and the need to take it for your condition, against the very real risks of using formula. This is not an exhaustive list or a substitute for seeing your PCP, but rather a list of the most common medicines that a breastfeeding mother might need to take (Hale, 2008; Schaefer, 2007).

- **Antibiotics.** Antibiotics are a very common drug used in the early postpartum period and most do not enter the milk in significant levels. Antibiotics can have an effect on the GI tract, mostly causing diarrhea and/or thrush. The Penicillins, Cephalosporins, and Erythromycins are safe to take. The Sulfonamides should not be used in premature babies or in the first 30 days after birth. The Floroquinolones should be used with some caution, and Metronidazole (Flagyl) is safe to take in either the oral or vaginal forms as the infant dose via breastmilk is less than the dose given to premature infants and children.

- **Pain Meds.** The NSAIDs (Non-steroidal anti-inflammatory drugs; Aleve, Motrin, Ibuprofen, Advil) are safe to use while breastfeeding, as the transfer into breastmilk is low. Acetaminophen (Tylenol) is safe, but do not use it long-term at high doses because it can damage your liver. Aspirin is not safe due to the potential to cause Reye's syndrome if your baby has a virus. Morphine, Codeine, and Vicodin are generally safe for major pain control. However, Demerol is not safe while breastfeeding. Use all pain meds sparingly and do not consume alcohol with them.

- **Antidepressants.** All antidepressants are secreted into human milk. However, they have been well studied and most are safe to take while breastfeeding. The tricyclic antidepressants have been around the longest and no long-term developmental delays have been noted. The newer SSRIs (Paxil, Prozac, Zoloft, Celexa, and Lexapro) are considered safe, with Zoloft, Paxil, and Lexapro considered the safest, as very little transfer to the baby. Celexa has shown some sedation in infants.

- **Cold Meds.** Cold and cough medicines are often not very effective at treating symptoms of the common cold or flu. The antihistamine and decongestants in many cold preparations can cause sedation, agitation, and hallucinations in some babies. It has also been shown that cold medicines with pseudoephedrine can lower a mother's milk supply. Nasal sprays can be used on a short-term basis and have been shown to be safe for breastfeeding mothers.

- **Dental Meds.** The primary medicines used by dentists are pain medications and antibiotics (see above), as well as local anesthetics. Local anesthetics, such as lidocaine, transfer into breastmilk in very low amounts, and it is unlikely they would have any side effects on a breastfeeding infant. To be safe, you can pump and dump for four to six hours after receiving the anesthetic to be sure it has cleared your milk, although it is probably not necessary.

- **Vaccinations.** Vaccines are safe for the breastfeeding mother. Vaccines are either the attenuated (weakened) or killed version. Killed version vaccines are safe. The only live, weakened vaccines that should be used with caution are the oral Polio vaccine (wait until the infant is six weeks old), Typhoid vaccine (use the killed version), and Yellow Fever vaccine (do not give if baby is less than six months old). The Smallpox vaccine is contraindicated.

- **Contraception.** Barrier methods, such as condoms and diaphragms, and LAM (see below) have no impact on breastfeeding. Oral or combination contraceptives, especially those with estrogen have been shown to decrease milk production--often dramatically--in breastfeeding mothers. Don't use these in the first six weeks if at all possible. And if you do use an oral contraceptive, use one that is progestin only. If you are on a patch, ring, or any type of contraceptive that has estrogen in it and notice increased fussiness, hunger, and decreased weight gain in your baby, stop taking the birth control immediately. Progesterone-only birth control, such as the Mini-Pill, Nuvaring, Norplant, and the Mirena IUD, do not cause decreased milk production. Some mothers have noted milk production problems after receiving the Depo-Provera shot, especially if it is given in the first six weeks after birth. The morning-after pill is safe for breastfeeding mothers.

  ° **LAM (Lactational Amenorrhea Method).** This is a very effective (98%) form of natural, non-hormonal, and temporary contraception that doesn't affect breastfeeding. It is **critical** that you meet all three criteria for LAM:

- You must be less than six months postpartum.

- Your periods must not have returned yet.

- You must be fully breastfeeding (no more than four hours between feedings/pumping during the day, and six hours at night-no more than one in every ten feedings can be supplements).

- *It is not fully understood what effect pumping and employment has on LAM. If you are at all concerned about becoming pregnant or any one of the above three criteria changes, choose another form of contraception.*

There are a few things to keep in mind when taking any medications that are prescribed to you. Take only medications that are absolutely necessary and take the lowest dose possible that is effective for your condition. Generally speaking, medications that are safe for your baby to take directly are safe for you to take while breastfeeding. It is best to take medications right after nursing so that it has peaked in your milk before the next nursing session, and once-a-day medications should be taken right before your baby's longest sleep period to minimize the amount he ingests. Do not take "no," or the recommendation that you need to wean, for an answer when it comes to medications while breastfeeding. Breastfeeding is the "best" medicine you can give your baby. So be adamant that breastfeeding is important to you and insist that your doctor take the time to research and find a suitable medication.

Postpartum Depression

Postpartum depression (PPD) is very real--and it hurts. It hurts the women who suffer from it and the babies whose mothers have it, as well as the family members who try to help the mother suffering from it. It is a very real condition, and it is not "all in your head." While many women may have a brief period of the "baby blues," a period of a few hours to days of weepiness, the baby blues are usually transient and over as quickly as they started.

Between 15%-25% of all women suffer from PPD, which is more severe than the baby blues (Kendall-Tackett, 2010). It can begin anytime after birth, with symptoms that last at least two weeks. It can occur anytime in the first twelve months after birth. Symptoms often include depression, an inability to experience pleasure in previously pleasurable activities, lack of or too much sleep, weight loss or weight gain, irritability, crying, loss of energy, indecision, lack of concentration, and feelings of being overwhelmed, worthlessness, or guilt, and thoughts of death or suicide.

A small number of women (1-2%) will suffer from postpartum psychosis, the most serious form of postpartum mood disorders. It involves hallucinations and can lead to a desire to harm your baby or yourself. Postpartum psychosis includes a range of diagnoses, but the most common form of postpartum psychosis is postpartum bipolar disorder with psychosis (Kendall-Tackett, 2010).

Risk factors for PPD include a previous history of depression or posttraumatic stress disorder (PTSD), a family history of depression, anxiety or depression during pregnancy, lack of social support, a recent stressful life event, psychological trauma, sleep disturbances, pain, an infant with health problems, a history of violence or abuse, and a difficult, negative, or life-threatening birth experience. Recent research also suggests that all of these factors increase stress, raising inflammation levels, which is at the core of all of these risk factors, and in fact, may be the underlying cause behind all the other risk factors (Kendall-Tackett, 2007).

It is not surprising then that women in the military might have higher rates of PPD than the general population (Appolonio & Fingerhut, 2008; O'Boyle, Magann, Ricks Jr, Doyle, & Morrison, 2005; Rychnovsky & Beck, 2006). Many of the risk factors for PPD are an everyday part of life for the military mother, and there are a few that are unique to the military: longer working hours, shorter maternity leave, childcare issues, family-work conflict, deployments, and previous trauma. Of the many risk factors, fatigue is of particular concern because inflammation is higher when a mother is fatigued, and research has shown that military mothers have higher levels of fatigue than civilian mothers (Rychnovsky, 2007).

With many women serving in combat zones coming home and starting families, there is a new concern of posttraumatic stress disorder (PTSD) and how that might affect new mothers, as trauma can increase the risk of PPD. Trauma and PTSD prime the body by keeping the inflammatory response on high alert. Combine that with normal postpartum fatigue and a lack of support, and a new mother is at prime risk for PPD. Further, both trauma and depression have a negative impact on sleep and can impact how tired mothers feel during the day. Mothers who are experiencing sleep issues related to depression and trauma are often advised to wean, especially at night, so they will get more sleep. But usually, the sleep problems are not related to baby care, and weaning the baby may actually make it worse because breastfeeding mothers actually get more sleep than mothers who supplement or exclusively formula-feed. Very little research has been done on the effects of combat and PTSD on women and how they cope once back home with families and small infants and children to care for.

Breastfeeding while suffering from PPD does not mean you need to wean. In fact, breastfeeding your infant will help you cope with the symptoms of postpartum depression, as research has shown that breastfeeding protects you from stress, lowers your inflammatory response, and increases both your mood and nurturing behaviors (Groer, Davis, & Hemphill, 2002).

Furthermore, breastfeeding also protects your baby against the effects of PPD by lowering the stress he experiences if you are depressed (Jones, McFall, & Diego, 2004). Mothers who breastfeed while suffering from PPD often report that breastfeeding is the one thing that keeps them going. They feel that because they "have to feed the baby" they make a connection with their infant, a bond. And that even in the depths of sadness, they are aware of and hold on tight to the life raft that breastfeeding provides.

This information isn't meant to scare you, only to make you aware that PPD can strike anyone, and it is treatable. Please seek help if you feel like life isn't worth living or that you want to hurt your child. These feelings are not normal and can be treated, often successfully, with anti-inflammatories (such as Omega-3s), medication, and therapy. And as shown above, antidepressants are safe to take while breastfeeding. Get the help you need and don't let the stigma of depression in the military, or the worry that your evaluations will suffer, stop you from telling someone you have PPD. You and your baby's health and well-being are at stake and are far more important than a promotion or an evaluation. (For further information and resources on postpartum depression, please visit UppityScienceChick.com.)

Tattoos

There is a long history between military service and tattoos. The art of tattooing goes back many centuries as a way for soldiers and sailors to mark their allegiance to a unit or ship, to remember important life events, or to commemorate a buddy lost in battle. Today's service members are no different. You may be sporting a tattoo yourself and wondering if it is safe to breastfeed.

Tattoos, both regular and cosmetic (which are now allowed in the U.S. Navy, see NAVADMIN 271/09), are created by injecting ink into the dermal layer of the skin. Tattoo artists use a hand-held electric machine that is fitted with solid needles of various diameters and number, and coated in the ink. The needles enter the skin from 50 to 3000 times per minute to a depth of up to a few millimeters. The process causes minor bleeding and is usually painful for the first 24 hours. The process of applying a tattoo can take from minutes to hours depending on the intricacy of the design and colors used (Roche-Paull, 2009).

Tattoos are a permanent form of artwork etched into the flesh and are not without risk; both local and systemic infections are the most prevalent risks of tattooing. Local infections can occur when the recommended aftercare regimen is not followed. Aftercare includes keeping the tattoo clean with mild soap and water, not picking at the scabs, and keeping the tattoo out of the sun (Reardon, 2008). Systemic infections, such as Hepatitis B and C, can occur when universal precautions are not followed by the tattoo artist. Universal precautions include sterilization of the tattoo machine using an autoclave, single-use inks, ink cups, gloves and needles, bagging of equipment to avoid cross contamination, thorough hand washing with disinfectant soap, and the wearing of gloves when performing the tattoo. Of course, it is important to screen the tattooist and the shop carefully, checking with the local health department for local laws and regulations. Reputable body artists support regulations and legislation to keep their customers safe and to legitimize the profession.

The AAP, ACOG, AAFP, and ACNM have taken no stance on the compatibility of tattoos and breastfeeding. Various sources state that already present tattoos, on the breast or elsewhere, do not impact breastfeeding. The possibility of the ink migrating into the mother's blood plasma, and then into the milk-making cells of the breast is negligible, according to several experts. It is, however, possible to have allergic reactions to the tattoo inks. The inks used may contain metal oxides or synthetic dyes, and in the United States are subject to FDA regulation as cosmetics. But none are approved for injection under the skin (FDA, 2008).

If you are thinking about getting a tattoo while breastfeeding, be aware that many, if not most, professional tattoo artists will not knowingly tattoo a woman who is currently breastfeeding or will actively discourage you from doing so. Most tattoo artists feel that the body needs time to heal the tattoo and that it is harder to do so when the body is also producing milk. There is concern that a disease "could" be passed to the baby from a bad tattoo, such as one done overseas or without following universal precautions (Hudson, 2009). This is really a judgment call for you, as the mother, to decide. A newborn baby is far more vulnerable to changes in the milk than a nursing toddler. Anecdotal evidence from various discussion boards related to body modification show that the majority of mothers go ahead and get tattoos while breastfeeding, with no ill effects on the baby or mother. Overall, you should feel safe in either getting a new tattoo (within military regs, of course) or breastfeeding your baby with tattoos in place.

Lt. Emily Nolan, USAF, and her daughter, Lucy

Photo courtesy Emily Nolan.
Used with permission.

Hopefully, this section has given you a good primer (or refresher) on breastfeeding so that you are comfortable with the basics and know where to go for further, more in-depth information should you need it. It may seem hard, or even overwhelming, to read about all the steps to a successful latch or how-to manage plugged ducts. But, for the most part, once you start breastfeeding, it really does fall into place. There are, of course, many other concerns, conditions, and problems that can--and do--crop up during breastfeeding that I simply can't cover in a book of this scope. I have tried to touch upon some of the more common ones that I feel may impact you more as a military mother. I trust that you will turn to a local breastfeeding support group, LLL Leader, or IBCLC if you have concerns not addressed here.

SECTION THREE

Duty Calls: Returning to Work

Diana's Story

I am in the fortunate, though unique, situation of being assigned to a permanent duty station in a non-deploying unit, one of the Army's "special" military bands (MOS 42S). I am an E-6 after 11 years of service.

Our schedule varies according to the season, so in order to ensure I could be available to my babies as much as possible for as long as possible, I planned both of my pregnancies to allow me to return to work during a "slow" season. By doing this, I was able to juggle my schedule such that I avoided any separations over four hours for the first six months of my babies' lives. If our day was to go longer, I would at least be able to get to my baby on a lunch break. This ended up being very necessary for me, as neither of my babies would feed from a bottle. One technique I used to extend the amount of time I could be home with my newborns was to save regular leave and take it in conjunction with the 42 days convalescence given by the Army after delivery. I was able to save and take an additional 50 days after the birth of each of my children, with the support of my commander.

In order to balance the needs of my family with the mission requirements of my unit, I needed to put in several hours each day from home after my children were asleep. Most of my extra-duty positions were computer-based, so I was able to write proposals, complete correspondence, and proofread publicity items from home. While this arrangement prohibited me from using that precious evening time to relax or do household chores, it allowed me to do the far more important job of being present for my babies as much as possible. The support I continue to receive from my husband (also a member of my unit) makes all of this possible. He does a great deal of the housework, as well as shares in the parenting of our children.

Another creative solution to the unique challenges of childcare and attachment my family has used is to take our children with us when we travel on TDY. The band takes several overnight trips each year. We do not live close to family, and my husband and I are both required to travel. Rather than leave my little nurslings home with a caregiver, we bring the caregiver and the children with us on every trip. This has resulted in enormous personal expense for us — but the investment in our children's physical and emotional health is priceless. For us, this arrangement has made extended breastfeeding and secure attachment possible. On the few occasions when I could not get to my children to nurse them, I have been able to secure an appropriate place to pump. This "appropriate place" has included major football stadium locker rooms, green rooms (performer's quarters), backstage at performance venues, or sometimes, my own car in the parking lot a mile away. I have always been able to ask for the flexibility I needed to express milk while accomplishing the band's mission.

Despite the efforts I have made to balance my family with my Army responsibilities, and the apparent success I have had in doing so, the reality is that many of my co-workers have a perception that I am "getting away with something" or "not pulling my weight." This perception has definitely hurt my opportunities for advancement and promotion. It would be ideal if this was not the case. However, I would make the same choices again on behalf of my children, knowing the impact they would have on my career.

Chapter 6
Planning Ahead

Military mothers who choose to continue breastfeeding while on active duty do so not only because it is good for their babies' health and it provides ease of feeding when off duty, but also because it makes them feel close to their babies, even when they are separated for long periods at work. It is well worth your time to plan how to combine breastfeeding with your military commitments. Some job specialties and ranks within the military will be able to combine breastfeeding and working better than others. Every situation is different, and this sections aims to help you evaluate your breastfeeding goals and work situation, while giving you practical information on military policies and pumping basics. The more prepared you are, the more confident you will be upon your return to duty.

Planning Ahead

The first and most important item of business to take care of, preferably before your baby is born, is to determine your work environment and facilities available to you. Do you have a separate room that is unused at your workplace, such as a supply room? Or will you be in field conditions in a tent, on a flight line, or in a medical facility? Do you have the option of on-site daycare where you can go to your baby on your lunch break? Military mothers have become very creative at converting areas into pumping stations: requesting a corner of an unused supply room with a curtain and couch or chair, cordoning off a corner of a tent, or using the back of an ambulance to pump.

Speak with your direct supervisor in your chain of command. You will need to let them know that you plan to continue breastfeeding when you return to duty and will need a clean, private area to pump and some flexibility in your work schedule to pump (lunch and two 15-20 minute breaks). If you feel uncomfortable speaking with your supervisor, you may request that another female be present with you when you make your case for breastfeeding upon your return to duty. You may work in a field that is mostly male. But do not let your feelings of embarrassment or shyness deter you from making the best choice for your baby. As this Air Force Captain says:

> *Don't be afraid to talk about it, especially with your supervisor—most men (if fathers) at least know that breastfeeding is an option. Your boss will probably be more uncomfortable with the conversation than you are. But in the long run, most bosses and coworkers will support and defend your right to breastfeed.*

You might be surprised at the answer you will receive and you won't know unless you ask! (See the section on Speaking with Your Supervisor later in this Chapter).

Bring in copies of your services' policy regarding breastfeeding and a plan for pumping that includes how often you'll need breaks and where you will pump. You can also ask your child's healthcare provider for a note stating that breastfeeding and breastmilk expression must take place for your child's health. You might also bring in an article or two regarding the benefits of breastfeeding (see Military Lactation Policies in Appendix E) and this book.

Talk to women at your workplace about their experiences with pumping and breastfeeding. Find out what worked and what didn't work for them. You may even decide to form an informal support group for one another to share tips and stories. Find a mentor who has breastfed on active duty and ask her questions about what did and didn't work for her. You can also look for formal breastfeeding support groups for active-duty breastfeeding mothers (many bases worldwide offer them) and some La Leche League groups meet on or near military bases as well (see Section Five-Support).

Purchase or rent the best quality breast pump you can afford. See Chapter 8 for more information on the various types, and advantages and disadvantages of each. If breast pumps seem expensive, remember that a year's supply of formula can be as much as $1500-$2300. Check with your MTF or clinic, as some military hospitals (mostly Army) either loan hospital-grade pumps or sell double-electric breast pumps. Local WIC (Women's, Infant's and Children's Program) offices on base, the New Parent Support Team, or Visiting Nurse programs (see Chapter 22) also sometimes offer low-cost or loaner pumps, or can point you in the right direction to locate one.

It goes without saying that getting breastfeeding off to a good start greatly increases the chances that you will be successful at breastfeeding once you return to work. Oftentimes, mothers assume that breastfeeding will go smoothly during their convalescent leave, and that all they need to do is learn how to pump, only to be blindsided by on-going problems that never resolve. Early breastfeeding problems, such as sore nipples or low milk supply, that are left unresolved can make it much more difficult to combine working and breastfeeding. All is not lost, however. With a little preparation, you can have breastfeeding well established before you go back to work. Remember the following:

- Take a breastfeeding-basics *and* a return-to-work class. Get as much information prenatally as possible.

- Practice skin-to-skin, nurse your baby immediately after birth, room-in with your baby, and feed him on demand.

- Get expert breastfeeding help while in the hospital and a referral to an IBCLC for additional help after discharge. Early help makes all the difference.

Delay your return to duty if at all possible. You can bank your leave time and, with your commander's permission, add it to the six weeks of convalescent leave you'll take after the birth of your baby. Every week that you can stay at home increases your chances of long-term breastfeeding success. When you do return to work, do so gently, and try to return at the end of the week. Easing into your new routine slowly makes it easier on you and your baby (see Chapter 10 for more information).

Policies and Regulations

Perhaps the most important information to know is your service's policy on breastfeeding. From this information, you can speak with your supervisor and co-workers and formulate your plans for continuing to breastfeed and/ or express breastmilk after your return to full duty. Overriding all the policies and forming the basis of the various regulations is the DOD Directive 1010.10 Health Promotion and Disease/Injury Prevention, which states that the Department of Defense and all of its employees must maintain military readiness by implementing and adhering to the goals of Healthy People 2010 (Department of Defense, 2003). One of those goals is exclusive breastfeeding for the first six months of life for the health of both the mother and baby. These policies vary widely between the services--from the Army, which has no policy and the shortest deployment deferment, to the Coast Guard with a two year "sabbatical" after the birth of a baby and the guarantee of return to the same job and pay grade.

These policies provide you with legal justification for making a request to breastfeed or express your milk while at work, while also allowing your supervisor to cite regulations when authorizing time for breastfeeding. However, none of these policies are fool-proof or ironclad. Keep in mind that operational commitments will ALWAYS have precedence over your right to breastfeed or pump: the mission always comes first. Links to full versions of the various policies are given in Appendix D and online at the companion website to this book. A chart outlining the highlights of each policy is provided in Appendix E. Below are excerpts from the pertinent sections of each of the policies for the Air Force, Coast Guard, Marine Corps, and Navy. The National Guard and Reserve components follow the policies of their parent services.

Air Force

The Air Force revised its policy in 2006, making clear the need for a private room and authorizing pumping breaks of 15-30 minutes every three to four hours. The deployment deferment period is 12 months. However, as an active-duty breastfeeding mother, you are not exempt from field training or mobility exercises, and you must plan your pumping needs with your supervisor.

Air Force Instruction 44-102

4.15. Breastfeeding and Breast Pumping

4.15.1. AF members shall be authorized 15-30 minutes every three to four hours to breast-pump. This should be allowed for approximately 12 months after delivery.

4.15.2. The obstetrician or PCM shall annotate on an AF Form 422 that the member wishes to breast pump and makes a request for a room or office that provides adequate privacy for breast pumping be designated to allow AF members to pump. The AF member must supply the equipment needed to breast pump and store the breastmilk.

4.15.3. The obstetrician, pediatrician or PCM shall annotate on an AF Form 422 a recommendation for deployment for those AF members who choose to exclusively breastfeed, i.e., the infant does not take formula at all.

4.15.4. Breastfeeding/breast pumping AF members may participate in field training and mobility exercises. Decisions to continue to breast pump must be made by the patient, in collaboration with obstetrician or PCM, supervisors, training instructors, and the MDG/CC in regard to having a place to safely express and store breastmilk.

Army

The Army does not have a breastfeeding policy in place at this time and only offers the standard six weeks of maternity leave. As a soldier, you will be worldwide deployable at six months postpartum. However, breastfeeding does not exempt you from going to the field. The Army does offer a sample letter to be used for educating, planning, and requesting a time and a place to pump after return to duty. This could easily be adapted for use by members of the other services. Within the Female Readiness Guide, there is a brief section on supporting the breastfeeding soldier.

Army- AR 614-30 Deployment and ALARACT 171/2008

Soldiers will be considered available for worldwide deployment 6 months after giving birth.

Breastfeeding Support Plan, Sample Memorandum (see Appendix F)

Provide information on breastfeeding to educate Commanders and postpartum Soldiers, and propose a support plan to assist Soldiers in breastfeeding on return to duty.

Section X of the TG281 (A Guide to Female Soldier Readiness)

It is critical that leaders support their Soldiers. The ability to successfully continue breastfeeding after returning to work involves space, time, and support. Leaders need to provide female Soldiers with social and administrative support if the decision is made to continue breastfeeding after returning to work. Providing a designated space in the workplace where mothers may express breastmilk is important since many active-duty mothers do not have private offices. If a designated room cannot be provided, the use of empty conference rooms or offices may suffice.

Coast Guard

The Coast Guard breastfeeding policy specifies that a private room is required. But it does not specify length or number of breaks allotted, instead leaving it up to you and the command to determine pumping breaks on a case-by-case basis. You will be deployable six months after birth. Coast Guardsmen, enlisted and officer, male and female, also have the option of taking a one-time, two-year, unpaid separation from active duty to care for a newborn, with a return to the same pay grade and benefits.

Coast Guard COMDTINST M1000.6A

Section 9.A.4 Breastfeeding.

a. Servicewomen should obtain information from their care provider relating to breastfeeding education, care, counseling, and support during the pregnancy, after delivery, and on return to work. If the servicewoman opts to breastfeed after returning to duty, the member and the command should communicate to address any concerns or issues.

b. When possible, the commanding officer or officer in charge will ensure the availability of a private, clean room for expressing breastmilk during the workday.

c. Requests to breastfeed infants during duty hours should be handled on a case-by-case basis; however, breastfeeding an infant is not a reason for granting excessive time for meals or away from work.

Section 9.A.3 Deployment

Servicewomen… will not normally be transferred to afloat units, aviation units, or OCONUS that are deploying during the period from the 20th week of pregnancy through six months after the servicewoman's date of delivery unless the servicewoman is medically fit and requests a waiver for an earlier resumption of duties.

Section 12.F.1 - Separation for the Care of a Newborn Policy

Under this policy, career oriented officers and enlisted members are allowed a onetime separation from Active Duty for up to two years to discharge parental responsibilities to care for newborn children (CNC). This policy allows a member to separate with a guarantee of reenlistment or a new officer appointment upon return to Active Duty on meeting physical and other qualifying standards.

Marines

The USMC has probably one of the better breastfeeding policies of all the services, with a 6-month deferment from deployment and the requirement of a clean, secluded space with running water for pumping. Break times are not specified, but instead are left to you and your supervisor on a case-by-case basis.

Marine Corps Order 5000.12E (MARADMIN 358/07)

Section 15 - Support of Servicewomen with Nursing Infants

a. Servicewomen who desire to continue breastfeeding upon return to duty will notify their chain of command at the earliest possible time to allow the command to determine how best to support them and facilitate the prompt evaluation of the workplace for potential hazards.

b. When possible, the servicewoman who continues to provide breastmilk to her infant upon return to duty shall be, at a minimum, afforded the availability of a clean, secluded space (not a toilet space) with ready access to a water source for the purpose of pumping breastmilk.

c. The time required for breastmilk expression varies and is highly dependent upon several factors including the age of the infant, amount of milk produced, pump quality, the distance the pumping location is from the workplace, as well as how conveniently located the water source is from the pump location. Supervisors and lactating servicewomen will collaborate to keep to a minimum the amount of time required for milk expression. Lactation consultants are available at the MTF to assist in this endeavor.

Section 8d. Deployment

Servicewomen will not normally be transferred to deploying units from the time of pregnancy confirmation up to 6 months from the date of delivery. The Marine may, however, waive the deployment deferment period.

Navy

The Navy policy is very similar to the Marine Corps policy, with a 12-month deferment from deployment and the requirement of a clean, secluded space with running water and refrigeration for pumping. Break times are not specified, but are left to you and your supervisor on a case-by-case basis, and you are required to have access to breastfeeding help and education if you need it.

Navy OPNAVINST 6000.1C

Section 103 -Deployment Policy

Servicewomen may… not be transferred to units that are deploying during the period from the 20th week of pregnancy through 12 months after the servicewoman's expected date of delivery.

Section 106 - Breastfeeding

a. Servicewomen should be provided access to educational information from didactic materials, a lactation consultant for breast care, breastfeeding education, counseling, and support during the pregnancy, after delivery, and on return to work.

b. When possible, CO shall ensure the availability of a private, clean room for expressing breastmilk. There should be ready access to running water and refrigeration for safe storage of breastmilk.

c. Requests to breastfeed infants during duty hours should be handled on a case-by-case basis; however, breastfeeding an infant is not a reason for granting excessive time for meals or from work.

Navy BUMEDINST 6000.14

Guidelines and resources for policy development to support commands with servicewomen with nursing infants are provided. Directs medical personnel to assist and educate fleet and shore workplace supervisors, COs, and OICs that have servicewomen who are breastfeeding, and directs workplaces to incorporate breastfeeding support into local policies. A focus on active duty workplace concerns, such as hazardous materials, a place and time to pump and resources for purchasing or renting a breastpump are highlighted. This instruction also directs medical personnel to consult with and address the needs of breastfeeding servicewomen with infants in military child development centers (CDC). Finally this instruction makes clear the need for qualified lactation consultants to provide education and support, and prohibits the provision of free formula samples to patients in MTFs.

Speaking with Your Chain of Command

The vast majority of respondents to an online survey of military mothers (Roche-Paull, 2010) stated that being upfront with your supervisor about your need to pump is the best policy. You need to be proactive about your need to pump, and in this case, it is better to ask permission beforehand than to hope for the best upon your return from convalescent leave. Don't be afraid to speak with your supervisor. Communication is essential! No one likes to be surprised, and you can't assume that your supervisor is thinking about how you are going to feed your baby.

The policies regarding pumping and breastfeeding have been out long enough that most, if not all, supervisors should have a passing knowledge of what is expected of them in granting you breaks and providing a place to pump. It doesn't hurt to have a written plan (see the Army *Breastfeeding Support Plan, Sample Memorandum*, Appendix F) ready that outlines your work schedule including: PT, lunch, and pumping breaks; a consult with Occupational Health, if needed; the private space you plan to use for pumping; a back-up plan for duty days, watch standing or emergencies; any required storage needs for your milk; and your POC information.

At least in the Navy, the policies concerning breastfeeding have changed (for the better!), so my advice to everyone would be to read up on what the policy states. Then you can go to talk to your supervisor BEFORE you start to pump at work. That way, he or she isn't blindsided and wondering where you are at certain points in the day. Petty Officer 2nd Class, USN

I told my supervisor my intent to pump at least two months prior to having my daughter. That way when I got back it wasn't a surprise. Just talking to them and having the policy printed out in case they do not know about it would be the first step. Senior Airman, USAF

When I was pregnant with my middle child, there was another nursing mother, so it was easy to tell my OIC. With my new unit, I told my

OIC I was planning on breastfeeding. The office is supportive of it, and once they got used to the sign on my office door, they call if they need anything instead of knocking on the door. Captain, USA

I was lucky in that my supervisor's wife had given birth to their second daughter the day before I gave birth. She was also active duty and planned on breastfeeding, so I basically just told him that I was going to "disappear" to take care of things twice a day. He didn't need any more info than that. Captain, USAF

Don't be afraid to ask for what you need--and you may have some unusual needs. I've found that if I treat it matter-of-factly, others do, too. You do what you've got to do. Major, USAF

When, Where, and How Long

How long you should breastfeed and pump is something only you can decide based on many factors, such as your work environment, schedule, possible deployments, and level of support you receive. No matter what, your attitude and commitment to breastfeeding is vitally important to whether you will be successful at breastfeeding on active duty for however long you choose to continue. Having a goal in mind for both breastfeeding and pumping (they may differ) will help you stay determined and focused. You'll need to decide what the minimum amount of time that you want to provide breastmilk to your baby is and see how that feels as a goal (remember to leave time to get any initial problems worked out). With that in mind, here are a number of goals in the first year that you may want to consider aiming for (also take a look at Appendix N, *What If I Want to Wean,* for a more in-depth look at weaning by age).

Birth to Six Weeks

Consider breastfeeding to at least the end of your six weeks (42 days) of convalescent leave. At six weeks, you will have made it over the initial hurdles of getting breastfeeding off to a good start, and given your baby an important boost by providing his or her first "immunization" via your milk. Having weathered the worst of the initial difficulties, you can better see how easy breastfeeding really is. Remember, if new moms had to decide whether to breastfeed for a year based on the first few days and weeks of breastfeeding, which can often be so difficult, many would never want to! If your military work environment or schedule will preclude any pumping, then you can know that you eased your baby through those critical first few weeks. From here on out, you can combine formula feeding while at work with breastfeeding while you are at home, or go straight to formula, if that is what you decide.

Six Weeks to Four Months

Because you'll be returning to work at six weeks, four months is a good first goal for pumping. Providing exclusive breastmilk for the first four months has been shown to have a significant impact on your baby's health. However, this is also the most challenging time, when most military mothers struggle with the demands of returning to active duty and managing a baby, home, and everything else. Your baby will be taking in a lot of nourishment during the day and having a few growth spurts as well. This can be the toughest time of all, so take it slowly, and try to keep your baby on exclusive breastmilk for as long as possible. If you can make it past this hurdle, it really does get easier!

Four to Six Months

This can still be a tough time for you as a working mother. Your baby's intake can be quite high (he is more active now) and you may be struggling with supply issues and being able to pump enough to keep up with his demand. If you are finding that you cannot keep up with your baby's demand at four months and have tried the suggestions later in this chapter on increasing your milk supply, you may want to speak with your lactation consultant and HCP about supplementing with formula to ease the stress of trying to pump enough. If you do supplement with formula, be careful, as too much supplementation can decrease your milk supply.

Six to Nine Months

The next goal to aim for might be your baby's sixth month of life. The AAP and WHO both recommend six months of exclusive breastfeeding to realize the **majority** of the benefits of breastfeeding. Your baby will still be drinking a lot of breastmilk. But you are no longer solely responsible for all of his nourishment, which gives you some flexibility and eases the pressure of pumping enough during the day. You can continue to pump at work (and begin to taper down how often) and increase solids while you are gone; or you can partially wean by combining formula and solids during the day at work and breastfeed at home. Breastmilk is vitally important to your baby and should remain the majority of his diet throughout the first year of life.

Nine to Twelve Months

Having a goal of nine months means that your baby will be eating a variety of foods that can substitute for more breastmilk, lessening even further the amount of pumping you'll need to do. Remember, though, that breastmilk remains an important part of your baby's diet. Most babies still want to and enjoy breastfeeding in the mornings, evenings, and at night (nighttime nursing equals higher milk supply). Continuing to breastfeed at nine months can help combat some of the separation anxiety he will be feeling and provides an on-going boost to his immune system. A note: some babies get so "busy" at nine months, especially if they have mastered walking, that they forget to nurse. This doesn't mean they are weaning. Rather, they need a gentle reminder from you that the "milk bar" is open. Don't hesitate to offer the breast if you are determined to make it to twelve months or beyond of breastfeeding. Most babies will happily oblige!

Over a Year

The final goal to aim for is your baby's first birthday or beyond. Breastfeeding for a year or beyond is recommended by the AAP to **maximize** the benefits of breastfeeding. Breastmilk continues to offer immunities from illness and provides proper growth and development well into the second year of life. By this point in time, your baby will be getting most of his nourishment from other foods, and breastfeeding will be more about comfort and reconnecting with each other.

Captain Courtney Power, USAF, and her breastfed son, Joey

Photo courtesy Courtney Power. Used with permission.

At this point, you can stop pumping completely, transition your toddler directly to cow's milk, and skip formula altogether. Breastfeeding to the age of one year or longer is the most pleasant time for working mothers. The hassle of pumping is over and gone and only the joy of nursing remains. A number of women have successfully breastfed, or even tandem nursed (nursing two children of different ages), for two or more years, as recommended by the WHO, while serving on active duty. It can be done!

> *My littlest son just stopped. He was three and a half years old.* Tech. Sgt., USAF

> *I have been on active duty, Marine Corps, and breastfed/pumped for my youngest daughter throughout my service time. I occasionally tandem nursed, too ... my youngest, now 4, occasionally nurses, and it has been an adventure!* Major, USMC

Your breastfeeding and pumping goals should be what works for you and your situation, both at home and at work. Set a goal that is doable for you, and then meet it. If you find that you are not ready to stop, set another goal. It feels better to set a goal and reach it, rather than set it too high and feel as though you failed. On the flip side, the breastfeeding goal you choose should never leave you feeling like you wished it had lasted longer. Studies have shown that women who feel forced or pressured into weaning (whether by circumstances out of their control or a goal set too high) tend to have ambivalent and guilty feelings about breastfeeding, while those that made a goal, met it, and are satisfied with their breastfeeding experience, have positive feelings when their breastfeeding relationship comes to an end (Hills-Bonczyk, Avery, Savik, Potter, & Duckett, 1993).

> *I think it is important for new moms to understand that ANY amount of breastfeeding is beneficial. It is OK to stop after one week, one month, one year. The decision is a completely personal one, and you should be applauded for even one day of breastfeeding.* Captain, USAF

It's Not All or Nothing

When deciding how *long* to breastfeed and pump, you also should consider how to *combine* breastfeeding and pumping in your workday. There is no right and wrong variation to this. Your decision will be based on the type of work you do, hours you will be away, what kind of time and place you have to pump, future deployments, and other factors. Whatever choice you make about pumping, you'll be surprised at how fulfilling it can be to nourish your baby with your milk. The decisions you make about expressing your milk will be as individual as you, your baby, and your work environment. Here are some various ways to combine breastfeeding and active-duty work that other mothers in the military have used successfully.

- **Exclusive breastfeeding:** With exclusive breastfeeding, you go to your baby at daycare or your baby is brought to you during the workday. There is no pumping during the day or use of expressed breastmilk or formula while at daycare. Exclusive breastfeeding is a luxury afforded to very few active-duty mothers, as it is just not practical given the work environment and hours.

- **Full breastfeeding and pumping:** Full breastfeeding and pumping means you will breastfeed at home and provide pumped breastmilk to your baby while at daycare. There is no formula use at all. You will need to pump at least two to three times during an eight-hour shift, if possible; more often for longer shifts. This combination of breastfeeding and pumping is most suitable for those military mothers who can pump on a regular schedule while at work.

- **Partial breastfeeding and pumping:** Much like full breastfeeding and pumping, with the exception of some formula given at daycare, in addition to pumped breastmilk. Mothers in this situation pump as often as possible at work and breastfeed while at home (a single pumping session at night can also yield extra milk for the next day). This combination is most suitable for those military mothers who cannot pump very often at work due to their schedules or environment. Mothers with a small storage capacity may find that their milk supply falters without regular expression (see Breast Storage Capacity in Chapter 9).

- **Partial breastfeeding:** With this combination, mothers breastfeed when at home and give formula while at daycare. There is no breast pumping or use of pumped breastmilk. This is the most practical option for those military mothers who cannot pump at work at all. It is important that breastfeeding remain unrestricted when at home to maintain a milk supply. This combination generally only works for mothers with a large storage capacity (see Storage Capacity in Chapter 8).

- **Reverse-cycle feeding:** Reverse-cycle feeding is a change in some babies sleeping and nursing patterns to better reflect mom's availability. You may find that your baby breastfeeds more in the evening and during the night, while taking fewer feedings during the day when he is separated from you. It is very normal for babies of working mothers to reverse-cycle and shows a deep, well-adjusted attachment between you both (Frederick & Auerbach, 1985). Most often, babies do this naturally by breastfeeding much more frequently when home with mom and sleeping when they are at childcare. A nice perk of reverse-cycle feeding is that you need to pump less, or maybe even quit pumping completely. If you are finding that day after day your baby is not drinking all the pumped milk you leave with the daycare provider, you may be able to adjust your pumping schedule. By five to six months, with the addition of solids foods, you may be able to reduce pumping further or quit pumping altogether. Reverse-cycle feeding works, in part, due to the higher hormone levels at night for milk-making. So it may or may not work for those whose shifts are on nights or mids. It is important that you practice unrestricted breastfeeding when you are with your baby, and co-sleeping facilitates mom getting some sleep and letting baby nurse often during the night (see Chapter 5, Safe Sleep).

Remember, when it comes to breastfeeding in the military, any breastmilk your baby receives is better than no breastmilk at all. It is OK to supplement and keep breastfeeding. It is not all or nothing. Your body is amazing. It learns when to make milk and when not to. If you can only nurse your baby in the evenings and at night, then your body will make milk at those times.

Chapter 7
Pumps

Choosing a Breast Pump

You might not, at first thought, think of your breast pump as a tool. But it is a very important and unique tool that will enable you to provide your precious breastmilk to your baby while you are separated. Just as with any tool, there are many factors to consider when choosing a breast pump, such as how and where you will use it, what options you will have available for expressing your milk at your workplace, and your budget. With so many pumps available with numerous features, including a range of cycle and suction settings, sizes, power sources, and prices, it can be confusing trying to determine which one will suit your circumstances best.

The type of pump you choose is as individual as you are, and what worked for your friend or co-worker may not be the best choice for you. Take your time and research all your options when choosing your breast pump. It can be very helpful to educate yourself on the various types of pumps and what their advantages and disadvantages are by talking with a lactation consultant who is familiar with breast pump technology. By choosing the proper breast pump, expressing your milk doesn't have to be a chore. As this Captain in the Air Force says, *"My pump and I became great friends!"* In time your pump will become a treasured tool and a reminder of all the goodness you faithfully pumped into those bottles day after day!

Cost of a Breast Pump

Cost is one of the first considerations many mothers make when choosing a breast pump. And while price is important, it shouldn't be the only, or even the first, factor that guides your decision. But with that said, it is understandable if you are junior enlisted and not making very much that the price of your breast pump might be a very important part of your decision making process. Given that the military workplace means you will be gone for more than 40 hours a week and may often be traveling, it behooves you to buy the best pump you can afford. Good quality breast pumps are expensive and usually non-returnable. So it is critical that you make the right choice. Here are some tips to help you get the most for your money.

Breast pumps are available seemingly everywhere: discount baby stores, drugstores, online retailers, hospital gift shops, WIC offices, even toy stores (yes, they sell breast pumps in Toys R Us ®). But before you run off to the nearest discount baby store or the base exchange to purchase your pump, you might consider seeing an IBCLC first. Lactation consultants are a fabulous choice for getting a well-informed recommendation on what type of breast pump would suit your needs the best. Furthermore, some lactation consultants offer breast pumps and accessories for sale, and they stand behind their products with follow-up and service after the purchase. They often will allow you to trial the pump (with your own kit) to see if it fits properly before you plunk down your hard-earned cash, and they can offer one-on-one support after the purchase should anything go amiss with the pump. Unlike discount stores, toy stores, and drugstores where you pull the pump off the shelf with no help or information, your local IBCLC is where you'll get help and support both before and after the purchase.

Most quality breast pumps range in price from about $150 to $350 for a personal-use, double-electric pump, depending on the accessories (extra bottles, cooler, gel packs, backpack, etc.) that come with it. Have you ever heard the old saying, "You get what you pay for"? This can be especially true in the case of breast pumps, where the cheaper models may state they are double electric, but, in reality, they are not nearly strong enough nor do they cycle fast enough to maintain your milk supply. Many women, unfortunately, buy a crappy first breast pump in the hopes of saving money, but find that their milk supply goes down the tubes, or the motor dies because it is not meant to be used more than two to three times a week. They then end up spending more money on a second, better pump a few months later (and may not recover their milk supply). Keep in mind that the cost of a good breast pump is about the same as two months of formula, but will last much longer. Despite the initial cost of a pump, pumping your milk is healthier and more economical compared to the cost of formula and increased illness for your baby.

Finally, you might want to consider whether the pump you are considering purchasing is returnable should something go wrong with it, how durable it is, and what the warranty covers, if anything. Most brands of consumer breast pumps, especially those bought in a store or online, are not returnable once the package has been opened. Unfortunately, you won't know if the pump will even work for you unless you try it out first, and by then you have voided the return policy. It is a bit of a catch-22 and is another reason to consider buying a breast pump from a lactation consultant (and trialing it first, if possible) or through a manufacturer that allows returns on their pumps, opened or not.

It is also a good idea to check on the durability of the pump you plan on purchasing. This can be a bit more difficult to determine as there are no independent reviews, as yet, of breast pump durability. You can, however, judge a breast pump's durability by the type of warranty that is offered. Look for a warranty of at least one year on the motor. Many "cheap" breast pumps have a short (90 days) warranty--or no warranty at all. In that case, if you bought the pump while still pregnant, the warranty might be expired by the time your baby is born. Another point to think about is how long do you plan to breastfeed and pump for this baby? Will you be breastfeeding future babies? Think about how long you want the pump to last and look for a quality breast pump with a warranty that matches your goals for breastfeeding and pumping.

New Versus Used pumps

Many mothers consider sharing a pump or buying a used pump as a means to save money. This is a potentially harmful practice for you and your baby for a variety of reasons. Personal-use pumps are considered "single-user" equipment by the FDA and are not to be shared or resold. Breast pumps of this type cannot be properly sterilized between users due to the way they are built (open versus closed systems). Even with new tubing and flanges, airborne pathogens in milk particles may have entered the motor from the previous user, and then are blown *towards* the bottles where they can possibly be passed onto you, the next user. This can present a small, but nevertheless very real risk of transmitting certain bacteria and viruses from mother to mother (a mother can be a carrier and not know it or show symptoms).

Another consideration is that many personal-use pumps are made to last about a year with full-time use (remember, even the best warranties are often only for a year). Buying a used pump runs the risk that the motor may not function correctly or at peak performance, which can negatively affect your milk supply. Furthermore, if the pump you borrowed from a friend dies, you may be on the hook to replace her pump, which will cost you the price of a new pump that you can't keep. Even if the pump keeps working, you still have shortened the life of her pump that she might want to use for future children. Warranties are also voided when pumps are shared or used by more than one user. Buying a new pump allows you to know exactly how the pump should feel and operate, and how effective it is straight from the box. This is very helpful later if you feel that the pump is not performing well, as you can troubleshoot it and determine if it needs new filters or if something more serious is going on. Buying a new pump also means you will know if the pump is working at full capacity if you use it with later children.

Having said all this, it is perfectly understandable why mothers go ahead and purchase a used pump anyway, especially if money is tight. So, is it ever okay to purchase a used pump? In a word, NO...but I know it will happen, so here are some guidelines to follow if you choose to go ahead and use a friend's pump. There are plenty of pumps out there that have never been out of the box they came in, for whatever reason. You may have a sister or a co-worker who bought a Pump In Style and used it for two weeks, and then quit breastfeeding. That is a perfectly good pump that is going to waste, collecting dust. So, if you know the person, know her health history, know the history of the pump (how long it was used), and are positive that the pump was kept clean, you may choose to take the risk and accept and use the pump. It is your decision. But be sure that you thoroughly clean and disinfect it, buy a new collection kit, and have the suction checked by a lactation consultant before use. Understand that if the motor starts to die or lose suction you may very well lose your milk supply. So keep an eye on your output. Legally, it is a no-no to share pumps. But reality says otherwise. Use your common sense and remember that I am not legally responsible if anything should go wrong because you followed the above advice!

★ Tip ★

The FDA considers personal breast pumps a "single-user" item, only to be used by one woman. Much like a toothbrush, breast pumps are personal care items, not to be shared by others.

Rent Versus Own

Should you rent or own your breast pump? Renting a breast pump is a good option for mothers who are planning to only pump for a few months, or who know that this will be their last baby. Renting is the way to get the best pump for the least money in the short-term. The cost of renting a breast pump will save you money on the initial outlay. However, with time, the rental fees combined with the purchase of the flanges, tubing, and other accessories will quickly cost more than a good quality personal-use pump.

If you do decide to rent, ask for a discount if you know you'll be pumping for at least three or six months, many places will offer price-breaks for a long-term contract. Rental pumps are considered multiple-user pumps because they operate on a closed system and have a filter that removes contaminants. They also pull the air *away* from the bottles, so your expressed milk is safe from contamination, and they have industrial-strength motors that can withstand years of use.

If you decide to buy your own breast pump, it will cost more in the beginning. But it is yours for as long as you own it, and it comes with all the accessories and parts you'll need. Many of the better pumps can see you through at least two babies, sometimes more, depending on how well you take care of it and how much you use it (obviously a pump that is used five to six times a day for 12 months is not going to last as long as a pump used two to three times a day for six months). If the initial price is still too much, remember that formula costs upwards of $2300/year. Looking at it that way makes the $350 you'll spend on a quality pump seem like a bargain (which it is).

Features to Consider

After deciding what your price level is and whether you'll rent or own, and looking at warranties and where to buy your pump, it is time to get down to the nitty-gritty of choosing your breast pump based on the various features of the pumps themselves. You can use the following basic guidelines for choosing the proper pump for your working situation. Make your decision based on these factors and what will work best for you.

Cycles and Suction Settings. Breast pumps are designed to empty the breast by mimicking both the suction pressure and frequency of a baby's suckling. Infants normally suck with a frequency between 40 and 126 sucks per minute (Zoppou, Barry, & Mercer, 1997). A pump that cycles automatically between 40-60 times a minute will be the most effective at removing milk, keeping your prolactin levels high and your milk production up. Babies breastfeed with a suction pressure between 50 to 220 mmHg. That suction pressure affects your comfort, the efficiency of milk expression, and the production of milk. Suction levels that are less than 150 mmHg are ineffective at emptying the breast, and those that are more than 220mmHg can cause nipple pain. It is very important that the pump be fully automatic. Most quality pumps will have either adjustable levels of suction and cycles (within the above specified ranges) that allow you to alter it to suit your needs, or pre-set controls that automatically create and release the suction. With many of the low-end pumps, you must regulate the suction and cycles manually by pressing a lever or placing and removing your fingers over a port.

Double Versus Single Pumping. A good pump will allow you to pump both breasts simultaneously, which is faster and increases the amount of prolactin released, leading to higher milk production. Once you become proficient at pumping, using a double pump can take as little as 10 minutes. If you will be limited to a single pump, such as during a FTX, you should switch the pump from breast to breast about every five minutes per session. Single pumping shouldn't take longer than about 15-20 minutes. Single pumping long-term can lead to lowered milk production.

Adapters and Batteries. What kind of power will you have available? Some pumps require access to electricity, while others come with car adapters. Some can run on battery power, while others are hand-operated only. If you are stationed overseas, make sure that you have the proper adapter for the outlet or you risk blowing the motor.

Carrying Case. Is the pump portable and easy to transport? Does it come with a carry bag and have a compartment to keep your milk cool (especially important if you won't have access to a refrigerator)? Many of the better pumps come with gel/ice packs that fit the compartment, and some have removable cooling compartments that allow you to leave unneeded sections at work. Some pumps are very large, bulky, and heavy, while others are small enough to fit in the pocket of your uniform (especially cammies or utilities). A professional looking "briefcase" or backpack will look better while you are in uniform. Many of the personal-use pumps come in a black, microfiber case with a shoulder strap.

Ease of Use. How easy is it to use the pump? Can it be put together quickly and easily, or does it have a lot of parts to put together every time you want to pump? Does it require that you maintain the suction-release cycle? How easy is it to clean? How noisy is it? Will you be in a noisy environment, such as a supply room off the hangar, or in a quiet office?

Other Features. There are a number of other features available on breast pumps that you may want to consider. Some of these features are useful and necessary, while others are a nice bonus, but not integral to your pumping success. One of the most important is whether the flanges or shields are interchangeable. You want flanges that fit you correctly, as this can impact your milk supply (see more on this in A Good Fit in the next chapter). Some pumps have a "let-down" feature that automatically sets the cycles fast and suction light to mimic the quick sucking your baby does to help the milk flow. Other pumps offer a "cry" feature that allows you to record your baby crying (laughing or cooing), as that has been shown to help the milk-ejection reflex in breastfeeding mothers. Many newer pumps offer LCD displays that show the speed and suction, as well as time and length of your last pumping session. Other extras may include soft "petal" inserts that massage the breast, timers, and other similar items.

Spare Parts. How easy is it to obtain spare parts for your pump, especially if you are overseas? It can be a real blow to your milk supply if you need a membrane or tubing and the only way to get it is from the manufacturer who states that it will ship in two weeks from the U.S. (or worse yet, they don't ship to APO/FPO addresses). Buying a pump from a well-known manufacturer who has a presence worldwide and parts that are carried by drugstores and lactation consultants can save you a lot of headaches.

Types of Pumps

With countless pumps on the market, each claiming to be the "next best thing to having your baby at the breast," it can be hard to cut through the hype and determine what the best pump is for your situation. Here then is a rundown of the four main categories of breast pumps--from hand-operated to hospital-

Medela Harmony
Photo courtesy Medela, Inc. Used with permission

Ameda One-Hand

Photo courtesy Robyn Roche-Paull.
Used with permission.

grade--with what they offer, their advantages and disadvantages, and the workplace situation they are best suited for.

Hand-Operated   Pumps. These pumps come in two basic types: cylinder and handle squeeze. Cylinder pumps have two cylinders: one inside the other, with a rubber gasket between them, and suction is created by pushing and pulling the cylinder in and out. Handle squeeze pumps create and release suction when the handle is squeezed and released. Both types of pumps are very portable, as they are lightweight, small, and quiet. Most hand pumps can be broken down into pieces and stashed in your uniform. These usually do not come with a cooler or storage case (the Ameda One-Hand and the Avent Isis are the exceptions), and they are easy to clean.

Some active-duty mothers buy two hand-operated pumps in order to pump both breasts simultaneously. Hand pumps are best suited for women who need to pump to relieve fullness or while in the field with no access to electricity. Very few women can maintain a full milk supply using a hand pump full-time due to the inability to cycle it at the speed a baby sucks. It can be useful to keep a spare hand-pump with you in case you are without your

regular pump or the electricity goes out. Examples of the better hand pumps on the market include the Avent Isis®, Ameda One-Hand®, and the Medela Harmony®.

> *I suggest purchasing a regular hand pump in addition to your double electric. Hopefully you will never have to use it. But I guarantee it won't seem like a waste of money if for some reason your double electric winds up out of commission. It's always a good idea to have a backup plan if you're a serious pumper.* Staff Sgt., USAF

> *I liked having the Harmony for those times that electricity was not available and/or I just*

Avent Isis Manual

Photo courtesy Robyn Roche-Paull.
Used with permission.

needed to "take a bit off the top" and did not have time to empty both sides. I tried other manual pumps, but none were as comfortable as the Harmony. Tech. Sgt., USAF

Avent Isis manual pump! I tried the Medela in the hospital and it worked as well as others professed, but I still prefer my Avent. I also tried the Avent battery/electric operated version and still prefer the manual and having full control. Petty Officer 3rd Class, USN

Medela Freestyle

Photo courtesy Robyn Roche-Paull. Used with permission.

Occasional-Use, Single or Double pumps. Occasional-use pumps, whether single or double, are generally "semi-automatic," meaning they require that you manually cycle the pump. Even if the pump is labeled as a double pump, most cycle too slowly to effectively drain the breast or provide the proper stimulation to increase your prolactin levels enough to maintain a milk supply.

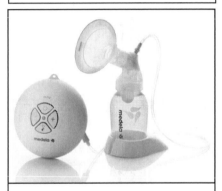

Medela Swing

Photo courtesy Medela, Inc. Used with permission.

These pumps can be battery operated or use an electrical adapter. However, the cost of batteries adds to the overall expense of the pump (and they eat through batteries quickly).

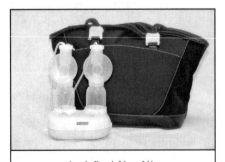

Ameda Purely Yours Ultra

Photo courtesy Robyn Roche-Paull. Used with permission.

The pump may need to be replaced if used frequently over a long time period because the motor is small and not meant for heavy-duty use. Most of the newer models now come with a cooler or storage case. And they are lightweight, small pumps. But they are not very quiet. As the name suggests, these pumps are meant for occasional use: no more than a few times a week. These pumps are best suited for those women who will not have access to electricity and need a portable, double breast pump. Some examples of the better pumps in this category include the Medela Freestyle®, Medela Swing®, Lansinoh®, Bailey Nurture III®, Whittlestone Expresser®, Avent iQ Duo/Uno®. A few of the pumps that are not effective include the Playtex Embrace®, Evenflo Elan® or Comfort Select®, and the First Years MiPump®.

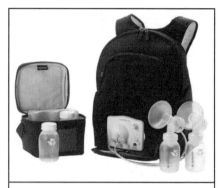

Medela Pump In Style Advance
Photo courtesy Medela, Inc. Used with permission.

I had a Medela double-pump that operated on both a plug and could also operate on batteries.... take extra batteries. Staff Sgt., USA

I have only used the Avent Isis iQ Duo, but it rocks!! It is about 3.5 years old, through two kids, and I have abused that thing! I would recommend it to everyone! Petty Officer 2nd Class, USN

I have only used a First Years pump.... used it for four months and now it's losing its suction...I wouldn't recommend the MiPump. Lt. Cpl., USMC

I tried the cheaper ones...they didn't work well. Tech. Sgt., USAF

Personal-Use, Electric, Double Pump. For active-duty mothers who will be separated from their babies for 40 hours a week or more,

Hygeia EnJoye
Photo courtesy Hygeia. Used with permission.

these lightweight, portable, highly effective, and fully automatic pumps are the best choice. All of these pumps double-pump (and can convert to single pumping if need be) and cycle 40-60 times a minute automatically. These pumps have dual-control mechanisms, allowing you to regulate the speed and suction to suit your comfort. And some models have a two-phase pumping action, a fast "let-down" phase and a slower milk-expression phase. Personal-use pumps are single-user (with the exception of the Hygeia EnJoye, which is FDA-approved as a multi-user personal-use pump), and most come in an attractive briefcase or backpack, with chill packs and a compartment for storing milk. They can be used with multiple power sources-electricity, AC adapters for use in a car/12v, and batteries or a battery pack. These pumps are best suited for use by those AD moms with a regular pumping schedule and someplace to pump and stash the breast pump when not in use. The most popular choices in this category include the Medela Pump In Style®, Ameda Purely Yours®, and the Hygeia EnJoye®.

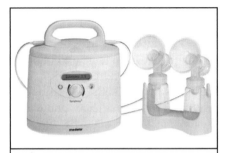

Medela Symphony

Photo courtesy Medela, Inc.
Used with permission.

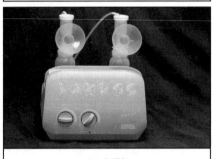

Ameda Elite

Photo courtesy Robyn Roche-Paull.
Used with permission.

Ameda Purely Yours for a double electric, I LOVED the Ameda because it is such a workhorse. I pumped for both of my kids using it and was even TDY for 5 months and pumped full time for her. Tech. Sgt., USAF

Medela Pump In Style. Love it and love the convenience of the bag and the two phase pump. Staff Sgt., USAF

Hospital-Grade, Rental, Double Pumps. These are the most efficient, effective, and comfortable pumps available. Hospital-grade rental pumps automatically cycle 40-60 times a minute with a very smooth action, can double-pump, and are the most effective at mimicking a baby's sucking

PJ's Comfort Limerick

Photo courtesy Robyn Roche-Paull.
Used with permission.

pattern. Like personal-use pumps, most hospital-grade pumps have dual controls for setting the speed and suction to your preference, and some also offer the two-phase pumping technology. These pumps are large and heavy, due to the industrial-size motor, and are not very portable, as most do not have a carrying case or a compartment to store expressed milk. They run on electricity, although a few offer battery packs for use when electricity is unavailable.

Hospital-grade pumps are multi-user pumps, so you must supply your own collection kit ($50-65), which must match the pump brand and is not interchangeable. These pumps are best suited for pumping within a workplace lactation center. Hospital-grade pumps are very expensive to purchase (upwards of $1000 or more) and are normally rented on a weekly or monthly basis ($35-70/month). Examples include the Ameda Lact-E®, Ameda SMB®, Ameda Elite®, Medela Classic®, Medela Lactina® or Medela Symphony®, Hygeia EnDeare®, and the Limerick PJ's Comfort®.

Types of Breast Pumps

Type of Pump		Suction & Cycles	Advantages	Disadvantages	Cost Range	Examples
Manual pump	Hand powered	Variable	Small, portable, quiet, inexpensive	Labor intensive Single-pumping May not be able to achieve proper cycling or suction *Not for maintaining supply*	$15-50	Ameda One-Hand Avent Isis Lansinoh Hand Pump Medela Harmony Simplisse
Battery-operated pump	Battery-operated motor	Variable	Small, portable, inexpensive Can double pump with two units	Goes through batteries quickly May provide inadequate cycling and suction Most models offer manual cycling only *Not for maintaining supply*	$50-150	Avent Isis iQ Uno Medela Swing
Occasional-use electric pump	Small electric pump	Variable	Small and quiet Double or single pumping	Semi-automatic cycling, Some models only offer manual cycling Difficult to achieve adequate cycling and suction Requires electricity or car adapter *Not for maintaining supply*	$50-200	Avent Isis iQ Duo Bailey Nurture III Evenflo Comfort Select First Years MiPump Lansinoh Double Electric Medela FreeStyle Playtex Embrace

Personal-use electric pump	Medium electric pump	40-60 cycles per minute 50-220 mmHg suction	Double or single pumping Automatic cycling Efficient and compact (carrying case or backpack)	Expensive Requires electricity or a car adapter	$150- 400	Ameda Purely Yours Hygeia EnJoye Medela Pump in Style
Hospital-grade electric piston pump	Large piston driven electric pump	40-60 cycles per minute 50-250 mmHg suction	Double or single pumping Automatic cycling Highly efficient Mimics baby's suction pressure and cycling rate	Large and heavy Very expensive, usually rented Requires electricity	Rental: $30-80 / month plus personal kit Purchase: $700 -1500	Ameda Elite or Lact-E Medela Symphony, Lactina or Classic Hygeia EnDeare PJ's Limerick

Adapted from (Biagioli, 2003) and www.breastpumps.com, www.ameda.com, www.medela.com, www.hygieababy.com, www.nursingmothersupplies.com, www.amazon.com, www.babiesrus.com

Breast Pump Maintenance

Remember that your pump is a tool, and like any good tool, you need to take care of your pump, so it can serve you well for many months--if not years. Part of taking care of your pump includes familiarizing yourself with all the parts and what they do, keeping your pump clean and operating at peak efficiency, and dealing with any problems that might occur.

Get to Know Your Pump. The first thing to do is become familiar with the various parts of your pump. Knowing what each piece is and what function it performs will greatly help you understand how a breast pump operates. It will also help you if a piece breaks and you need to replace it, or if you need to clean your pump and put it back together.

Every electric breast pump has the same basic parts and works in the same general way: there is a motor to create suction, tubing that attaches the flanges or shields (that are placed on the breast) to funnel the expressed milk down into the collection bottles, a valve or membrane that releases the milk and then shuts back in place to create a vacuum, and the collection bags or bottles. Some pumps also have diaphragms or filters to keep contaminants away from the milk, various ports for plugging tubing and adapters into the pump, and dials or knobs for adjusting the suction and cycles. Read through the instructions when you first receive your pump to be sure you understand what parts come with your pump and what they do (and in some cases, how to assemble your pump). If you bought your pump from a lactation consultant, have her review the pump's proper use and care with you before you take it home.

Keep it Clean. Regardless of the type of pump you purchase, you should follow the manufacturer's directions in caring for your pump. Before you use your pump for the very first time, take it apart and sterilize all the parts that will come in contact with your milk by boiling them as instructed. In general, all pump cases need to be wiped down with a damp cloth when they are soiled.

If you are using a shared pump in a workplace lactation room, you might want to wipe the pump down before and after you use it with a disinfectant solution. Flanges and other pump parts that contact the milk, such as the valves or membranes, should be rinsed after each use and then washed in hot, soapy water at least once a day. However, many working mothers purchase multiple collection kits for their pump (the flanges and tubing), so they do not have to clean them at work. Or they put the used flanges in the refrigerator until the next use (see Chapter 10 for more information).

Some parts may be put in the dishwasher (flanges, bottles), while other parts cannot (tubing, valves, diaphragms). All parts should be air dried after washing. There are cleaning cloths available that allow you to wipe the pump and parts down when you are without water, as well as steam bags that provide sterilization of the parts and tubing. However, you will need a microwave for the steam bags to work (see Resources). If you should get condensation inside the tubing (a major problem with some brands of pumps), you can either force the water out by swinging the tubing around like a lasso or by running the pump with just the tubing attached. The air flow will evaporate the water.

Troubleshoot and Address Problems. Your pump should be comfortable to use and work effectively. And just like breastfeeding, using a breast pump should NOT hurt. As mentioned above, it is a good idea to know how your pump operates normally, so you can be aware if it is acting up. Don't automatically assume that a milk supply issue is "your" fault; it might be your pump. Even the best pumps can have problems or be defective, although it is not very likely, and cheap pumps often tend to break or lose suction quickly.

If your breast pump is not working correctly, malfunctions, or you are having trouble learning to use it, your first call should be to an IBCLC. She can help you determine if it is the pump or something else that needs attention and point you in the right direction for further help. If the pump is still under warranty and you've determined that the pump is malfunctioning, call the manufacturer for help. Sometimes, the retailer you purchased the pump from may be of assistance as well, particularly if that is their only business. But if you bought it from a big-box retailer, don't expect any help at all. See Chapter 11 for more information on troubleshooting pump problems.

Chapter 8

Milk Expression Basics

Expressing or pumping your breastmilk is one way of connecting to your baby. It provides him with your precious milk, along with all the antibodies and nutrition that is so important for his growth and development. But more than that, it also keeps your milk supply up, so you can breastfeed and remain close when you are together.

The frequency with which you express your breastmilk is the key to stimulating and maintaining a good milk supply. You should aim to have a pumping routine that simulates, as closely as possible, your baby's feeding schedule when you are together. Pumping or expressing breastmilk is not a natural process; we are not meant to be hooked up to machine for this very natural process. So it does take time and a learning curve to get the hang of it and become successful at expressing milk. Follow the tips and suggestions in this chapter to get off to a good start with milk expression for your sweet baby.

Hand Expression

Regardless of your method of expressing your milk, everyone benefits from becoming familiar with this technique. Hand expression is a very useful skill to know, especially for the active-duty mother who may have to unexpectedly leave her baby for a Temporary Duty Assignment, training exercise, or anytime where taking a pump would be impractical. It's also really helpful when you forget your collection kit, your pump breaks, or the power goes out. Hand expression requires no electricity or extra gear besides your own two hands and a container to collect the milk (in field conditions you could express your milk onto the ground, if needed).

Many women find hand expression to be easy, free, and convenient. There are no pumps or parts to worry about. It is portable and natural. Hand expression can relieve fullness and keep your milk supply stable until your return. Some women can express as much, or more, milk by hand as they can by using a pump, and once mastered can completely drain both breasts in 15-20 minutes. Using hand expression before and after pumping can increase the amount of milk you remove compared to pumping alone.

Some women find practicing hand expression in the shower to be helpful. The warm water helps with let-down, and the spraying milk doesn't make a mess. You can also practice on one breast, while nursing your baby on the other. Just be sure to have a towel handy. When you are at work, you'll want to lean forward slightly when expressing and collect the milk in a clean cup or wide-mouth container (unless you are in the field). Try not to let your milk dribble over your fingers or get on your uniform (this is easier said than done!). If you need a visual on how to do hand expression (and most women do), go to http://newborns.stanford.edu/Breastfeeding/HandExpression.html for a fantastic video that shows the steps of hand expression, using both real mothers and animation. Hand expression takes practice, so be patient with yourself and take your time learning!

> *I learned really quick how to manually express my milk one night on CQ duty when I didn't have a pump at all and I was engorged.* Staff Sgt., USA

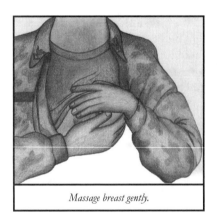

Massage breast gently.

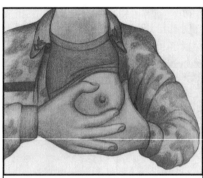

Place thumb and index finger 1-2 inches from nipple.

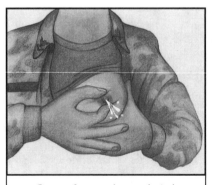

Compress fingers together towards nipple.

★ How to Hand Express ★

1. Massage breasts gently to encourage let-down.

2. Place thumb and index finger on either side of your areola about one to two inches back from the nipple. Your hand should form a 'C' shape.

3. Press back towards the chest wall.

4. Compress your fingers together towards the nipple (like making fingerprints, do not slide or squeeze).

5. Relax.

6. Repeat around the breast to empty all the ducts.

7. Repeat steps on other breast.

8. Most mothers express from each breast for 3-5 minutes or until the milk flow changes from a stream to a trickle. Express from each breast two to three times. The entire process should take about 20-30 minutes.

Learning to Pump

One of the first questions military mothers ask is when they should start pumping while on convalescent leave. There is quite a bit of controversy regarding when the best time is to start pumping before heading back to duty. Some books will tell you to wait until four weeks, while others suggest you should start pumping as soon as your milk comes in.

The first couple of weeks are the most important time for calibrating the breasts to the amount of milk they need to make for the long-haul. Because of your short convalescent leave, you'll probably want to begin practicing with the pump as soon as your milk comes in. This will calibrate your breasts to make more milk than needed and may help to increase your storage capacity as well. By doing this you will build up a superabundant milk supply and be better able to compensate for the inevitable dip when you return to duty. This practice will also help you begin to stockpile breastmilk for your return to work. Do NOT, however, spend so much time and effort trying to pump extra that you don't spend time just being with your baby, bonding, and falling in love with one another. These six weeks will fly by, and while maximizing your milk production is important, spending time *breastfeeding* your baby is more important.

★ Tip ★

The best time to learn to use your pump is when you are calm and unhurried and your breasts are full. Usually after the morning feeding is best when your supply is at its highest. You may be able to express milk more easily, especially from the second side, if it wasn't drained as well.

A good time to begin learning how to pump is in the morning. Most mothers find that their milk supply is at its highest in the morning, and they are the most relaxed at that time as well. You can pump after your baby has breastfed. Even if he took both breasts, there should be enough milk from the second, less drained breast to collect and store. You can also set your pump up to single-pump, and pump one side while simultaneously nursing your baby on the other side. This is a great way to have a quick and strong let-down and boost your prolactin levels.

Pumping is a skill that must be learned, and it takes time to master this skill. Do NOT be alarmed if you get only drops or even nothing at all the first few times. The point of pumping in the early days is to tell your breasts to make more milk. But it will take time. Pumping is as much a physical process as it is a psychological process, so try not to become discouraged. Your body is used to letting-down to a warm, cuddly baby and must get used to letting-down to a cold, hard plastic pump instead. Effectiveness at pumping improves with practice!

First read and follow the manufacturer's directions for your pump. After washing your hands thoroughly, you can set-up your pump and bottles at a table with a comfortable chair. Expose both your breasts (as you become proficient you won't need to undress!) and begin to lightly massage your breasts. Gentle massage helps stimulate your let-down reflex. You may also want to put a warm cloth or heating pad against your breasts as well. Looking at your baby while you pump or smelling an article of his clothing can also be helpful. Once pumping becomes routine, your breasts will become used to the pump, let-down will occur more easily, and you won't need to do all this preparation.

Center your nipple in the breast flange (some mothers find that lubricating the flange with water or olive oil helps to create a stronger seal and reduces friction), and start the pump. If you are using an automatic pump, turn it to its lowest setting and gradually increase the speed. If you are using a manual pump, start with a gentle, slow rhythm. If pumping is painful at anytime, check that your nipple is positioned correctly and your flanges are the correct size (see below). You may also need to adjust the suction, as it might be too strong. Remember, pumping should not be painful. If it is, something is wrong.

It is normal for one breast to spray while the other drips. Very often, one side produces more than the other. Whatever the amount of milk you get these first few times, keep in mind that it is not a reflection of how much your baby gets at the breast. A baby's suck is more effective than a pump. Here are some further tips for getting off to a good start with pumping and throughout your pumping career.

A Good Fit. The flanges (or shields) are the part of the collection kit that fit over your nipple.

Since women's nipples can vary from small to large, and most pumps are packaged with a standard, one-size-fits-all sized flange, it is important that your flanges are properly fitted to your anatomy. The way to tell if your flanges are properly fitted is to watch your nipples when you pump (large breasts do not always mean large flanges,

A good fit is essential.

Used with permission, B. Wilson-Clay, K. Hoover, Normal Breastfeeding Photo Set, www. BreastfeedingMaterials.com, 2009.

it's all about the nipple!). After centering your nipple in the flange, you should see extra space around your nipple.

During the suction phase, your nipple should move in and out of the "tunnel" without rubbing the sides. If pumping is painful or uncomfortable, your nipple fills the tunnel on the flange or seems to be stuck, you see a white ring at the base of the nipple where the tunnel opens into the flange, or your nipple turns a dusky, dark color, you may need larger flanges.

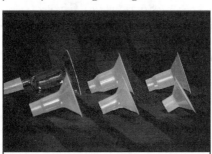

Medela PersonalFit Shields

Photo courtesy Robyn Roche-Paull.
Used with permission.

Using too small of a flange will cause tenderness. But more importantly, it presses against the milk ducts in the nipple, limiting the amount of milk you can express. It can also possibly lead to plugged milk ducts, mastitis, or a lowered milk supply. On the other hand, if the flange does not form an airtight seal or a large portion of your breast tissue is being pulled into the tunnel of the flange, you may need a smaller flange or a reducing insert.

See an IBCLC for help in properly fitting yourself for flanges. Some, but certainly not all, breast pump companies have multiple-sized flanges for their pumps. You may need to try out several flange sizes before finding one that fits correctly. You can't always go by the size of your nipples at rest either. Women with small nipples at rest may find that they swell considerably with suction, while other women have differing flange sizes for each breast.

Ameda Custom Flanges

Photo courtesy Robyn Roche-Paull.
Used with permission.

Sometimes, even after a few weeks of pumping, you may find that your flange size needs to be changed again. All of these are normal occurrences and another reason why it behooves you to buy a pump that has interchangeable flanges. If you can't find flanges for your pump or you are having trouble finding flanges that fit properly, you may want to take a look at a company called "Pumpin' Pals." They

Pumpin Pal Angled Flange

Photo courtesy Shannon O'Donnell.
Used with permission.

make an insert called the "Super Shield Plus" that is angled and has a gradual slope from the flange to the tunnel. It is very forgiving when it comes to size and allows you to sit back, rather than lean forward, while pumping. See Resources for more information on this product.

Suction and Cycles. You'll want to start on the lowest suction setting, if you have one, combined with a rapid cycle rate to trigger your let-down (some pumps do this for you with the two-phase technology). Then you can switch to a slower cycle rate and gradually increase the level of suction to the highest level you are comfortable with.

Using higher, painful suction settings are counterproductive, as it could affect your let-down reflex. When breastfeeding, you probably only notice the first let-down; however, most women can have multiple let-downs during a nursing or pumping session. You can trigger them yourself by increasing the cycle rate and lowering the suction to mimic what your baby does at the breast. Once the let-down has started, decrease the cycles and increase the suction to draw the milk out.

With practice, when using a fully automatic double pump, you should be done in 10-15 minutes. If you are using a single pump, expect it to take about 10-15 minutes per breast, switching about every five minutes. Continue to pump for two to five minutes after the last drops have flowed. In general, it should only take as long to pump as it does to nurse your baby.

Any milk you collect should be stored, not fed to your baby yet (see Chapter 9). Every bag you collect is another two to three ounces of liquid gold for your stockpile (see below). To increase the amounts you collect, grab your pump anytime he only takes one breast and pump the other side. Wait until about four weeks to introduce the bottle. It is important that your baby is exclusively breastfed in these first weeks, so he can become an expert nurser (see Chapter 10, Introducing the Bottle).

Stockpiling Your Milk

The term "stockpile" means to keep a large amount of frozen expressed milk in the freezer for later use. Since you will be separated from your baby on a regular basis, it is a good idea to build up a supply for later use. Begin to stockpile a reserve supply of frozen milk when you start practicing with the pump. Since you will be pumping after several feedings each day in order to calibrate the breasts to make more milk than needed, you will begin collecting a fair amount of milk. By creating an "oversupply" of milk, you will compensate for the dip in production upon your return to work, and your frozen stockpile can be a wonderful back-up for unexpected growth spurts, missed pumping sessions, or other variations in supply.

You'll want to decide how much milk to stockpile. Some mothers choose to keep a small reserve of about three days' worth of milk for "just in case" reasons. Calculate how much your baby eats at daycare and multiply that by three days (if he takes three 3-ounce bottles, you'll need to store nine 3-ounce bottles). However, a number of women who start pumping and collecting their milk early on find that they can manage to stockpile enough to continue giving their babies frozen milk long after they have stopped pumping or even breastfeeding. One active-duty mother had so much milk stockpiled that she was able to give her baby her expressed milk until she turned 18 months old. She breastfed at home and sent breastmilk bottles to daycare.

A couple notes of warning: don't become obsessive about how much milk you can or cannot stockpile. For some women who let down easily to the pump or have an abundant supply, stockpiling milk may be easy. Other women may find it next to impossible to squeeze out even an extra ounce of milk for the freezer. Enjoy your baby while you are together and don't worry if you have to supplement with formula because you couldn't store enough milk in the freezer. Also, while it is important to calibrate your breasts to make more milk than needed in the first weeks, don't pump so much that you end up with plugged ducts or mastitis when you return to work and you can't pump as often. Finally, you should remember that your extra store of frozen milk is for emergencies only. Don't assume that you can rely on your stockpile once you return to work. If you regularly use your stored milk, you'll quickly deplete your stockpile, and every bottle that you give in place of breastfeeding or pumping reduces your milk supply.

★ Tip ★

Low milk supply is the number one reason employed women give for why they stop breastfeeding. Pumping during your convalescent leave and building a "superabundant" supply can guard against low milk supply and keep you breastfeeding for as long as you wish.

Pumped Milk Quantities

Another very common question from mothers who must pump is how much milk they should expect to get at each pumping session. How much milk you pump depends upon many variables, such as the age of your baby, how long it's been since your breasts were last emptied, the time of the day, your stress level, and how established your milk supply is. Pumped milk quantities vary from mother to mother, and even throughout the day and week (kind of like breastfeeding).

Because you can measure how much milk you are pumping, any increase or decrease is more obvious and worrying, even when it is a normal variation. Also keep in mind that your baby can almost always get more milk from your breasts than even the very best breast pump! And that some women never get much out with a pump, even though they have a full supply. Here are some of the factors that make the biggest difference for working mothers in how much milk you can pump.

Normal Quantity. Mothers who are nursing and pumping are able to normally pump between one-half and two ounces total for both breasts per pumping session. Many mothers think they should be able to pump four to eight ounces, but that is unusual and probably due to an oversupply, large storage capacity, or responding better than average to the pump. It is also normal to have to pump two to three times to get enough for one feeding.

At Home Versus Separated. If you are still at home on convalescent leave and are pumping on top of nursing full-time, don't expect to get a lot of extra milk for your freezer stash. Milk pumped during this time is "extra" milk, over and above what your baby needs (remember you are trying to build a superabundant supply). Don't get discouraged. Once back at work, you should be able to pump more per session because you are not also nursing at the same time.

Baby's Age. Pumping for a six-week-old baby is far different than pumping for a six-month-old baby, and so too are the amounts of milk you can expect to express. Before six weeks, your milk supply is still becoming regulated and is controlled by how much your baby demands to nurse. By the 6-week mark your milk supply (and pumped milk quantities) will be at its highest (Kent et al., 2006). Around six months (with the addition of solids), some mothers may notice that their supply and, hence, pumped amounts of breastmilk, begins to drop.

Regularly Scheduled Pumping. Pumping at the same time everyday can greatly affect how much milk you can express. Your body learns when to make milk. If you pump at certain times of the day, your body will become accustomed to producing milk at those times of the day. Exceeding those times can cause fullness and disrupt the hormones responsible for milk making. Furthermore, if you stick to a regular schedule, your breasts won't get too full, which slows milk production (see below).

Breast Storage Capacity. As was discussed earlier in the Basics of Breastfeeding, every mother has a set storage capacity for her breasts. This storage capacity varies widely from mother to mother and does not always correlate with the size of her breasts. What this means is that your breasts can hold a certain amount of milk before the pressure of the milk causes a chemical inhibitor to be released that tells the breast glands to stop making more milk.

For some women, that capacity is small (e.g., two ounces). A woman with a small storage capacity must nurse or pump more often to drain the breasts and keep the pressure down or the chemical inhibitor will be released. She can produce an ample supply, but must nurse or pump every few hours to keep her supply up. For other women, their storage capacity is much higher (e.g., six to seven ounces), and they can go longer periods between nursing or pumping before the pressure causes the chemical signal to stop production of milk. A woman with a large storage capacity might be able to pump once or twice a day and maintain a great supply. Both women will produce the same amount of milk in 24 hours, but those with the smaller storage capacity must remove it more often to keep production up.

This can affect pumping in a number of ways, good or bad, depending on your work environment and demands. If you are a mother with a smaller storage capacity, you'll need to pump more often, but will not get as much at each pumping session. Yet overall, you can pump the same amount in 24 hours as a mother with a larger capacity, *if* you are allowed to pump as often as needed. If you are not allowed to pump often and have a small storage capacity, you may find that you need to supplement in order to have enough milk for your baby.

Many, many women feel guilty or bad that they somehow aren't doing something right when it comes to not being able to pump enough, when in fact it is nothing more than a mismatch between storage capacity (which you cannot control) and a lack of adequate pumping time (which you may or may not be able to control). It can be a relief knowing that it is nothing you are doing wrong, yet a tough pill to swallow, knowing that if you were allowed to pump as often as needed, you'd have enough milk for your baby. On the flip side, mothers with a large storage capacity can get away with pumping erratically once, maybe twice a day, and get six to eight ounces per breast at a sitting and still have oodles of milk. For these mothers, the demands of the work environment do not affect their milk supply nearly as much.

Time of Day, Time of Week. Your breasts produce more milk at night and during the early morning hours than during the late afternoon and evening. You can then expect to pump a greater quantity in the morning sessions than later in the day. Similarly, after a weekend of breastfeeding your baby on demand, you'll probably find that you can pump more milk at the beginning of the week, but by Thursday or Friday your supply is waning.

Milk Ejection Reflex (MER). It is essential to have a let-down or milk ejection reflex in order to breastfeed or pump successfully (even if you don't feel it happening). However, it can be hard to have a let-down with a pump, especially if you face any kind of time pressures or a stressful work environment that is not conducive to pumping. Research has shown that the let-down or MER is 52 seconds when breastfeeding (Kent, Ramsay, Doherty, Larsson, & Hartmann, 2003), yet it can be as long as three minutes when pumping (Mitoulas, Lai, Gurrin, Larsson, & Hartmann, 2002). This can certainly limit the amount of milk you can pump if you've only got 10 minutes to pump.

Chapter 9
Collecting, Storing, and Using Your Milk

Collecting Your Milk

Your expressed breastmilk is a unique fluid, a combination of both nutrition and antibodies, which protects your baby against illness and promotes proper growth and development. Expressed breastmilk can be thought of as a fresh, living substance; it is more than just a food. Therefore, you will need to take good care of the milk you pump, as how it is stored will affect how well the nutritional and anti-infective qualities are preserved.

Containers for Storage. Follow these guidelines to safely collect and store your breastmilk.

- **Hard-sided containers,** glass or plastic, protect your milk, and are a one-time expense. However, they are bulky and can take up a lot of room to store. Research has shown that there is less fat loss with glass or plastic bottles, and the fat that does stick to the walls of glass or plastic bottles is more easily redistributed back into the milk than with breastmilk storage bags (Tully, 2000). If you are concerned about Bisphenol A (BPA) in plastic bottles, there are many manufacturers that carry BPA-free bottles. Any bottles you choose should have well-fitting, airtight, solid tops (not a nipple), and be washed in hot, soapy water and rinsed well before use. Not all hard-sided containers are a universal fit for various breast pumps, so check carefully before buying. Finally, expressing your breastmilk directly into the feeding container greatly decreases the likelihood of contamination.

- **Plastic (polyethylene) milk storage bags,** made for freezing and storing human milk, are convenient and take up less room for storage (especially if you are accumulating a large stockpile). However, they are a one-time use product and cannot be reused, and they are expensive. They can be attached directly to the breast pump for easier collection and storage in the same container. However, pouring milk out of them into a bottle can be awkward if they don't have a pour spout. Moving the milk between storage and feeding containers also increases the possibility of contamination. The fat loss found with using bags for breastmilk storage can be minimized by double bagging (Tully, 2000) to reduce air exposure. If your baby gets most of his breastmilk at the breast, the fat loss from using milk stored in bags is probably insignificant. However, if he drinks mostly pumped breastmilk, you might want to consider hard-sided containers for storage.

• **Disposable plastic nurser bags or liners for bottles** should not be used for storing expressed milk. They are not as durable, are prone to bursting or tearing, are not designed for freezer use, and are not designed for long-term storage. If you choose to use them, double-bagging can help prevent accidents. Never use plastic sandwich bags for storing breastmilk.

• **Do not fill either hard-sided containers or milk storage bags more than three-fourths full** to allow the milk to expand as it freezes. If you express into bottles, leave the cap loose before freezing, and then tighten once the milk is frozen. Squeeze out the air in milk storage bags before sealing. This also helps to prevent freezer burn and your milk from absorbing the odors from other foods.

• **Label every container of milk** with the date of expression and your baby's name, using a sticky label or non-toxic marker. Labeling ensures that your baby gets your milk at childcare.

• Many mothers find a rack, such as the Mother's Milk Mate Breast Milk Storage System® for storing bottles of milk (it dispenses bottles from oldest to freshest), or a plastic container, such as a bin or box to hold the bags of frozen milk (to prevent them sliding around and tearing), to be helpful. Make sure to mark the larger container with the month and year of milk collection (*August 2010 #1, August 2010 #2*).

Mother's Milk Mate Breast Milk Storage System
Photo courtesy of Mother's Milk Mate.

• Store expressed breastmilk in "feeding sized" quantities (two to four ounces) to minimize waste and make thawing easier. Some mothers use an ice-cube tray to freeze their milk. A new take on the old stand-by of using an ice-cube tray is MilkTrays®, a reusable, BPA-free, medical-grade plastic tray that freezes breastmilk in one ounce "sticks." It holds up to eight sticks (that fit in the mouth of bottles) and comes with a lid.

- It is fine to "layer" or combine milk from different pumping sessions on the same day. You can add freshly expressed milk to frozen milk after chilling it in the refrigerator (or cooler compartment) for at least 30 minutes. Avoid adding more freshly expressed milk than the amount already frozen in the container.

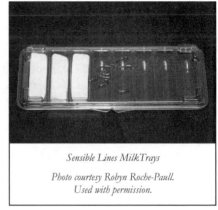

Sensible Lines MilkTrays

Photo courtesy Robyn Roche-Paull.
Used with permission.

Milk Usage Guidelines

In the perfect world, your freshly expressed breastmilk should be given to your baby as soon as possible to have the maximum benefit. The vitamin content of expressed breastmilk degrades and the bacteria count increases the longer it is stored.   Anytime you express milk, some of your skin bacteria will get mixed in with it. Fortunately, breastmilk is full of immune properties that help to prevent these bacteria from multiplying. Refrigeration of breastmilk preserves most of the immune properties, but not all of them. And freezing destroys the white blood cells that protect against illness, but preserves some of the other immune properties.   Despite all of this, expressed breastmilk that is properly collected and stored is far superior to formula.   The following guidelines for storing expressed breastmilk are based on research, expert opinion, and the common practices of mothers like you.

Room Temperature

It is best if you can provide freshly expressed breastmilk to your baby. Antioxidant activity in breastmilk, important for fighting infection and mopping up free radicals, has been shown to decrease slightly with both refrigeration and freezing (Hanna et al., 2004). If you can pump once in the morning before work, you can leave a bottle of freshly expressed breastmilk in the diaper bag for the first feeding at daycare. If, by chance, you forget and leave a bottle of freshly expressed breastmilk sitting on the counter or table (we've all done it at least once), it will remain safe to use for four to six hours at temperatures up to 77°F or 25°C.

Insulated Cooler

If you don't have a refrigerator at work (or don't feel comfortable leaving it in the workspace refrigerator), freshly expressed milk can be kept cool in an insulated container with freezer gel packs or ice packs when no refrigeration is available for up to 24 hours at 59°F or 15°C.

Refrigerated

Refrigerated, not frozen, milk is next best, if at all possible. There is no need to freeze the milk you pumped on a Friday if you will be using it on Monday. Most of the anti-infective properties are preserved when breastmilk is refrigerated (Williamson & Murti, 1996). If you don't use it within five to eight days, add it to your freezer stash. Always place your expressed milk in the coldest part of the refrigerator, usually at the back, away from the door. Freshly expressed milk can be refrigerated for three to eight days at 39°F or 4°C.

If you do store your milk in a refrigerator at work during the day, or your childcare provider has questions about storing your milk around other food, you can let them know that the Centers for Disease Control and the U.S. Occupational Safety and Health Administration have both made statements that human milk is **not** a body fluid that requires special handling or storage in a separate refrigerator as a bio-hazardous material. It can be stored in a common refrigerator at work and childcare facilities (Centers for Disease Control, 2009; Occupational Health & Safety Administration, 1992).

Frozen

If you know you won't be using your refrigerated milk within three to eight days, it needs to be frozen as soon as possible after collecting. Place containers of breastmilk at least an inch away from the walls of a self-defrosting freezer to prevent defrosting and refreezing. Do not store containers in the door of a freezer where the temperature fluctuates. Always maintain a temperature of 0° F or -18°C. Frozen breastmilk will remain safe to use for three to six months in a self-contained refrigerator/freezer unit.

When using frozen breastmilk, always use the oldest stored breastmilk first for two reasons. One is so you don't exceed the storage duration guidelines (see table) and the other is because the properties of your milk are specific to the age of your baby. It is best to use milk expressed when your baby was two months old when he is nearer to two to three months of age than when he is 10 months old. Remember, though, that your frozen breastmilk, no matter how "old," is always a healthier choice than formula! Try to rotate in a few frozen bags per week (two to four), along with your refrigerated supply, and freeze some of the freshly expressed milk to replace the milk you defrost. This ensures that your milk is rotated, and your baby still receives mostly fresh milk at feedings.

Some mothers pump enough everyday to accumulate a sizable freezer stash that quickly exceeds the limits of their regular freezer. You can store your milk in a deep freezer for 6-12 months at -4°F or -20°C. Having a huge stockpile allows you to continue feeding your baby expressed breastmilk long after you may have stopped pumping or breastfeeding (see Stockpiling Your Milk in Chapter 9).

Human Milk Storage			
Type of Milk and Storage Area	Temperature	Storage Time	Comments
Freshly Expressed Milk			
Countertop or table	Room temperature Up to 77°F or 25°C	4 hours (ideal) 6 hours (acceptable) 8 hours (maximum)	Keep containers covered and as cool as possible
Insulated cooler & frozen gel packs	5-39°F or -15-4°C	24 hours	Keep ice packs in contact with milk; limit opening the cooler bag
Refrigerated Milk			
Fresh	32-39°F / 0-4°C	3 days (ideal) 5 days (acceptable) 8 days (maximum)	Store milk towards back of main part of refrigerator
Thawed	32-39°F / 0-4°C	24 hours	
Frozen Milk			
Freezer compartment inside refrigerator	5°F or -15°C	2 weeks	Store milk towards back of freezer
Freezer compartment with separate door	0°F or -18°C	3-6 months	
Separate deep freeze	-4°F or -20°C	6-12 months	
Adapted From: (Academy of Breastfeeding Medicine, 2004; La Leche League International, 2008)			

Transporting Expressed Breastmilk

Transporting your expressed milk to and from work to home and daycare generally isn't a problem. Pop your collection bags or bottles into an insulated cooler or container with frozen gel packs if they've been in the fridge at work, and off you go. Some mothers drop the expressed milk off at the daycare for the next day, and others take it home to add to their stockpile.

If you are one of the lucky few who may be away at school or training and will be shipping milk back home, there are a few guidelines to follow in order to keep your milk safe. When shipping expressed milk, you will need to make sure that your milk is completely frozen. Place the bags or bottles into a cooler, using lots of newspaper around and between the containers. The frozen milk will act as its own ice pack and newspaper is a fabulous insulator. Tape it very well, making sure the address is clear, and ship using the fastest speed possible. Have your caregiver check for any thawed or leaking containers when it arrives (See Chapter 13 for more information on shipping breastmilk).

Thawing & Warming Frozen Breastmilk

There are several safe methods for thawing frozen breastmilk. The best, yet slowest, method is to leave it overnight in the refrigerator. It will take several hours to thaw three ounces of frozen milk. You can thaw milk quickly by holding the bottle or bag under warm (not hot) running water or by placing it in a bowl of warm water. Make sure the top of the container remains above the water at all times and change the water when it cools.

Do not leave human milk out to thaw at room temperature. Nor should you leave thawed milk at room temperature. Place it in the refrigerator where it can remain for 24 hours or feed it to your baby. And just as you wouldn't refreeze thawed meat, do not refreeze thawed milk. The ability of the milk to inhibit bacterial growth is diminished in previously frozen milk.

Some babies don't care whether their milk is cold or not. Others create a huge fuss if it isn't warm like when it comes straight from you. If your baby prefers his milk warm, there are a few ways to warm it safely. Much like with thawing milk, you can warm milk by running warm (not hot) water over it or by placing it in a bowl of warm water. You can also use a commercial bottle warmer. Just be sure not to overheat it.

Never use the stovetop or the microwave to warm expressed breastmilk. Unintentional overheating, or "hot spots," may occur that can burn your baby's mouth. High temperatures can alter the composition of breastmilk and destroy many of its beneficial properties, including antibodies and other immune properties, as well as lipase, the part of your milk that helps your baby digest fats (Tully, 2000).

Reusing Thawed Breastmilk

Ideally, each day you will send the amount of milk your baby is likely to eat. If he is still hungry, some additional milk can be added to the bottle to complete the feeding. The problem is it doesn't always work out that way. Oftentimes, another full bottle is prepared, and then when your baby only takes an ounce, the daycare provider is left with an almost full bottle of milk, which she tosses out. After all the hard work of pumping and storing your breastmilk, it can be very discouraging to find that your daycare provider has been throwing your precious breastmilk away when your baby doesn't finish his bottle--especially if your milk supply is low and you struggle to provide enough each day.

It is not generally recommended to save the breastmilk left in a bottle for a later feeding, mostly due to the lack of studies on its safety. Whenever a baby drinks from a bottle, bacteria from his saliva can enter and the contents will be exposed. Left at room temperature, they multiply like crazy. This is a real problem with formula, which promotes bacterial growth and can make babies very ill. However, breastmilk has properties that kill bacteria. It is reasonable to recommend that any breastmilk that is leftover from a feeding can be saved for the next feeding, provided it is used within just a few hours and the bottle is returned to the refrigerator. Don't, however, reuse a bottle of expressed milk a second time. You can find further information on reusing expressed breastmilk at http://www.kellymom.com/bf/pumping/reusing-expressedmilk.html. You may also want to talk with your IBCLC or HCP about this if you have further questions.

Colors, Smells, and Separation, Oh My!

Human milk can vary in its color, depending on what you have eaten. This is normal, and if you weren't pumping, you'd never see the color. The usual culprits include prenatal vitamins (bright neon green milk), foods or drinks with lots of artificial colors (a whole rainbow of colors), and foods that have naturally deep colors, like spinach, carrots, or tomato sauce in large quantities (pale green, orange, or pink).

Sometimes mothers will notice blood in their milk. Generally, this is caused by cracks in the nipple (which means your baby's latch or the size of your flanges need to be looked at) or minor bleeding in the ducts. Blood will also give your milk a pale pink shade. Differently colored milk isn't anything to worry about unless it lasts for more than a few days or gets worse. Furthermore, drinking the strangely colored or blood-tinged milk will not harm your baby.

Fresh breastmilk has a slightly sweet, mild scent and taste, and depending on what you eat or drink, will echo the flavors found in your diet. Much like during pregnancy, your baby is being fed a steady diet of interesting flavors through your breastmilk. If you like a lot of garlic or curry, then your baby will too! This comes in handy when it is time to start solids because your baby is already used to a varied diet of flavors and smells.

Unfortunately, while not common, some mothers notice that their thawed breastmilk may have a soapy or rancid smell. It is most often caused by the enzyme lipase, which breaks down the fats in milk, so babies can digest it easier. The breakdown of fat occurs more easily with refrigeration and freezing. Some women produce breastmilk with more lipase than others, which causes the changes in smell or taste to be stronger and occur more quickly (Mohrbacher & Stock, 2003). The soapy smell and taste do not affect the nutritional quality of your milk, so it is safe to feed to your baby. Most babies, especially younger ones, will not object to the taste. However, older babies may reject the flavor.

You can try offering the unpleasant tasting milk with fresh milk to dilute the flavor and see if your baby will accept it. For most mothers with milk high in lipase who must use stored breastmilk on a regular basis, your best bet is to scald the milk. Scalding the milk *before* storing it inactivates the lipase (it won't have any affect if you scald after it has turned rancid) (Lawrence & Lawrence, 2005). To scald your milk, you need to express it, pour it into a pan, and heat the milk until it is bubbling on the sides, but do **not** bring it to a full boil. Remove it from the heat and quickly cool the milk in the refrigerator or freezer.

Unlike cow's milk or formula, breastmilk is not homogenized, so it separates into a "milk" layer and a "fat" layer when stored. When you or your childcare provider are ready to feed it to your baby, you should swirl it gently to mix the layers of separated milk. This will also redeposit the fat that has adhered to the sides of the container. Never vigorously shake your breastmilk. Shaking breaks and splits apart the proteins, a very important part of your milk (Smith, 1998). Remember, human milk is a living tissue!

Chapter 10
Back on Duty

Introducing a Bottle

After "When do I start pumping"?, the next-most-often asked question is, "When do I introduce the bottle"? Quickly followed by, "How do I introduce the bottle"? Just as is true with pumping, there are ways to do it so it is least likely to cause problems in your breastfeeding relationship. Some babies can switch back and forth between your breast and a bottle nipple with no problems. Other babies object to anything but the real thing.

There are a lot of opinions about when the best time is to introduce the bottle. The consensus seems to be between three to four weeks is best for a mother who has to go back to work at six weeks. This gives your baby time to have mastered breastfeeding, and you time to master expressing your milk. But it isn't so long that your baby becomes resistant and refuses to take the bottle.

Choose a nipple with a gradual flare from tip to base

Photo from (Peterson & Harmer, 2010).
Used with permission.

Before you introduce the bottle, you need to select the proper nipple. It can take a bit of trial and error to choose the right nipple that will help, not hinder, breastfeeding. Maintaining and protecting your breastfeeding relationship is priority number one, so the type of nipple you choose is very important and needs to allow your baby to switch between bottle and breast easily.

There is an excellent method for choosing the best nipple for your breastfeeding baby developed by Amy Peterson and Mindy Harmer in their book, *Balancing Breast and Bottle: Reaching Your Breastfeeding Goals* (Peterson & Harmer, 2010). The SIMPLE Method is included in the textbox below. Keep in mind that there is more to combining breast and bottle-feeding than just selecting and introducing the bottle, these topics are further explored in their book, which I highly recommend.

★ SIMPLE Method ★

The SIMPLE Method is an acronym that identifies the various steps in choosing a bottle nipple for a breastfed baby. Each letter stands for a phrase describing one step of bottle introduction. Every step is important in determining the best bottle nipple for your baby.

S   **Select a nipple**: Start with a slow-flow nipple that gradually flares from length to base and has an appropriate texture.

I   **Interest the baby**: Beginning when your baby is three to four weeks of age, introduce the bottle to your baby when he is alert and calm, allowing him to latch onto a bottle nipple that isn't dripping.

M   **Maintain a wide latch**: Make sure your baby's mouth is widely opened, accepting the nipple length in addition to a portion of the nipple base.

P   **Position of tongue**: Check that your baby's tongue stays over the bottom gum ridge, with the sides cupping the nipple, moving in a wave-like motion visible under your baby's chin during swallowing.

L   **Lips**: Make sure your baby's lips stay flanged, which means the top lip is visible and the bottom lip flips outward. Both lips should gently rest on a portion of the nipple base. After your baby latches onto the bottle nipple, adjust your baby's lips.

E   **Effortless swallow**: Listen for a rhythmic swallow pattern. Your baby should swallow after every one or two sucks, without gulping or gagging.

Excerpted from *Balancing Breast and Bottle: Reaching Your Breastfeeding Goals* (Peterson & Harmer, 2010). Used with permission.

When you first introduce the bottle, much like the first time you pump, you'll want to choose a relaxed, unhurried, and calm time. Usually, the mornings seem to be best, between feeds, as you don't want your baby either too full or too hungry. You might want to offer small amounts of two to three ounces, so you don't waste any of your breastmilk.

It is not a good idea to offer formula. It tastes completely different than breastmilk, and he may refuse the bottle on taste alone. Let him learn on a familiar tasting and favorite food! Try the breastmilk warm, room temperature, or cold. You'll really just have to see what your baby prefers. You may need to warm the nipple, too.

Most books suggest that someone other than you should be the one to introduce the bottle. And in some cases, this makes sense. Some babies will

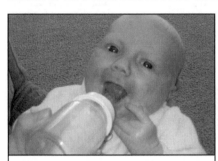

Introducing a bottle to your baby

Photo from (Peterson & Harmer, 2010).
Used with permission.

refuse to accept a bottle from mom because they can smell the milk and will constantly turn and root at the breast. If that is the case, you may need to have your partner, baby's grandmother, or caregiver give the bottle. However, you are most familiar with your baby. You know his latch and suck, what his lips look like when latched properly, and how long your let-down lasts. So you really are best suited to teach him how to take a bottle. Once your baby is comfortable taking a bottle from you, you can teach another caregiver how to do it.

To begin offering the bottle, hold your baby as you would to nurse him, rest the bottle on his top lip or stroke his lips and wait for him to open his mouth. Do not push or force the bottle into his mouth. He can pull it in on his own, just as he does at the breast. He may only play with or mouth it the first few times. This is OK. Let him learn at his pace.

Some babies will only take a bottle if they are facing out, away from the breast, with his back to your chest. Sometimes, movement can help. Try swaying, walking, or putting him in a sling. It is not a good idea to sit in the same place where you normally nurse. He'll want to breastfeed, not try the bottle! Once he begins to suck, let him control the rate. And when he signals that he has had enough, stop! Don't force him to finish the bottle. Whatever you do, introducing the bottle should never be a battle of wills. If you or your baby, your partner, or the caregiver is feeling upset, STOP. If it is not working, try again later.

It is important to practice consistently in order for your baby to remember and readily accept the bottle when you go back to work. Many times, mothers have introduced a bottle at four weeks, and then quit using the bottle, only to find at six weeks when they return to work, their babies won't take the bottle at all. Once he has accepted the bottle, continue to offer it once every two or three days to maintain his acceptance of it. Your baby should have his breastfeeding "meals" at the breast and practice bottle-feeding during "snack time," with one-half to one ounce of expressed breastmilk in the bottle.

Breastfeeding for meals makes sure that your breastfeeding relationship and milk supply are preserved. Once the practice sessions are going well, go ahead and teach another adult. You'll want to do this so that your baby doesn't learn to associate breast and bottle-feeding only with you, and then won't accept the bottle from anyone else. After your baby is readily accepting a bottle from others, you should only breastfeed to reinforce that breastfeeding is done with you, bottle-feeding is done with others.

There are some major differences between bottle-feeding and breastfeeding. One of the biggest worries of breastfeeding mothers is that their babies will prefer the bottle over the breast and wean. Understanding and controlling the differences can go a long way towards making bottle-feeding more like breastfeeding.

Difference 1. No waiting for the let-down. One of the first differences you'll notice is the lack of non-nutritive sucking before the let-down occurs when babies are bottle-fed. If you remember back to the Basics of Breastfeeding chapter, I explained the difference between non-nutritive sucking (NNS), or the light "flutter" sucking that occurs to trigger the let-down, versus the nutritive sucking (NS) that happens when your baby is actively sucking and swallowing.

When a baby is bottle-fed, the milk begins flowing as soon as the bottle is put to his lips. There is no NNS. Furthermore, with breastfeeding your breasts have numerous let-downs during a single feeding. Your baby begins breastfeeding by triggering a let-down using non-nutritive sucking, and once the milk begins flowing uses nutritive sucking. Then when the milk flow slows, he goes back to NNS to trigger another let-down. This can happen many times during a single feeding. Not so with bottle-feeding, where the milk flows non-stop.

You can mimic breastfeeding (and the let-downs) by offering a bottle that is not dripping and by controlling that first huge amount of milk that most bottle-fed babies receive. You can do this by making sure that the pressure in the bottle is equalized before offering it to your baby. If the bottle will not equalize and keeps dripping, position your baby in an upright position and offer the bottle with the milk below the tip of the nipple. Once he takes the bottle and begins sucking, you can tip the bottle so the milk is over the holes. During the feeding, you can mimic let-downs by having your baby pause and rest after every 25-30 swallows by either taking the bottle away or resting it so that no milk flows (the milk is below the level of the holes) for 10-30 seconds.

Difference 2. Speed of flow. The flow from a bottle is faster than the flow from your breasts, and when babies are fed with a bottle, they tend to eat faster and eat more, which can be a problem for a variety of reasons. Babies can easily begin to prefer the "fast" flow and quick feedings and get frustrated by the breast and how "slow" it seems in comparison. Or they learn to "stop" the flow by pushing their tongue against the bottle nipple. When your baby goes back to the breast, he may want the "fast" flow. If the flow doesn't happen fast enough, it may lead to a frustrated, fussy baby who doesn't even stay at the breast long enough to trigger a let-down. Eventually, this can affect your milk supply and lead to weaning. Having learned to put his tongue against the bottle nipple to stop the flow, he may put his tongue against your nipple, which can lead to sore nipples. Finally, bottle-fed babies can easily be overfed. Overfeeding leads to the perception that you need to pump and send more milk to daycare (putting way more pressure on you). He also won't nurse as much when he is with you because he is full (both of which can lead to weaning). And overfeeding can lead to obesity problems as he matures.

You can control all of the above by using slow-flow nipples, even when your baby is older. Slow-flow nipples require that your baby work harder to get the milk out, much like he does at the breast.

Difference 3. Lack of infant/caregiver interaction. This is a big one. It is really easy to have bottle-feeding turn into an independent feeding method, where your baby feeds himself. Far too many caregivers (and parents) prop the bottle for young babies (so they can do other things) or allow the older baby to feed himself the bottle. When this happens your baby misses out on very important human interaction, which is integral to his growth and development. It also means that bottle-feeding is no longer anything like breastfeeding. Your baby may learn to prefer the quick, I-do-it myself approach and squirm and fuss when being held for breastfeeding.

★ Making Bottle-feeding More Like Breastfeeding ★

Make it a rule that your baby MUST be held in a caregiver's arms when being given a bottle. To further mimic breastfeeding, you or your caregiver should make eye contact, talk, touch, and switch sides when holding him. The caregiver should control the flow of milk as outlined above to mimic let-downs and burp your baby halfway through the feeding. And by all means, continue holding your baby, even as he gets older. It is vital to their well-being.

The typical feeding from a bottle of three to four ounces should last about 10-15 minutes. If he feeds any faster (less than 10 minutes), he won't realize that he is actually full yet and may continue to be fussy. Or because he has gulped the feeding down, he may actually have an upset stomach and be fussy.

Signs that the flow is too fast include a sputtering, gagging, or choking baby who pulls off frequently. Feedings that take longer than about 15-20 minutes may be due to him being uninterested in the bottle or frustrated due to having difficulty with the nipple. Remember that you should hear or see one to two sucks for every swallow when using a bottle. You may need to adjust the nipple size to find the right flow rate for your baby, and adjust it as he gets older.

Back at Work

Your first days back on duty are going to be hellish. There is just no way around this fact. No matter what kind of soldier or airman you are, no matter what horrors of war you've seen, there is nothing like leaving your baby in the arms of someone else the first time and marching into your workplace. You've fallen in love with a new little person, who is completely dependent upon you, and now you're supposed to leave him? This will be one of the hardest things you will ever have to do (after deploying without your child). But it can be helpful to know you aren't alone in feeling this way. Virtually every mother-- civilian or military--has had to come to grips with leaving their precious baby to go to work. Even if you are feeling a little sigh of relief to be back in the adult world, it can still come as rude shock the first time you drop your baby at daycare and walk away.

Becoming a mother changes you. From now on, you are tied to another human being in a very intimate bond. Breastfeeding, for good or bad, makes that bond extra tight. You have hormones that are coursing through your body that make you want to be with your baby and that set off alarm bells when you are apart. These hormones are not in the bodies of mothers who do not breastfeed.

AD mother reconnecting with her baby at the end of a long day.

Photo courtesy Leah Bailey. Used with permission.

Accept the reality of the situation and build on it. Use the hormonal bond to your advantage. It will help you to stay closer to your baby when you are at home. Realize too, that you will shed a few tears and that your mind is going to be elsewhere the first few days, until you get into a routine. Your baby is also going to go through some adjustments in these first few days, and this will be no cake-walk for him either. Do not be surprised to find that he wants to nurse more than ever when you pick him up. It is his way of reconnecting with you and making sure that you are really back. Take it as a compliment of your attachment to one another.

The first couple of days are the hardest, so try to schedule, if you can, to return to work on a Thursday or Friday. This allows you a chance to get back in the swing of your new schedule and pumping at work, and learn to deal with the tiredness, emotions, and hormones for only a few days, rather than have the whole week looming ahead of you.

It is also a good idea to give it a trial run a few days before your return to full duty. Take your baby, with a bottle of expressed milk, to your caregiver and leave him for just a couple of hours the first day. Go run errands or go to the Starbucks on base and relax (remember that?) for a few hours. This gives your baby and caregiver a chance to get to know one another. And you can still be "on call" if he really isn't handling it well. The next day you may want to leave him for a longer period of time, or even the full day, and pump on a schedule you think will mimic what you can do at work. This will give you an idea of how much milk you can express and how much your baby will take in the course of a day.

Once you are back at work on a full-time basis, you will find that how you plan your day can make a huge difference in how well pumping goes for you. You will find that your day is controlled by your pumping schedule, and having a routine in place helps to make the workday go by more smoothly.

At Home. If at all possible, try to start your day by breastfeeding your baby. Hopefully, he will either stay or go back to sleep, so you can finish getting ready without him in your arms. Since your milk supply is highest in the morning, try to fit in a pumping session before you leave to drop him off at daycare. If you have to PT first thing in the morning, nurse beforehand (which you'll want to do for comfort anyway), and then when you come back home to shower, try to squeeze in a pumping session. Either way, that bottle of freshly expressed milk can be sent to the daycare for your baby's first meal later in the morning.

Hopefully, the night before, you packed both your bag and your baby's diaper bag and cleaned your pump parts, so they are ready to go in the morning. Here is a list of useful items to be sure you have in your bag (this list is also in Appendix I).

- Breast Pump with all parts and tubing
  - ° Extra set of flanges, tubing, membranes
- Two bottles or collection bags for *each* pumping session
  - ° Extra set of bottles/collection bags
- Power supply, extension cord, batteries
  - ° Adapter if overseas
- Hand pump

- Ice packs and tote or cooler

- Breast pads or Lily Padz©

- Cleaning supplies

  ° Steam bags

  ° Ziploc bag with water & dish soap

- Extra set of uniforms

- Hands-free bra/bustier or Pumpin Pals strap (optional)

- Baby pictures

- MP3 player or iPod with music/photos/baby's sounds

Dropping/Picking Up Baby. When you drop off (and pick up) your baby, that is your time to communicate with your daycare provider about your baby's feedings. It is important that you do this on a regular basis. Your daycare provider needs to know what amounts to feed your baby, how he is feeling, and what is going on developmentally. This also gives your daycare provider a chance to fill you in on how your baby is doing while you are apart and whether you need to send more or less milk every day. See Chapter 11, Childcare, for more information on speaking with your provider about feeding amounts, how-to feed a breastfed baby, end-of-day bottle, etc.

Pumping Scenarios. Because the military is such a unique work environment, there is no one-size-fits-all scenario for pumping. Section 4 of this book covers how to manage pumping in some of the military work environments in detail. However, this portion of the book will give you an overview and general idea of how you might want to schedule your pumping sessions. You can adjust it to suit your circumstances. There are a number of pumping scenarios for the workday that may or may not work for your situation.

Military Pumping Scenarios			
	Morning	Lunch	Afternoon
Scenario One *Best (Unlikely)*	Breastfeed at CDC	Breastfeed at CDC	Breastfeed at CDC
Scenario Two *Very Good (Possible)*	Pump 10-15 minutes	Breastfeed at CDC	Pump 10-15 minutes
Scenario Three *Good (Most Common)*	Pump 10-15 minutes	Pump 20 minutes	Pump 10-15 minutes
Scenario Four *Good (Common)*	Pump 5 minutes to relieve engorgement	Pump 10-20 minutes	Pump 5 minutes to relieve engorgement
Scenario Five *OK (Common)*	? Pump ?	Pump 10-20 minutes	? Pump ?
Scenario Six *Not Good (Likely)*	No Pumping	Pump 10-20 minutes	No Pumping
Scenario Seven *Worst (Likely)*	No Pumping Breastfeed at Home, Supplement on Duty		

Using Scenario Three from the above chart, which is probably the most common scenario for you as a military mother, you can work out an individual pumping and nursing plan for your entire day. At a minimum, you need at least eight pumping or nursing sessions in 24 hours to maintain your milk supply.

One of the ways to make sure you are getting enough breastfeeding and pumping sessions in during a 24-hour period is to keep your baby with you. Wear him in a sling or front carrier and do your household chores with him in it. Take him with you to the store. Go to the movies and dinner. Sleep with him. Let him nurse as often as possible. Remember the mantra that when baby is with you, he gets the breast. When he is away from you, he gets the bottle. If he is with you when you are not at work, you can be sure that he will get the breast often, and that can only help your milk supply and your attachment to one another! Here is an example of how to fit nursing and pumping into a typical 24 hour military day.

★ **Sample Plan for a Pumping, Active-Duty, Breastfeeding Mother of a 4-month old** ★

- 0500 Nurse
- 0600 PT
- 0700 Pump and send milk to daycare
- 0730 Drop baby at daycare and nurse briefly
- 1000 Pump 15 minutes
- 1230 Pump at lunch
- 1500 Pump 15 minutes
- 1730 Nurse at daycare
- 1800 Nurse at home (longer)
- 2100 Nurse
- 0100 Nurse (and sleep)
- 0500 Nurse

Cleaning Up. When you are planning your pumping scenario, make sure you calculate clean-up time of your pump parts as well. While pump manufacturers and HCPs recommend that you wash any pump parts that contact your milk (flanges, filters, and bottles) in warm, soapy water after every use, there are alternatives. Some military mothers will not have access to a sink. Others may not have the time to wash their parts *and* pump.

You can shorten your cleaning routine and have more time for pumping by using some of the following suggestions. Many mothers buy an extra set or two of flanges and bottles to use during the day, and then clean everything in the evening at home. Another idea is to use sanitizing wipes (they kill up to 99% of germs) made for cleaning pump parts. This is especially useful when a sink is not available, such as out in the field, as no water is required. If you use sanitizing wipes, be sure to let your pump parts dry for at least 10 minutes before using again. If you do wash your pump parts at work, you can save drying time by hanging them in a mesh bag to dry.

A final technique to consider is refrigeration of your pump parts. Rather than cleaning your pump parts after every use, you can keep your pump parts assembled in the refrigerator between pumping sessions. Refrigeration can keep the milk from drying on the filters--especially if you put the parts in a Ziploc bag. Bacterial growth is retarded due to the antibacterial properties of your milk and the cold temperatures. Refrigeration of pump parts is considered safe, and research backs this practice. Breastmilk is safe at room temperature for several hours and refrigerated for up to eight days (Academy of Breastfeeding Medicine, 2004; Biagioli, 2003; La Leche League International, 2008). An Air Force Major, who flies long-distance flights of 8-10 hours and pumps in the back of the aircraft while her co-pilot flies the plane, has this to say about refrigeration of pump parts:

> *At first I thought I needed to clean my pump parts after every session. But then I realized that I could just put everything in the fridge on the plane. If breastmilk is good for up to eight days in the fridge, then my pump parts are probably okay… in between cleanings as long as they're kept in the fridge. When I did clean them, I used the Medela wipes and the Medela steam bag for the microwave.*

No matter what cleaning option you use at work, you must clean the pump parts that come in contact with your milk by using warm, soapy water at least once a day. If you want to be extra thorough, you can sterilize your pump parts by either boiling them briefly (check your pump instructions) or using microwave-sterilizing bags. These can be purchased at most stores (including the base or post exchanges). The bags can be used multiple times and are useful for sterilizing nipples, bottles, and tubing.

Timesavers, Tips, and Tricks. There are any number of tricks and tips that pumping mothers the world over have used or found helpful when pumping at work. Here are just a few that have been suggested to me while working with military mothers and during the writing of this book. One of the most often repeated pieces of advice has been to listen to a recording of your baby cooing, crying, or making whatever special noise he makes. With the rise in popularity and availability of electronic gadgets, you may want to make a slideshow with photos and sounds of your baby to play on your iPhone, iPod, mp3 player, or Smartphone, and then play it while pumping to stimulate your let-down.

> *I started using my iPod, and that was the greatest help ever! I set it up to have calming music play over headphones while I looked at my iPod and viewed pictures of the baby the whole time. It's a compact, private way to block out your surroundings and view pictures of your baby to relax while pumping in even the most uncomfortable situations.*
> Captain, USAF

Some women find mental imagery (such as flowing water or milk) or childbirth breathing helpful, as is keeping a piece of clothing which smells like your baby with you. It is helpful to minimize distractions and follow the same routine each time you pump, if you can. However, this isn't always possible in some environments, such as during field training exercises.

Setting up all your pumping equipment as soon as you get to work, so you won't have to do it later, can also save you some time. This is only possible if you have a dedicated pumping space. Some mothers pack Ziploc bags (gallon-size) with soapy water/fresh water for cleaning their pump parts. This is particularly handy if you are pumping in the field or your POV.

Some women find a "hands-free" bra or kit helpful when pumping. These devices allow you to hold your flanges in place, through the use of straps and hooks or slits that the pump flanges fit into, so you can continue to work. They are most suitable for those personnel who have a private office and have administrative type work to do, as they require that your uniform blouse be unbuttoned and open while pumping. Most of the major nursing bra companies make hands free bras that work with the major pump brands. Or you can buy a bustier that zips in the front to hold the flanges in place (see Appendix B for resources). You can also make your own hands-free bra by taking a sports bra and cutting a cross (+) over the nipple area, slide the flanges into the slit in the bra, and the snugness of the sports bra will hold it in place. Another way to make a "hands free" device is to take two to three hair elastics and chain link them together to form a figure eight. Then wrap one end of the chain around the funnel portion of the flange and

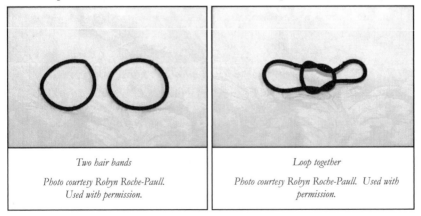

Two hair bands	*Loop together*
Photo courtesy Robyn Roche-Paull. Used with permission.	*Photo courtesy Robyn Roche-Paull. Used with permission.*

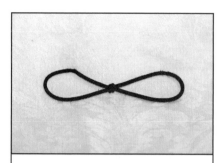

Form a figure eight

Photo courtesy Robyn Roche-Paull.
Used with permission.

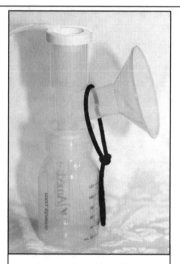

Loop one end on flange funnel

Photo courtesy Robyn Roche-Paull.
Used with permission.

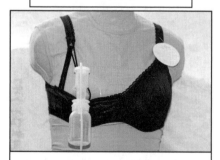

Hook other end on bra hook or strap

Photo courtesy Robyn Roche-Paull.
Used with permission.

attach the other end to the hook on your nursing bra strap. The bottom portion of the flange slips inside the flap of your open nursing bra, and with the suction of the pump, the flange should stay in place.

It goes without saying that keeping extra parts (flanges, valves, tubing) with you at work will be a life-saver if you can't clean them, you lose one, or something breaks. There is nothing worse than finding that your tubing has a leak in it at 0900 hours and you can't leave until 1700, and have no way to pump until then. In the same vein, make sure you have extra bottles/bags to express milk into if you must stay late for an unexpected watch, late mission, or maintenance that must be performed. Finally, keep extra batteries for your pump in case of power failure and learn how to hand express! If you will be sent, or are, overseas, be sure that you have the proper adapter for your pump. More than one military mother has blown out the motor on her pump due to the voltage difference from the U.S. to foreign countries.

And a Surprising Benefit. Many mothers find that they actually look forward to pumping during the work day and are more productive at work, knowing they will have a chance to relax for 30 minutes and get some "me" time to de-stress during the hustle and bustle of the day.

With all the stress of the day, I knew that no matter what I was going to have some calm moments for 30 minutes twice a day because of pumping. That helped me stay productive during the other times because I knew that I would have "me" time with my pump later.
Captain, USAF

Milk-Supply Issues

One of the biggest issues that employed breastfeeding mothers who are separated from their babies face is low milk supply. In talking with other active-duty mothers, you may think that a low milk supply is inevitable because it's such a common issue. Some mothers find that while their milk supply is great on a Monday after a weekend of nursing, it is faltering by Thursday. Or they hit a slump at around the three-or six-month mark. A low milk supply is not inevitable. But if your supply does dip, here are some possible reasons why.

Your pumping frequency determines a lot about whether you'll have milk supply problems. It has been repeated often throughout this book that milk supply is based on breast drainage. That's easy enough to manage when you are just breastfeeding. But it can get a bit trickier when you throw pumping into the mix. Removing milk from your breasts tells your breasts to make more. If the milk remains in your breasts and they become overly full, that tells them to slow down production. Pumping maintains your milk supply by keeping your breasts empty. But pumping enough times to maintain your supply can be difficult to manage in the military.

It is really easy to start out pumping three or four times a day when you first start back on duty. But a few weeks down the line, you may find that you are only pumping one or two times a day on busy days--and the busy days are increasing. That's a sure-fire recipe for a faltering milk supply. Another item to think about: when do you determine it is time to pump again? Do you go by the clock or do you wait until your breasts feel full? If you are waiting for your breasts to feel full, you are telling your breasts to make less milk, and it will take longer and longer for them to feel full. It is a vicious cycle that eventually ends with a dramatically lower supply.

Is your baby sleeping through the night? It may seem to be a godsend that your baby is sleeping at night. But that also means that he is nursing less when he is with you. He'll make up those feedings while at daycare, which will require you to pump more milk to leave for the next day. You can do this by adding more nursing or pumping sessions during the day, or you can encourage him to nurse at least once at night, or even reverse-cycle his feedings. If you choose not to (or can't) pump extra or manage nighttime feedings, your milk supply may decrease.

Are you offering a pacifier? It is far too easy to give a pacifier when you are busy trying to get dinner on the table By offering a pacifier, you are limiting the amount of sucking at the breast that your baby is doing, which stimulates the hormones that make milk. If your baby "needs" a pacifier when you are NOT separated, what he really needs is to be held (or fed) more often. Pacifiers can often be the root cause of milk-supply problems (see Chapter 5 on Pacifiers).

Resist the urge to offer a bottle when you are not separated. When you offer a bottle, even of expressed breastmilk, you have just decreased your milk supply by that amount. You also run the risk of breast refusal (see below) if your baby gets more bottles than time at the breast. When you are together, all sucking needs to be at the breast!

Stress can affect your let-down and pumping output. And while there isn't a whole lot you can do about stress in the military, try not to sweat the small stuff. Concentrate on your baby and your job, and let someone else pick up the slack (your partner can do the chores and buy groceries). Also, stressing about how much milk you are or are not producing is a sure-fire way to lower your output. As this mother says:

> Pumping was much easier if I didn't worry about it. I had friends that would stress over how much they were getting out of pumping sessions. But if I didn't worry, then I found I got more milk and my let down was much easier.

If you've been ill lately, especially if you've had mastitis, a fever, or been dehydrated, you may find your milk supply temporarily decreased. A few days of nursing should turn your supply around, though. Bear in mind that some medications, especially decongestants and cold medicines, can lower milk supply.

There are some hormonal causes of lowered milk supply to consider. Some women find that once their periods resume, they have a slightly lowered supply near ovulation and/or during their period. If you find that this is a problem, try to pump a little extra ahead of your period, or realize that you'll be raiding your freezer stash during that time of the month. Hormonal contraceptives, especially those with estrogen in them, can wreak havoc on your milk supply as well. A new pregnancy can also lower your milk supply.

A drop in your pumping output or supply could be due to your pump. It may seem obvious, but check the easy things first. Double check that your pump settings are correct. Check that the tubing is attached to the pump and the flanges are correctly positioned. Also, check the tubing for any leaks, cracks, or tears (blow through one end, you should feel air coming out the other end). Check that the valves or membranes are not ripped and are attached correctly as well. On the Ameda pumps, the valves are the "duckbill" shaped white cones, while the Medela membranes are flat, white discs. Check the flanges for hairline cracks, as that can affect suction. Also make sure that the bottles or bags are attached securely to the flanges. You can test the suction yourself by putting a flange to your cheek and starting the pump. You should feel a strong, almost painful, pulling sensation (have the suction checked by an IBCLC with gauges to be certain).

Parts can get worn out and may need replacing every three to six months (tubing, valves, flanges). And clean all your parts. Parts that are gummy with dried milk can affect the suction as well. Depending on how old your pump is, and how often it was designed to be used, the motor may be wearing out. Of course, if the pump is making weird noises, has strange smells, or smoke pouring out of it, you can be sure that something is wrong with it. If it is new and under warranty, send it back. If it is used, you may be looking at purchasing a new pump.

Finally, growth spurts are another possible culprit for milk-supply issues. Unlike those early growth spurts when you were at home (and could stay on the couch for hours on end while your baby nursed), a growth spurt while you are working and pumping is harder to cope with. There is no doubt about it. How will you know a growth spurt is starting? Generally, you will have a day or two where all the milk you leave for the sitter is gone by noon (plus some), and when you get home, he wants to nurse non-stop. During a growth spurt, he will want (and need) more milk than usual until it passes. Fortunately, growth spurts usually only last a few days at most. And then he'll be back to his usual routine.

The best way to manage a growth spurt while pumping is to mimic, as much as possible, the frequent nursing you would be doing if you were at home. Try to squeeze in extra pumping sessions at work, add five minutes to your normal pumping sessions, or just nurse more frequently when you are at home to boost your supply. Remember that you won't see the extra milk right away, as it takes a few days for your production to ramp up to meet his needs. If you simply can't pump extra, then this might be a good time to raid your freezer stockpile. But keep in mind that using your stockpile will NOT boost your milk supply.

Maintaining and Increasing Milk Supply

Even if you are not facing a decreased milk supply, it is super important that you remove the milk from your breasts often while working to maintain your supply. Research has shown that mothers make between one-half to two ounces per breast per hour, and the "emptier" the breast, the faster it makes milk (Kent, Mitoulas, Cox, Owens, & Hartmann, 1999). The key to maintaining or increasing your milk supply is to NOT go longer than five to six hours without nursing or pumping. And you must nurse or pump at least eight times in a 24 hour period. Milk left in your breasts tells them to make

LESS milk. It can be a challenge to keep your supply up. This is especially true in the military, where you might work an odd schedule and certainly can't just take a day off to stay home and breastfeed in order to boost your supply. Here are some tips that have proven helpful to other mothers (both in and out of the military) in maintaining and boosting their milk supply:

- Breastfeed often and exclusively (no bottles or pacifiers) when off duty and at home. This includes evenings, nights, and weekends. Remember: *"When my baby is with me, he gets the breast. When he is at daycare, he gets the bottle."*

- Try a **nursing vacation** every few weekends (or off-duty day) to super-charge your milk supply. A nursing vacation means that you don't do anything but breastfeed your baby very frequently, pump often, and rest as much as possible over a 24-48 hour period.

- Try **cluster pumping**, or nurse and pump every half hour for several hours instead of a regular nursing session.

- Pump in the middle of the night, since milk-making hormone levels peak around 0200 and your milk supply is highest then.

- Double pump after breastfeeding.

- Tandem pump by pumping one breast while your baby nurses on the other breast.

- Pump more often by adding a session, either at work or during the night. If time is short, even a **power pump** (a quick, five-minute pumping session) whenever you get the chance is helpful.

- Pump at least every three hours while separated. This may not be practical, given your work environment. But try to aim for this goal if at all possible. The longer you go without pumping, the fuller your breasts will become. Full breasts signal your body to slow production. It may seem like you get more milk to begin with, but over time it will lower your supply.

- Use a high-quality, double-electric, fully automatic breast pump, as described in Chapter 7. Using a less-than-best pump may affect your milk supply in the long run. Switching to a better one may turn your milk supply right around.

- Adjust your pump settings while pumping to stimulate a let-down. Do NOT turn the vacuum setting higher. This will not increase your milk supply. But it will most certainly give you sore nipples.

- Pump for at least 10-20 minutes and continue for about two to three minutes after your milk stops dripping.

- Breast massage and/or breast compressions (as explained in Chapter 4) before and during pumping can be very helpful in increasing milk output during a pumping session. Research has shown that compressions or massage can increase the amount pumped by 40-50% (Jones, Dimmock, & Spencer, 2001) by further emptying all the milk glands.

- Try different sized flanges or inserts (such as the Medela Soft-Fit®, Ameda Flexishield Areola Stimulator®, or Avent® petal massager insert) or rearrange the flanges after five to six minutes to help stimulate different parts of the breast and areola, which may result in more let-down reflexes, thereby increasing milk output.

- Try reverse-cycle feedings with your baby (see Chapter 6). The combination of nursing more at night, and your baby not needing as much expressed milk during the day, can help you to maintain, if not increase, your milk supply.

- Breastfeed your baby at drop-off and pick-up from the daycare provider and ask that they do not feed your baby within one hour of you picking him up. It may not seem like much, but those one to two extra nursing sessions during the day may be just the ticket to boosting your supply. This is particularly helpful when there is a long commute between the daycare and home. Once home, you can nurse him again, further boosting your supply. Breastfeeding your baby at daycare will also lessen the amount of milk you need to pump and leave with your caregiver.

- Drink to thirst (too much can actually decrease your milk supply) and eat a well-balanced diet.

- Discuss galactogogues (prescription or herbal) with your IBCLC and HCP as options for boosting your milk supply (see Appendix A for books on the subject). These herbs and medications work best when combined with increased breastfeeding and pumping. They don't work as well used by themselves. Some of the more popular options include:

    ° **Herbs**. There are too many herbs to cover in this book, and some are targeted towards specific low milk-supply issues. However, some of the all-purpose herbs for milk production include: Alfalfa, Fenugreek, Goat's Rue, Nettles, and Shatavari.

    ° **Medications**. Domperidone (Motilium®) and Metoclopramide (Reglan®) are the favored prescription drugs for boosting milk supply. Domperidone increases prolactin and has an excellent safety profile. Unfortunately, due to the FDA review process, it is not approved for use as a galactogogue in the U.S. But you may be able to get if from a compounding pharmacist (availability varies by location). Metoclopramide also boosts prolactin levels, but it can cause depression in some mothers. It is approved for use as a galactogogue in the U.S.

Pumping for your baby takes a huge commitment. You should feel very proud of your accomplishment, no matter how little or how much milk you provide for your baby. Remember, that while providing your milk IS important, your breastfeeding relationship is more important. And pumping allows you to be able to breastfeed when you are at home. If you are finding that you are having issues with persistent low milk supply, and the tricks and tips in this book aren't enough to improve the situation, take a look at the book *The Breastfeeding Mother's Guide to Making More Milk* by Diana West and Lisa Marasco (2009). It is devoted solely to milk-supply issues and has a full section on working and breastfeeding.

Bottle Refusal

You've done everything right, followed the directions, and now it is week five and your baby still won't take a bottle. Or maybe you've been back at work for a few months, and suddenly he refuses the bottle. What is going on? And what can you do? Bottle refusal can occur for two reasons: it is either due to a late introduction to the bottle (after four weeks) or to a bottle strike that can occur at any time and for no particular reason in a baby that formerly accepted a bottle. A common age for bottle strikes is around three months, when babies become more aware of what's going on around them.

One of the most important things to remember when dealing with a bottle strike is to remain calm and patient. Babies pick up on your emotions. If you feel frustrated, he will too. Before you start trying to introduce a bottle again, rule out any physical problems, like teething, colds, or earaches. Offer the bottle twice a day during happy, relaxed times. Practice for only 10-15 minutes, and stop if he becomes sad or upset. Wait to breastfeed for about 10 minutes, so he doesn't associate "winning the breast" with refusing the bottle. Keep using the same bottle nipples you were using previously. Consistency is key. Here are some more tips to try to help your baby overcome a bottle strike. Many of these ideas involve distraction and repetition. So give these suggestions two or three tries before giving up and moving on to something else.

- **Try different positions:** Have your baby on your lap, either facing you or with his back against your chest.

- **Try different places:** In the swing, in the car seat, in a bouncy seat, on the couch, in the bathtub.

- **Go outside** and offer the bottle (both in your arms and out), while looking at the trees, cars, clouds, etc.

- **Try offering the bottle when he is hungry,** when he is sleepy (just after waking up-still groggy), or in the middle-of-the-night.

- **Try offering the bottle after the first let-down** while breastfeeding or after the first side. If he nurses to sleep, remove your nipple and slip the bottle nipple in.

- **If he uses a pacifier,** try replacing it with the bottle nipple. You can also try having him suck on your finger, and then switch to the bottle while he is sucking.

- **Sing a song while offering the bottle.** Hide the bottle in a washcloth or stuffed animal (have more than one that looks exactly the same).

There are some don'ts, as well, that you need to be mindful of when dealing with a bottle strike. Don't make Dad the bad guy by having only him deal with the strike. You both need to work on this together. Don't offer the bottle in the "nursing" corner or chair. Don't starve your baby into taking a bottle. It is cruel and often doesn't work anyway. Don't put juice or formula in the bottle. That only confuses your baby into learning a new taste, and his tummy isn't ready for it yet (you're setting him up for allergies and tummy problems).

Don't leave it up to your caregiver to figure it out. That isn't fair to them, and you'll be worrying all day about whether your baby is eating or screaming his head off. Finally, don't go to a higher-flow nipple. All that will do is force-feed your baby, which won't teach him to take the bottle. In fact, it may make it worse and might cause him to choke or aspirate. Take a deep breath and relax.

There are a few babies out there that simply will NOT take a bottle, no matter what you do or try. If this is the case for you, there are a few pointers to keep in mind. You can try alternate ways of feeding him, such as a sippy cup, eyedropper, medicine cup, or finger feeding. They are all very time-consuming and messy methods, but they have been used successfully with infants as young as six weeks old. You may also find that your baby simply doesn't eat while separated from you, but "tanks-up" when you are together (especially if you practice reverse-cycle nursing). This is OK as long as you carefully monitor his growth and development to be sure that he is growing appropriately. Being a working mother with a baby that refuses a bottle can be a scary experience; however, your baby is smart and knows he wants the "real thing" and won't settle for anything less. Take it as a compliment, Mom!

> *My son wouldn't take a bottle at all, we tried everything that the LLL Leader and the LC suggested. My daycare provider assured me that he wouldn't starve, and he didn't. I suppose I was lucky, he reverse-cycled his nursing and my daycare provider carried him in a sling and said*

he slept most of the time. The hardest part was that he nursed ALL THE TIME when I was home, but he stayed on track on the growth charts, and the pediatrician was fine with his weight gain. Still it was a scary experience knowing that he ate nothing from 0600 to 1600 everyday. Petty Officer 3rd Class, USN.

Breast Refusal

Breast refusal, or a "nursing strike," is when a formerly happily breastfeeding baby suddenly refuses the breast. There can be any number of causes for a nursing strike: illness, teething, thrush, or even a new laundry detergent. Many comprehensive breastfeeding books have an expanded section on nursing strikes, with tips and tricks for overcoming them. However, most suggest avoiding artificial nipples and bottles. But for working mothers, whose babies must have a bottle, avoiding bottles is not an option.

Unfortunately, babies who have multiple bottle-feedings do have a higher risk of nursing strikes. This is usually due to nipple preference, as result of bottle-feeding with a nipple that flows too fast. Babies learn to prefer the bottle with its fast flow and don't want to "work" at the breast, with its natural and normal slower flow. You can reduce the risk of a nursing strike by following the advice given above on choosing the proper nipple (using the SIMPLE Method outlined in Introducing the Bottle), and by waiting three to four weeks to introduce the bottle.

If you have ruled out other causes for a nursing strike, you might want to consider your milk supply. A lowered milk supply can cause some babies to refuse the breast. Can you pump your normal amount of milk? If not, re-read the section above on milk-supply issues. If you feel that your milk supply is fine, keep pumping to maintain your supply, while you encourage your baby back to the breast.

When your baby is having a nursing strike, practice lots of skin-to-skin contact. You can try offering the breast while bathing together or when he is asleep. Forcing the breast on your baby will only make it worse. Do NOT confuse a nursing strike or breast refusal with weaning (especially if your baby is under a year old). Very few babies wean suddenly; weaning occurs gradually, while nursing strikes come on suddenly. Keep calm and remain patient. Contact a La Leche League Leader or IBCLC if you need more help on overcoming a nursing strike.

Deciding When to Wean from the Pump

If you are finding that pumping is just too much to handle, and you are thinking about quitting, there are some things to think about and try first. Are there other things going on in your life, not related to breastfeeding, making pumping the proverbial "straw that broke the camel's back," so to speak? We tend to think of ourselves as supermoms who can do it all. And we often don't want to ask for help. Do you need help around the house? Is there a volunteer position or collateral duty you can drop? See if there isn't something in your life that you can let go or have someone else do for you. And then rethink whether quitting pumping will still make a difference.

If you feel that weaning from the pump is still the best answer, then you may want to set a timeline or goal and see if that makes your situation better. It's really easy to decide to quit when the going gets tough. But rash decisions are never a good idea. Make a reasonable goal, such as next Saturday or the end of the month. And if it is not better by then, you'll quit. Whatever you do, don't make a decision to quit on a Friday night after a long week. Instead, wait until Sunday, after a weekend of rest, to decide when and how to move forward.

Would supplementing on a partial basis help? Sometimes, removing the pressure of having to provide every last drop of your baby's nutrition is just enough to make it workable for you. I can't stress enough that any breastmilk you can provide is better than none at all. Formula can be a reasonable substitute, especially for an older baby. You can supplement and continue to breastfeed. It is not an all-or-nothing proposition.

If your baby is younger than six months when you stop pumping, you will need to supplement with formula, even when you are at home, as it can be a challenge to keep your supply up, while working with a baby that age without pumping. You should breastfeed as often as possible when you are at home and have someone else offer the supplemental formula. Remember, that your baby gets the breast from you and the bottle from others. If your baby is over nine months, you can supplement with more nutritious foods, and encourage your baby to nurse a lot when you are together and at night to keep your supply up. Be sure to keep a close eye on your baby's developmental milestones and growth curves to be sure that he is getting enough to eat.

Ultimately, of course, the decision of when to wean from the pump is up to you. When you do decide to stop expressing your milk, you'll want to do so slowly, especially if you have a well-established supply built up. Much like weaning from the breast, weaning from your pump too quickly can lead to plugged ducts and mastitis. You should expect to take about two weeks to wean completely from the pump.

There are a couple of ways to wean from the pump: eliminate one pumping session for a week to ten days, and then when your breasts have adjusted, pump half the time for another week or so, after a few more days you can probably stop pumping altogether. Another option is to keep pushing your pumping sessions back until the last one "falls off" at the end of the day (if you pump at 1000, 1300, and 1500, then push it back slowly to 1130, 1400, and 1630. The 1630 one can then be "dropped"). Keep doing this until all your sessions have dropped off. You can also decrease the duration of your

pumping sessions, while keeping the sessions at the same time. Finally, you can wait to pump until you feel full, bearing in mind the storage capacity of your breasts. Mothers with a large storage capacity will take longer to feel full, while those with a small storage capacity will feel full sooner. By pumping only when you feel full, you will tell your breasts to make less and less milk. The downside is that you may end up weaning completely, not just from the pump. But it doesn't have to be that way.

Whatever you decide, don't beat yourself up over it. No matter how long you have managed to pump, you have given your baby a wonderful start in life. Be proud of what you HAVE accomplished. Remember that weaning from the pump does not mean weaning completely. You can continue to breastfeed for as long as you both desire long after you've stopped pumping. And in fact, many mothers do, because it provides you both with all the joys of nursing minus all the hassles of pumping. "Hanging up the horns" is a milestone in your nursing career. Whether it is at three, six, or 12 months, weaning from the pump is a transition for you. Take some time to reflect on the sacrifices you made to provide your milk to your sweet baby, and the pride you rightfully deserve to feel in meeting your goals.

Chapter 11
Childcare

Choosing a Breastfeeding-Friendly Provider

While you are still pregnant is a good time to start looking for a caregiver. This is especially true if you plan to use the military Child Development Center on base, as the waiting period can be a year or more. First and foremost, you'll want to select a caregiver who is supportive of breastfeeding. They should be an unwavering ally in your effort to breastfeed your baby.

You should also think about whether to choose a caregiver who is close to work or close to home, whichever works best for you. One of the advantages of having a provider near your workplace is the ability to drop in during the day and breastfeed. You might also want to breastfeed there in the a.m. or p.m. or both, so your baby can get one last feeding at the breast before you leave and first thing when you arrive. There are a number of choices for childcare: Child Development Centers, commercial daycare centers, home daycare, family, or a nanny. No matter who you choose to care for your baby, young babies do best with a single, nurturing, and consistent caregiver with whom they can build a relationship.

CDC/Daycare

Daycare centers and Child Development Centers (CDC) on base are licensed to provide childcare and must follow strict rules and regulations. They are staffed by trained personnel and often have rooms designed specifically for infants, with a low caregiver-to-infant ratio. Daycare centers have strict rules about bringing in babies and children who are sick. Most don't allow ill infants, so you'll need to have a back-up plan for the few times your breastfed baby does become ill. CDCs on base generally offer care on a sliding scale (based on rank), and many also offer after-hours care, which is Godsend to active-duty parents who may work nights or have duty on the weekend.

According to mothers surveyed, most CDCs on base are breastfeeding-friendly and know all the regulations and handling needs of breastmilk and breastfeeding babies. Some CDCs also have "nursing rooms" available for breastfeeding mothers to use when they come in on a break from work. If your CDC is not familiar with breastfeeding babies or how to handle breastmilk, you can direct them to this website http://dhs.wi.gov/health/physicalactivity/pdf_files/BreastfeedingFriendlyChildCareCenters.pdf (or you can print it out and bring it in) for a PDF of a "Ten Steps to Breastfeeding Friendly Child Care Centers" Resource Kit.

> *One of my most-proud moments was when Joey transitioned from the 6 weeks – 6 months room at the base daycare (CDC-child development center) to the 6 months – 12 months room. I was the only parent (eight kids to a room) who was still providing breastmilk!* Captain, USAF

I breastfed my first daughter for 15 months, and was even able to visit the CDC once or twice a day to nurse her until she was a year old. Senior Airman, USAF

I usually would forgo the office lunch outings, opting, instead, to go to see my baby at the daycare so that I could nurse her. SSgt, USA

The base daycare (CDC) is extremely breastfeeding-friendly and had a nursing room right next door to my son's room, so I could come by and nurse him during the day if I had time. They also allowed me to bring in two weeks' worth of frozen milk, which they would thaw daily. I knew that all I had to do was make the milk, the ladies at daycare would take care of the rest. Captain, USAF

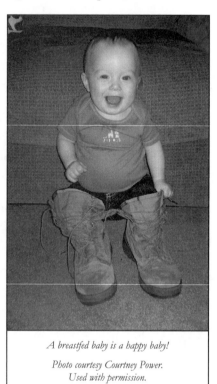

A breastfed baby is a happy baby!

Photo courtesy Courtney Power.
Used with permission.

Home Care

Home care is another option for childcare. Many parents like this option because of the "home-like" atmosphere. With home care, you drop your baby off with an individual who provides care in her home. Generally, home-care providers are mothers themselves who are trying to earn some extra money while staying home with their own children.

Most states require that the home care be inspected and the provider licensed. But there are plenty out there who are not. Home-care providers generally do not cost as much, since there is no overhead to pay for. And some home-care providers, especially those near military bases, will offer only after-hour care, as a specialty for parents who must work nights and weekends.

Caregiver-to-infant ratios can be a little more lax, and it is important to find out how your baby's day will be spent (in front of a TV or with lots of one-on-one interaction and tummy time?). It is also important to determine what the back-up policy is if the provider is sick, as well as what the policy is if your baby is ill. As with any caregiver, you'll want to determine what, if any, experience she has with breastfeeding babies.

Family/Nanny

Not as likely, due to geographical distance or expense, is the option of having a family member or a nanny care for your baby in your home. If you choose to have a family member watch your baby, she probably will not be licensed and may or may not be CPR certified. Family members generally don't charge for watching their grandchildren. But they may have their own ways of doing things (like feeding your baby Cheetos or watching Jerry Springer) that clash with yours. If your mother or mother-in-law didn't breastfeed, you may have a struggle on your hands with continuing to breastfeed your baby due to simple mismanagement. On the other hand, if she did breastfeed, you'll be all set.

Nannies must be licensed and bonded, and CPR-and First-Aid qualified. And they may, or may not, also do housework for you. However, it is a real toss-up as to what kind of breastfeeding knowledge or experience she'll have.

Breastfeeding and Your Care Provider

It is vital that you choose a care provider that understands how important breastfeeding is to you and who is willing to support your efforts to breastfeed. They may not understand just how much their support can make or break your efforts to be successful. So feel free to explain how much breastfeeding means to you and how they can help. When you are interviewing care providers, ask whether they have breastfed their own children or cared for other breastfed babies. If they haven't, are they comfortable handling breastmilk and coping with breastfed-baby behaviors? Are they encouraging and make you feel normal? Or do they think it is weird or gross? Do they seem receptive to learning more about breastfeeding and willing to go along with your requests?

Once you have chosen your care provider, you'll want to go over the basics of breastfeeding, breastfed-baby behavior, and the handling of breastmilk with them. Whether they have cared for breastfed babies before or not, review and make sure that your caregiver understands the following concepts:

- Discuss with your caregiver your need to breastfeed your baby at both drop-off and pick-up times in order to help maintain your milk supply. Ask whether they use their own bottles or the ones you provide (and be prepared to request that they use the ones you have chosen). Also find out if your caregiver will allow you to keep a small amount of frozen breastmilk in their freezer for emergencies, in addition to the breastmilk that you provide every day.

- Be sure to go over the storage and handling of breastmilk, in particular the storage times, the need to swirl not shake the milk, and how to properly thaw frozen milk (see Chapter 9). It doesn't hurt to explain that breastmilk looks very different from formula or cow's milk, and that it separates. You might want to also explain the difference between breastfed versus formula stools, so your caregiver is not concerned at the appearance or odor.

- Caregivers tend to like to feed babies on a schedule. But breastfed babies don't do schedules. Breastmilk digests quicker than formula, so your baby may want smaller and more frequent meals. Do they know what cues to look for that your baby is hungry (rooting, gnawing on fists) and that crying is a late sign of hunger? Make sure that your care provider understands and is willing to feed your baby whenever he is hungry. Just like adults, sometimes your baby will want just a snack. Other times, he'll want the whole four-course meal. If your baby is fussy (and has just been fed), will your care provider be willing to hold or carry him, possibly even in a sling, to soothe him? On the flip side, be sure that your caregiver will hold your baby at times other than feedings, so he doesn't associate feeding with the only time he gets held.

- You will want to explain how to properly bottle-feed your baby, so your breastfeeding relationship stays intact. Teach your caregiver how to do "paced bottle-feeding," which begins by holding your baby in an upright position and stroking his upper lip with the bottle. The caregiver needs to wait for him to open his mouth wide, and then allow him to "accept" the bottle. Do not force or push the bottle in his mouth. Your caregiver should mimic breastfeeding by encouraging plenty of pauses after each 25-30 sucks, as this mimics your let downs and helps prevent nipple preference. The bottle should be held level throughout the feeding, and your baby should be burped after every ounce. It is important that he be switched from one side to the other midway through the feeding, much like when he is breastfed. Feedings should last about 10-20 minutes, which also mimics the usual breastfeeding experience by allowing his stomach to feel full. It also discourages guzzling and overfeeding (see below).

- It is extremely important that you are clear that your baby is not to have his bottles propped, for a number of reasons. He is a breastfed baby and is used to being held while feeding, so he may object to being left by himself. Furthermore, your caregiver cannot properly use paced bottle-feeding (see above) if the bottle is propped. Propped bottles can lead to choking, overfeeding, and a baby who quickly learns to prefer the bottle rather than the breast.

- Overfeeding is a major concern, as too many bottles at daycare can make your baby so full that he doesn't want to nurse at home with you (leading to a lowered milk supply). It increases colic and fussiness (due to an over-full stomach), and makes it much harder for you to be able to keep up with the demand for expressed milk (which often leads to weaning). Be sure to go over how much to feed your baby with your caregiver. It can be tricky trying to figure out how much to give your baby. But it is determined, in part, by weight and age. Here is a quick way to estimate how much your baby is likely to take at each feeding: Multiply your baby's weight by 2.7, and then divide by how many times he eats in 24 hours. That number is about how many ounces he'll need at each feeding for the first few months. This isn't foolproof. Your baby may take more or less. But it does give you a starting point.

- Remind your caregiver that your baby is in charge of how much he eats. Babies are great at regulating how much food they need. There is no need to make him finish the bottle (you don't make him finish the breast). When he is done, he is done. By forcing him to finish a bottle, your caregiver is ignoring his cues, overfeeding him, and contributing to possible obesity in the future. Again, it is all about paying attention to the cues he is giving. If he turns his head away, closes his mouth, or is drowsy and releases the nipple, he is telling the caregiver he is finished. Stress that the caregiver is not to force the nipple into his mouth, massage his throat, or reawaken him to finish the bottle. If there is milk left in the bottle, you can explain that due to breastmilk properties, it is okay to save the milk and re-use it for the next feeding if it is within a few hours. Repeated bottles that are not finished may signal a need to reevaluate how much pumped milk to send.

- You'll want to explain growth spurts and how to manage them by feeding him extra from your frozen stockpile. And it is important that your caregiver keeps track of how much he eats, so you know how much to pump. You should also cover what to do if you're unable to pump enough for a feeding, or the caregiver runs short of frozen milk to add to the freshly expressed milk you have left. There are two options: your caregiver can add formula to the bottle of expressed milk equal to the amount your baby would eat. However, keep in mind that it all must be thrown out if it is not finished (potentially wasting breastmilk). If you would rather that no breastmilk go to waste, you can ask that your caregiver give the breastmilk first, and then offer a bottle of formula as a top off.

- You may or may not want to request that your caregiver separate your expressed milk in order to manipulate how full your baby feels during the day. This is done by adding extra hindmilk to a bottle of expressed milk, making a higher fat (double cream) feeding to help space the daytime feedings; and the remaining foremilk bottle of expressed milk, which is lower in fat (skim), is given at the end of the day to quench his thirst, but not fill him up. Be very careful if you do this. The natural balance of foremilk and hindmilk that your baby receives is perfectly balanced for his growth and development. It shouldn't be tinkered with unless you have considered it thoroughly and have the assistance of an IBCLC.

- It is vital that you make clear to your caregiver that you need to be able to feed your baby when you pick him up. In order for you to be able to do this, your caregiver must not feed your baby in the hour or so before you arrive. If they do, he will be too full to nurse, and your breasts will be not be emptied. This can lead to a lowered milk supply over time. To avoid this very common scenario, you may want to have a few "end-of-day" bottles with only one ounce or so of expressed milk stashed in the daycare freezer. These can be used to tide your baby over until you arrive, as they will be just enough to keep him happy, but not fill him up. Another idea is to offer a pacifier, if he will take one.

Finally, it is very important that you and your caregiver have good communication with one another. Whether verbal or written, be sure that you review your baby's eating, sleeping, elimination, and behavior with your caregiver every day. This will help you determine how much to pump and send, and your caregiver how much to feed, as well as letting you know how your baby is doing. See Appendix H for a sample childcare provider list that you can fill out and give to your caregiver with a return handout for your caregiver to give to you.

SECTION FOUR

In the Field: Dealing with Workplace Issues

Beth's Story

I've been in the USAF since 2000. I fly C-17s, and I was stationed at McChord AFB when we had our first baby in September, 2006. I already had orders to PCS to RAF Brize Norton to fly C-17s with the Brits through an exchange program. I was quite lucky in the fact that after I came off maternity leave, I didn't have a standard 0730 to 1700 job since I was trying to out-process and get everything ready for the move overseas.

I had massive problems feeding William. I never had thrush or mastitis. But for about two months, I had cracked, bleeding nipples, and every time he latched, I would cry and curl my toes in pain. I never would have made it through that time without the support of my husband and the lactation consultant at Madigan. My first overnight separation from William was my first flight back when he was about seven or eight weeks old. It was supposed to be a local training mission, but we got picked off to do something else. When I made it home the next day, there were only two bags of milk left in the freezer. Talk about stress for me and my husband. Of course, I brought home almost 20 bags of milk.

When William was three months old, I started going on trips again. My husband is a stay-at-home dad and that has given me peace of mind to be able to leave. My trips were sometimes just overnighters and other times, up to 10 days long. At first, I pumped every four hours and that was hard. I would pump right before I left the house, and then it just worked out that when we hit cruise, it was four hours later. Our crew rest area was dubbed the "crew breast area" by my squadron mates. I was never shy about pumping, and I think that put my squadron at ease about it. People would sit there and talk to me while I was pumping, maintenance would be doing work on the aircraft while I was pumping, etc.

I faced some logistics issues during this time. At first, I thought I needed to clean my pump parts after every session, but then I realized (after reading lots at LLLI) that I could just put everything in the fridge on the plane. If breastmilk is good for seven days in the fridge, then my pump parts are probably okay for a couple of days in between cleanings, as long as they're kept in the fridge. When I did clean them, I used the Medela wipes and the Medela steam bag for the microwave. The other problem was getting my milk home when I was on long trips. Luckily, because of the way my squadron worked, I would always see other crews (who were going home) while I was out. I would leave my milk with them, and they made sure it got back to the fridge in the squadron and my husband was notified. Without their understanding and help, it would have been quite difficult.

Eventually, pumping every four hours turned in to pumping every six, then eight, then 12. I breastfed William till he was two years and four months old (and I was four months pregnant). I stopped taking my pump on trips with me when he was a little younger than two. At that point, my breasts could handle being away for 10 days without needing to empty them.

In June, 2009, we had our second child, Joshua. I started going on trips when he was about two months old. Luckily, I was an "old hat" in the squadron, and I could pick and choose what trips I would go on. Then we moved back to the States when he was almost six months old, and it's taking a while to get up and running in my new squadron. I'm back to flying with the USAF instead of the RAF, and I have some serious fears since the trips are much longer and I won't necessarily be able to get milk home. I'm also going to a four-week long school when Josh is nine months old. I'm not worried about the pumping (which should only be three to four times a day), but I am scared he won't come back to the breast after a month. These are all new adventures in pumping/feeding, and I'm sure I will get through them with the support of my husband and the understanding of my new squadron mates.

Breastfeeding my children has been the hardest thing I've ever done in my life, but it's also been the most rewarding. I LOVE feeding my kids and am always amazed by my body.

Chapter 12
Unique Workplace Environments

While all working mothers have to find a place and time to pump, many military mothers have unique working environments that make it more difficult to do so. There are a myriad of workplace issues for military women to consider that your counterparts in the civilian world do not share. Where else are you expected to perform maintenance on the deck of a pitching aircraft carrier or go on a 20-click march with a 100-pound pack on your back? This chapter will begin with finding a place and time to pump that are common to all women in the military, and go into more detail about some of the more unique workplace situations, such as aviation, maintenance, medical, and security that cut across all branches of the armed services. Pumping in field conditions and aboard ship is also covered in this chapter.

You'll also be dealing with deployments and TDY assignments, hazardous materials in the workplace, physical readiness tests and weight standards, career and rank concerns, as well as co-worker issues. The following chapters will go over those issues in more detail. While you may not have to deal with all of these issues, it is important to be aware of what you may face as a breastfeeding mother returning to the active-duty workplace. This section aims to arm you with knowledge of what to expect in various military workplaces and give suggestions and tips to make breastfeeding in the military a reality.

A Place to Pump

Finding a *place* to pump may be one of the more challenging parts of returning to active duty as a breastfeeding mother! You are not alone in this quest. Mothers in certain civilian jobs have a difficult time finding a place to pump as well. Not everyone has a cushy private office with a locking door or an employee lactation room. Just like many mothers in non-traditional jobs, such as police officers or firefighters, military mothers have become very creative in creating, finding, and using places to pump at their commands. As stated in the Policies section, the Air Force, Coast Guard, Marine Corps, and Navy are *required* to provide a secluded place to pump with running water. This can be a private office, an unused room, a converted supply closet, or a lounge or locker room with a cloth drape. It is convenient to have an electric outlet nearby, and a sink as well. However, the reality is that you may be pumping out of the back of an ambulance, in the back of an aircraft on a long flight, or sitting on the edge of your cot in a tent. Unfortunately, more often than not the only place available to pump is in the restroom.

The first order of business is to speak with your supervisor about possible locations that would be suitable for pumping in your workplace. These do not need to be fancy or big. Any place that provides some privacy, an electric outlet, and is close to running water is sufficient. It is helpful if there is a refrigerator that you can use, but not necessary. Be creative and don't overlook an area because it isn't an obvious first choice or someplace you think isn't suitable for pumping.

Many women end up using the restroom because it is the only place available, and it is semi-private. However, don't resort to using the restroom unless there really isn't any place else to go. It is unhygienic, noisy, and uncomfortable, and akin to eating your own lunch while sitting on the toilet. You'll probably find it difficult to "let-down" and relax while in the restroom with other people walking in and out--as well as all the smells. As this Captain in the Air Force says:

> I tried a couple times pumping in the bathroom, but it was quite uncomfortable trying to "find a happy place" so I could have a good letdown, while listening to the sounds (and smells) of the bathroom.

There are as many different scenarios for finding a place to pump as there are job specialties in the military. This chapter cannot begin to cover every possible scenario, but here are a few ideas from mothers in the field that may help you find a place to pump:

- Conference room
- Office, unused
- Storage closet, converted
- Clinic room, unused
- Lounge
- Locker room
- Stateroom (onboard ship)
- Medical (onboard ship)
- POV

> I didn't have a private office, so I found a storage closet in the building's gym room and claimed it as my pumping room. I told the SMSgt (E-8) and TSgt (E-6) that I worked with where I was, but not many other people knew. Because the main room was a gym area, there was a fridge, so I could store my milk and take it home in the afternoon, and it was right across from the women's bathroom, so I could rinse my pump stuff off when finished. The closet didn't have a lock, so I put up a sign that said "occupied-do not enter," I also started locking the

main door to the gym so that I could rest a little easier because I didn't have to worry about getting walked-in on. Captain, USAF

At my last unit I had an office and was asked to pump in a restroom instead of my office (in a corner), I refused and pumped in my office. At my new unit, there isn't anywhere for me to pump and I use my POV. I was told I could pump in the restroom and told them I'd rather pump in my vehicle in the freezing Maryland cold than to pump inside of a restroom and that's where I pump now. Sergeant, USA

When my second daughter was born...I was not embarrassed to demand a room to pump in. Although I no longer use the room, I am proud to say that it is still in use by other nursing mothers in my squadron. Captain, USAF

I had to ask my Commanding Officer (a male) for a place to pump and without hesitation he allowed me to use the conference room. My commanding officer was willing to allow me to use that space because I approached him with a solution. I searched for a place I thought would work. I found a few in my building, but the other two were storage closets. The conference room was the ideal place for me. Petty Officer 2nd Class, USN

You can also look into having an employee lactation room set-up if there are enough breastfeeding mothers in your command. Write a memo, citing the regulations and policies of your service, the various statements put out by the AAP and WHO regarding the importance of breastfeeding to you and your baby's health, and outline what you need in the way of a room and supplies (locked door, chairs, electrical outlet, sink/running water), and then send it up your chain of command for approval. It may seem as though this isn't possible in the military, but as this mother's story proves, it can be done.

Lactation room in a USAF dental clinic

Photo courtesy Christine Luna.
Used with permission.

I am fortunate enough to work at a medical facility, specifically a dental clinic, in the United States Air Force. There are always plenty of rooms not being utilized that could be used as a pumping room. I forwarded the information (AFI 44-102) up to my chain of command, and stressed the importance of a proper place for me and a few other co-workers to have a go-to place to pump, not to mention breastfeeding mothers in the future. After only a couple of months of bouncing around, my Commander approved an unused treatment room to be our employee lactation room. We are still in the process of decorating the room to make it more "mommy-time" friendly. Also, I donated a mini refrigerator to store our milk and a locked cabinet was installed to keep our pumps safe. All of these things put together have made pumping while on active duty so much simpler. Without the support of my co-workers and my chain of command, it just would not be possible. I highly encourage any other active-duty mom to stay headstrong and go through whatever chain of command you have to in order to ensure you have the capability of providing the best for your child. It can be done! Senior Airman, USAF

Having a place to pump makes all the difference for AD moms.

Photo courtesy Christine Luna. Used with permission.

A final item to think about is how or even whether to let others know when you are leaving to pump and what you are doing behind those closed doors. It can be embarrassing to announce that you are going to pump. However, you also don't want to run the risk of being unaccounted for. While some mothers feel that it isn't necessary to announce they are pumping any more than they announce they are using the restroom or going to the snack bar, it is appropriate and recommended to let someone in your shop or workplace know where you are going.

The majority of mothers in an online survey suggested that you be upfront and not ashamed of your need to pump. The more comfortable you are (or at least pretend to be) about the need to express your milk, the more comfortable those around you will be. Another thing to think about is signage for the door of your pumping area or room. If you aren't clear about why the door is locked, someone might assume that a meeting is going on or call security to open the normally unlocked door. Your sign can range from a to-the-point "Breast Pumping in Progress" to the more discreet "Meeting in

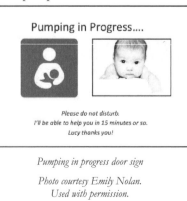

Pumping in Progress....

Please do not disturb.
I'll be able to help you in 15 minutes or so.
Lucy thanks you!

Pumping in progress door sign

Photo courtesy Emily Nolan.
Used with permission.

Progress," it all depends on what you (and your command) are comfortable with. Here are some interesting ways other mothers have made their pumping intentions known.

> *One of the airmen in my shop signs out on our board with "Operation Backpack" and that lets everyone know that she is pumping without announcing it.* Staff Sgt., USAF

> *I use to just pick up my "Backpack" and everyone would just say "Oh, you're going to pump." It was funny to hear guys say that.* Staff Sgt., USAF

> *I used to have a sign that said "Mommy Thing... leave a message" until someone decided they didn't like it and replaced it with one that said "Meeting in Progress"* Captain, USA

> *Finding the right sign was challenging for the room I pump in. I first just put a "Meeting in Progress" sign up, but people thought they were missing out on some important meeting they weren't aware of and would constantly knock. Then I put a "Do Not Disturb" sign up, and people still constantly knock, or question what I'm doing.* Petty Officer 2nd Class, USN

> *The building custodian made a sign for the door that said, "Room in Use; Do Not Enter" that was magnetic, so I just threw that on the door and for the most part people left me alone.* Captain, USAF

> *We generated a sign that said "Breast Pumping in Progress!" That way everyone knew not to bother us for 30 minutes.* Captain, USMC

> *Our room has the international breastfeeding symbol on door.* Lt., USN

> *Basically when people saw me walking down the hall with "the bag" they knew where I was headed and were respectful enough to give me time. Be proud of the fact that you are pumping and providing the best form of nourishment for your children.* Staff Sgt., USAF

A Time to Pump

Another challenging aspect to breastfeeding in the military is finding the *time* to pump. The military is a 24/7 job in and of itself, and many of the specialties within the military do not lend themselves well to pumping breaks. Ideally, as explained in Chapter 11, you should pump at least three times in an eight-hour shift, that's one lunch break and two other breaks (mid-morning and mid-afternoon). If you work longer hours or a different shift, you'll need to adjust your pumping schedule accordingly. Military policies state that flexibility in allotting breaks for pumping is granted, but no extra time may be given for pumping. As with finding a place to pump, your first plan of action should be to speak with your supervisor about scheduling breaks in your workday. Explain how often and for how long you'll need to pump each day, two to three times for 10-20 minutes (that includes set-up and breakdown) and see if something can be worked out.

> *I have a set schedule of the times a day that I pump, but life gets in the way and not every single day am I able to pump right when I planned to, but if you can get a schedule that works for you and your job, that would be best, so that way no one can accuse you of "trying to get out of work." Talk that over with your supervisor as well.* Senior Airman, USAF

> *As for pumping, I only tell people where I am going if asked. It's not like I have to tell people when I am going to the bathroom, so I don't need to tell them when I go pump for 15 minutes. I just set the expectation with my chain of command that I pump at 9, 12, and 3. If they look for me around those times, I am covered.* Lt., USN

> *We just informed our boss that we were planning on breast pumping and that it was pertinent that we keep to our pumping schedules.* Captain, USMC

There are many roadblocks to finding time to pump on active duty, and operational commitments top the list with flight schedules, maintenance workloads, consoles that require continuous monitoring, and patients overruling your need to pump. Extended or late shifts, especially when unexpected, can wreak havoc on a pumping schedule, as can watch standing duties after a full shift. These are an unfortunate reality of military life. It will be up to you to be proactive and pump ahead of time, rather than wait for the "scheduled" time, especially if you can see that an additional shift or change in mission is headed your way. Keep extra bottles or bags handy if you must stay late, so you don't have to pour your milk down the drain to make room for another pumping (there is nothing worse than watching your hard-earned milk go down the drain).

If it seems that you will not or cannot be given breaks or operational commitments overrule your need for breaks, you'll need to get creative. Even a quick 5-10 minute pumping is better than nothing. You may find that there will be times when you have to choose between eating and pumping or using the restroom and pumping. While your friends and co-workers break for lunch, you'll be heading off to the lounge to pump instead. Finding the time to pump can be a real struggle, but if you are committed, there is almost always a few minutes in the day to pump a few precious ounces of breastmilk for your baby.

> *Sometimes it was difficult to find time to pump. I would have meetings with male commanders that would last a while, and I would have to*

run to my car to grab my pump and either pump in the car, or bring it in to the office and ask strangers if I could use their office to pump. Or if I had a hearing that would last all day, and they would only give 10 minute breaks, I would run to the bathroom and pump, sometimes foregoing using the restroom all together. Captain, USAF

I had just finished working a 12-hour shift at my squadron and the four bottles I had with me were full from the four pumping sessions I'd managed during my shift. The person who was supposed to take the next eight hour watch was sick, and I was next on the duty roster, so guess who got to stay? I was going to need to pump at least twice more and had no more room in the bottles, and no more empty bottles. I very reluctantly poured the milk down the drain (it was that or stand at the sink and pump), so I could pump and fill the bottles up again. I learned my lesson that night and always kept a spare bottle or two in my locker after that! Petty Officer 3rd Class, USN

As with anything there were days when meetings and work interfered with my normal lunchtime appointment to pump, and I would be so engorged I thought I would burst. But for the most part, I made a commitment to get home, so I could take care of myself and my son. There were definitely times when I almost resented pumping because it controlled so much of my "free" time—I couldn't go out to lunch with friends from work because if I did, I'd miss pumping. However, when you put it in perspective and realize that you have an inconvenience for a short while to give your child the best start possible, it made it much easier to manage. Captain, USAF

Whatever you do, try not to go too long without pumping, as you greatly increase your risk of plugged ducts and mastitis. You'll notice that your breasts are sore, hard, and you may have unexpected let-downs (as your breasts try to relieve the fullness). As noted in Chapter 5, some women are more susceptible to plugged ducts and/or mastitis. If you are one of those women, it is very important that you maintain a regular pumping schedule, and even a quick hand expression to relieve the fullness can help to ward off a plugged duct from forming. If find that you've gone eight, 10, or more hours without pumping or breastfeeding, either due to operational commitments or you just plain forgot to pump (it happens); hand express to relieve the fullness until you can pump or nurse your baby, and then pump again to be sure your breasts are fully drained.

If not being able to pump regularly is becoming a way of life at work, it is time to speak with your supervisor again about your pumping schedule. Repeated days and weeks of not being able to pump **will** lower your milk supply. If this happens you have a number of options, you can pump more on the weekends and evenings/nights to build up your supply, you can take an herbal supplement to boost your supply (although they are not as effective without regular stimulation by breastfeeding/pumping), or you can partially wean your baby and introduce formula or solid foods, depending on the age of your baby (see the chapter on Weaning later in this section). Remember, any breastmilk is better than none at all, and a stressed out mother isn't good for anybody: herself, her baby, or her command.

One final note for those women who work mids, nights or swing shifts, your body as well as your breasts will become accustomed to your sleep-and-wake cycles and when to produce higher amounts of milk (usually at night when prolactin levels are higher). If you work swing shifts, where your shift changes every few days, from days to mids to nights, you may find it takes a few days for your breasts to adjust to making enough milk once you are on the new shift schedule. As for any pumping mother, regular emptying of the breasts is crucial to maintaining your milk supply.

Aviation

Women working in the aviation field, such as pilots, flight officers, and aircrew, will require careful planning for pumping, due to the various challenges posed by the nature of the job. For these types of jobs, you really must plan your pumping around the flight schedule, keeping in mind that flight schedules are notorious for changing, depending on the weather, maintenance on the aircraft, and other factors out of your control. You'll want to take the opportunity to pump as soon as possible before your flight, and again as soon after you land as possible, bearing in mind you'll also have pre- and post flight briefs to attend to as well.

Major Beth Lane, USAF pilot, pumping in the crew rest station of a C-17 transport aircraft.

Photo courtesy Beth Lane. Used with permission.

Depending on your aircraft and mission, you may be on 24-hour standby, in the air for many hours, or have back-to-back flights, and will need to be creative in finding time to pump. You may be able to quickly express milk in the onboard restroom, at the back of the aircraft, or during refueling. Again, this is dependent upon your aircraft type and the familiarity you have with your flight crew (and realize you may have to endure some comments from your crew mates). Stash your pump in your helmet or gear bag and keep a small insulated lunch bag with cold packs available to transport your milk in. It is a good idea to wear nursing pads to control leaking (flight suits are pretty unforgiving with wet milk stains) and plan to take a battery or hand-operated pump with you as back up or for an emergency should your aircraft require maintenance and you cannot get back to your home base.

I was a crew member on E-3s and had to get an extension cord to plug in my pump from a crew chief before we flew, and then I had to pump in the galley with a blanket over me while everyone hung around getting coffee and food all the time hearing the pump and knowing what I was doing under the blanket!!!! That sucked, crew dogs are not nice when it comes to comments, but you just have to crew dog up and tell them to keep their comments to themselves. Staff Sgt., USAF

I'm a C-17 pilot and I breastfed my first for over two years. My second son is seven months old and we're still going strong. We have a crew rest area that has two bunks and two seats and a fridge in the galley. It's located right behind the cockpit, which is up the stairs from the rest of the plane. I pumped in the seat in the crew rest area while the copilot flew and talked on the radios. I only did this while at cruise if there wasn't an extra pilot to jump in the seat for me. I'm quite lucky to be in an airplane where I can get up and pump when I need to. Major, USAF

I'm a SH-60 pilot and when I know we're going on a SAR mission and I have a few minutes to prepare for the flight, I'll run to the restroom and pump to empty my breasts beforehand. I also always take my pump with me and try to express whenever we get a break—usually during lunch or when we're fueling the helicopter. Lt., USN

Some other minor items of interest to breastfeeding mothers who fly are the effects of altitude decompression sickness (ADCS), dehydration, and the gear that is required to be worn when flying. Altitude decompression sickness can occur in pilots and aircrew who fly above 18,000 feet, particularly in unpressurized cabins. It is similar to the decompression sickness that occurs in divers (the "Bends") in that nitrogen is released into the bloodstream causing joint pain, and in worst-case scenarios, neurological and lung involvement resulting in death. Military aircraft and flight crew breathe oxygen at altitude, which is effective in combating ADCS. However, it can still occur. Breastfeeding mothers do not need to worry about the nitrogen released into the bloodstream, as it will not pass into the milk or the baby (Federal Aviation Administration, 2010; Divers Alert Network, 2010).

Female aircrew need to be mindful of dehydration and the possible effect on milk supply. With flights that can last anywhere from 30 minutes to 8-10 hours, depending on the platform, it is imperative that hydration is maintained. While a breastfeeding mother doesn't need to take in great quantities of water to maintain a good milk supply, not drinking enough liquids can have a deleterious effect on your milk supply. Couple that with infrequent pumping, and you have a recipe for lowered milk output. Dehydration can be a factor when flying for a number of reasons, you may not be able to take in fluids due to the constraints of flying, or you might choose not to drink due to the lack of suitable (or any) relief tubes or restrooms onboard. It is important, as a breastfeeding mother, that you maintain adequate hydration while flying (even if it means wearing a piddle-pak or diaper) so that you can continue to provide your milk to your baby.

Finally, it is wise to keep in mind that all the flight gear you must wear when flying is heavy and a lot of it rests right over your breasts. Some women, not all, are susceptible to plugged ducts from pressure on or near the breasts and armpits (breast tissue extends up into your armpit area). If you find that you are suffering from repeated bouts of plugged ducts, take a good look at how your flight gear fits and where the various straps and buckles are resting. You might find that a simple adjustment is enough to take the pressure off your breast tissue. If not, you'll have to be sure to practice the suggestions given in Chapter 4 on treating plugged ducts, including lots of massage and drainage, to keep from having it turn into a case of mastitis. Breastfeeding and flying are compatible; it just takes a bit of creativity and dedication.

Field Conditions

Many women, particularly those in the Air Force, Army, and Marines, are often sent on field training exercises (FTX) that may range in duration from days to weeks. Since they are training maneuvers and not deployments, you won't necessarily be exempt from them due to breastfeeding. You will be eating, pumping, showering, and sleeping in the field, conditions will be dirty, and you'll have virtually no privacy. You will be on the move constantly and most likely you will not have any electricity or refrigeration available. Despite all this, you can continue to pump while in field conditions and will want to do so if you won't be away for very long, or to keep from developing mastitis if you'll be gone for an extended period of time and must wean abruptly. There are a number of items you will want to think about and prepare for before you leave on your FTX.

First and foremost, talk to your supervisors, both the one at home base and the one at the FTX (if they will be different). You are not asking to be taken off the FTX, but rather you will be reminding them that you are breastfeeding and will need time to pump throughout the exercise. You might also want to find out if your command has adopted a similar program to the one started at Joint Base Lewis McChord where a courier service is available to take your milk back to the main base once a day (see Chapter 19). If it helps, you can also let your command know that pumping while in the field is necessary in order to keep from developing mastitis (and if a note from medical would help, then don't hesitate to request one).

Speaking with your leadership is vital. Don't go into the FTX hoping that you can pump without anyone knowing about it. You might be exposed to chemicals that can pass through breastmilk or any of a number of other situations that can affect breastfeeding. The last thing you need is to fall out with a raging case of mastitis and no one, including the medics, is aware that you are a breastfeeding mother. Your leadership needs to know your requirements for pumping, even if it is just that you will disappear for 10-15 minutes a couple of times a day. It is also important to mention the need to eat and drink regularly in order to help maintain your milk supply. Do not forgo

Pumping during a FTX

Photo courtesy Rachel Davis.
Used with permission.

drinking enough water because you can't relieve yourself in the field due to the conditions or a lack of time. It is vital that you not become dehydrated as it can affect your milk supply.

Finding a suitable place to pump in field conditions can be tricky. You'll very likely be living in primitive conditions with other women, and possibly men, in a tent. Other women in this situation have created some privacy behind a strung-up towel around their cot, or in a corner of the tent, and some have just stuck the pump under their shirt or rain poncho and pumped regardless of privacy. For some women, it is just easier to hand express their milk directly on the ground, especially if you are only expressing enough to relieve fullness.

Realize that you probably will not be able to pump nearly as often as you would back at your home base and that your milk supply may drop. Try to aim for at least four times in 24 hours, but there are no hard-and-fast rules here. It is all about what kind of time you can eke out during the FTX. If you are on a hard march, it's going to be pretty difficult to manage any type pumping at all. However, if you have a chance during meal breaks, you should go and pump. Upon your return home, frequent nursing and pumping should increase your supply back up to its normal level. Some mothers have also found that herbal supplements, such as More Milk Plus (a tincture you add to water), and Fenugreek or Blessed Thistle taken in capsules, can help keep your milk supply up. Be sure to check with an IBCLC and your HCP before taking anything not authorized by the military (the last thing you need is to pop positive on the urinalysis).

In preparation for leaving, many mothers pump and store extra milk in order to leave a good supply of expressed milk at home for their baby. Pump as much as possible, including when you are at home (your baby will still be able nurse afterwards and get enough milk), to build up a good stockpile. For a short-duration FTX, you should have no trouble leaving enough milk behind. If it will be a longer exercise, your caregiver may need to supplement your baby with formula. Be sure that you have introduced a bottle (if you haven't already) and whichever formula you will be using well before you leave to be sure that your baby will tolerate it (see the Chapter on Weaning later in this section).

Here are a couple of final items to keep in mind. If you will be wearing heavy gear or packs, be sure that the straps are not pressing into your breast tissue as it may increase the risks of plugged ducts. It is important to wash your hands and your pump parts while in the field, and keeping some hand sanitizer and/or hand wipes in your cammies is a good idea. Practice hand expression, so you are comfortable with the process and are proficient with it before you leave on the exercise. Battery-operated and manual pumps do break. You don't want to be miserable with rock hard, sore breasts during your FTX because you can't express your milk. Breastfeeding while on a field training exercise is doable. However, it will take a lot of perseverance and dedication on your part. But as the mothers below attest, it is definitely worth it.

When I went to my nine week Nursing Officer basic, I took my daughter with me as my husband was PCS\'ing to Europe. Her first birthday was during my one week in the field...and yes she was breastfeeding then. I stored as much milk as I could before I left her in my parent's wonderful hands. The first night in the field I discovered my battery operated pump was broken. I was miserable in my cold mummy bag with my breasts feeling like rocks on my chest, sharing a huge tent with males and females and no privacy curtains. I went to the medics to see what assistance they could give me... none. Their officer, said, "You can have some Tylenol, but that's poor planning Lt." I toughed it out, and was eventually able to manually express my milk. So, the remaining part of the week, every time we got a break for meals, I lifted my shirt and manually expressed my milk on the ground. Lt., USA

Pumping in the field

Photo courtesy Julie Kellogg.
Used with permission.

When I went to the field for four days, I took my pump. I had planned to send the milk back to the OB floor via a daily runner, but conditions in the field were too dirty. So, I just pumped and dumped. I took Reglan and More Milk Plus (a supplement with Fenugreek and Blessed Thistle) to maintain my milk supply. I could only pump about four x a day. I pumped in the tent that I shared with about 20 other people, both male and female, and used my rain parka to keep covered. My milk supply did decrease, and it took some extra nursing to increase it again. Major, USA

When my baby was seven months old, I was sent to a Combined Artillery Campaign Exercise in 29 Palms for about eight days. I was assigned to something called a "Shock Trauma Platoon." I brought two manual pumps (Avent Isis) and "double pumped" while at base camp... and then the next day when we got on the convoy and went out to the middle of nowhere in the desert, I brought just one, broken down into pieces in the pockets of my cammies. I tried to pump as much as possible, including once over night. It was very sad dumping my milk into the desert sand after each pumping session. I missed my baby very much every day. Because he was a "reverse-cycle nurser," I had tons of milk stored up in the freezer. He was able to have expressed breastmilk the whole time we were separated. Lt., USN

I had to be out in the field, and there was nowhere for me to pump, so I had to walk about a mile to go to a hard-wall building to pump. So there I was, twice a day, with my chem-gear helmet and breast pump. The first time I mentioned it to the people out there, they didn't expect for a nursing mother to be in that type of environment. One thing I always did was make sure my leadership was aware of my situation, and it was always the same answer, just let someone know when you get there. It's hard when your schedule isn't flexible, and you don't know what's going to come next, or when you'll have a chance to pump. I was glad it was only for a week. But that was a hard week. Senior Airman, USAF

Once at Fort Bragg, I had a 20k qualifying ruckmarch with my unit scheduled. Usually when events like this came up, my daughter's father would be the one to take her to daycare or whatever needed to be done so that I could participate. As odds would have it, he also had a qualifying 20k ruckmarch scheduled for the same day at the same time. So I arranged for one of the NCOs in my section who was not doing the ruckmarch, but would be setting up the water station at the halfway point, to care for my daughter until I completed the ruckmarch. Even though he was a single soldier and didn't have any kids of his own or much experience with small children, I entrusted my daughter to him on that dark Friday morning at 0500. She was still sleeping and I prayed that we would be done before she ever woke up. We loaded up our packs, put on our kevlars, picked up our weapons, and the march began. We marched 6 miles out to the water station and the half way point. While all the other soldiers got water, ate a piece of fruit, and changed their socks, I was the only soldier that changed my socks and a dirty diaper. I gave my awake but groggy Sweet Pea a hug and a kiss, handed her back to my fellow NCO, picked up my alice pack and weapon, and started off on the last 6 miles. After the 12 miles were completed in under 4 hours and we were all sitting on the curb in front of our building removing our boots and socks, I hurriedly picked up my gear, my boots, my wet socks, and hustled up the stairs to my waiting daughter. I took my gear and my daughter into my office, closed the door, settled on the floor sitting cross-legged, removed my soaking wet shirt and bra, and let my hungry baby latch on. She waited for me for 4 hours and 12 miles and I dropped the soldier gear to pick up my mother's mantle so my Sweet Pea could nurse. Staff Sgt., USA

Maintenance

Mothers who work in maintenance-related jobs, either as aircraft maintainers or as part of a motor pool, face some unique challenges of their own. Finding a place to pump shouldn't be too difficult. Most hangar bays and motor pool maintenance areas have administrative offices and unused storage closets or a locker room that can be used for pumping. Be sure that whatever area you are in is not near Hazardous Materials, and be certain that you have made your breastfeeding status known to your supervisor and Occupational Health, particularly if you are working with fuels, oils, solvents, and other HAZMAT (see Chapter 14 on HAZMAT for more information). Finding time to pump can be problematic. Some breastfeeding mothers in the maintenance field find that it is difficult to find time to pump because fixing the aircraft or the deuce-and-a half takes priority over the allotted break time. You'll need to pump when you get a chance, rather than wait for a scheduled break.

Working as a jet mechanic, we were always tied to the flight schedule and the need to have the "birds" up and ready to fly the missions. Many times I would soak through my coveralls, even with breast pads, because I wasn't allowed to pump when I needed to…the maintenance came first. Petty Officer 3rd Class, USN

Medical and Dental

Medical personnel run the gamut from enlisted corpsman in administrative positions to flight nurses and trauma surgeons. Being able to pump while working in the medical field depends very highly on your job and not so much your rank. Finding a place to pump is fairly easy. Most medical and dental personnel should not have any problem finding an unused space to pump in.

Hospitals and clinics have spare examining rooms and offices, and oftentimes a pumping or lactation room has already been set up.

In the hospital setting, you also have the option of visiting the Mother/Baby unit and using the pumps there, as long as you have your own collection kit. Finding the time to pump depends very highly on your specialty within the medical department. Personnel working in administrative positions or as providers in clinics (especially OICs) will find pumping easier to manage than a nurse working in the ER or an EMT. It is more difficult to find the time to pump simply due to the chaotic nature of the job and the constant stream of patients. Twelve-hour shifts are the norm in medical as well, making it important to add another pumping to your schedule if at all possible. Like many of the other job specialties in the military that often have unexpected changes in schedule, it is important to pump when you get the chance and not necessarily wait for your next scheduled break. Some women are able to be successful and pump enough to keep their milk supply up, and others are not as these examples show.

> *I went home many a day without having the chance to pump and my shirt soaked!* Captain, USAF

> *I am a Navy nurse, so I squeeze in pumping at work about every three to four hours during a 12-hour shift. Since I am at a large hospital with a NICU, there are private pumping rooms available. The Navy also has a policy that requires members to have a place to pump that is private and not a bathroom, as well as a place to store milk and adequate time to pump. They emphasize that allowing mothers time to pump will decrease the likelihood of the mom having to take off work for sick children. I have been in the Navy for 11 years, have had three children, and breast fed and pumped at work for all of them.* Lt. j.g., Navy

> *My experience with breastfeeding was good. I breastfed my daughter for 13 months. I think being a provider in the Navy helped my experience go smoothly because I had my own office, and I could lock the door when I needed to. All of my support staff and colleagues were supportive of my decision, which also made things easier. Almost every day that I pumped at work, I would shut my door for lunch, strap on the hands-free contraption, and keep working at the computer while I pumped. Working in the clinic setting is probably the most convenient for pumping moms because there is almost always a room with a sink that can be utilized.* Lt., USN

> *I was an OIC of a clinic. I was very busy seeing patients and going to meetings. I pumped every morning and afternoon. It was routine for me to pump and talk to my staff at the same time. They would come to my office to ask questions or to get a signature on some form. I*

didn't mind. I used a hands-free device and my shirt covered everything. I just couldn't take the time to sit and concentrate on pumping; I had to document patient care or do administrative work while pumping just to keep up and on schedule. I rarely had to pump in the middle of meetings at the hospital...I remember going to a corner and covering myself up. Some meetings lasted too long for me to wait until after the meeting to pump. Plus, I usually had something scheduled right after the meeting. My colleagues didn't seem to mind. Of course, they may have minded and just didn't tell me. Overall, they were very supportive and not freaked out by the thought of my pumping. Major, USA

Medical personnel work with various drugs and other agents that can be harmful to your baby if passed on through your breastmilk. Be sure to check with your Occupational Health representative, especially if you work with anesthetic gases (nitrous oxide, halothane), antineoplastics, or radioisotopes, as all can pass through breastmilk (see Chapter 14 for more information). Finally, if you are a flight medic or part of an EMT unit, keep a spare hand or battery operated pump with you for pumping on the go and try to pump as regularly as possible when you are at the hospital and between runs. Medical personnel can certainly continue to breastfeed while on the job, and in fact, can be at the forefront of modeling this healthy behavior to their fellow co-workers and patients.

Security Forces and Firefighters

Firefighters and security personnel have a few challenges of their own to deal with, including frequent patrols, guard duty, emergencies, and fires to respond to. You'll have to be ready to find time to pump whether you have a day in the office doing paperwork or a four-hour shift on patrol with a partner. At the firehouse, you might just be getting ready to pump when the alarm sounds, and there is no chance you'll be able to pump. Many personnel in these jobs work rotating shifts, which can wreak havoc on your milk supply, so breastfeed as often as possible on your days off to help keep your milk supply up. Talk with your partner if you'll be on patrol together and need to pump, or schedule your pumping right before patrol and right after, and then stick to it. If you have guard duty, you should be able to squeeze a quick pumping session in as you rotate on and off duty at the gate. Mothers in the fire station need to pump whenever possible, as you won't know when you might get a chance or if the next alarm will sound in 10 minutes or two hours. Try as much as possible to stick with a schedule, but squeeze in a pumping whenever you can.

Security personnel and firefighters have to wear or carry a lot of heavy gear, including bullet-proof vests and turnout gear, which can put pressure on the breasts. Make sure that you do not develop any plugged ducts from the constant pressure. If you will be handling weapons or spending a lot of time on the firing line as part of your daily job, be sure to check Chapter 14 for more information about lead exposure and follow the precautions listed.

Firefighters come into contact with any number of hazardous materials, including carbon monoxide in fires, and while you will be wearing a breathing apparatus, the toxic smoke invades your clothes, hair, and skin. Be sure to thoroughly shower before going home, and wash all work clothes separately from your family's laundry. Wash your hands thoroughly before pumping. As with most hazardous materials, some will transfer into breastmilk. However, the benefits of breastfeeding outweigh the risks of the possible exposure. See Chapter 14 for more information on the various hazardous chemicals in the military environment.

Shipboard

While it may seem that this is an area where it is highly unlikely you will be able to pump, especially if you are out to sea for extended periods of time, it can be done with some planning. The Navy has extended its deferment from deployment to one year. However, that doesn't exempt sailors from training exercises that are only a few days to weeks long. Should you be a mother who is breastfeeding beyond a year you will be rotated back to sea-duty and may face a deployment. Much like soldiers who are sent away for field training exercises of a few days to a few weeks, shipboard sailors face many of the same challenges. You will be faced with a lack of privacy, limited time to pump, and a lack of a place to store your milk.

Old style enlisted shipboard racks

Photo courtesy Robyn Roche-Paull.
Used with permission.

Finding a place to pump can be problematic for some, especially enlisted sailors in berthing where there is no privacy. You can pump in your rack with the privacy curtains pulled shut if you are on a ship outfitted with the newer racks. The old-style shipboard racks are not made to sit up in, which leaves sitting in the lounge area where everyone in the berthing can see and hear you pumping. You will have to decide how comfortable you are pumping "in the open." Pumping in your workplace is not likely to be doable either, as ships' spaces are small and privacy is nonexistent. Officers can use their staterooms to pump in, while enlisted staff may need to find an unused space on board or go to Medical to pump.

There will be limited time for pumping, as most ships go to a 12-hour shift rotation, with all personnel working non-stop except for meal breaks. During a 12-hour shift, you'll want to aim for four pumping sessions, and then pump one to four times during your "night" hours, depending on the age of your baby. There will be times when you'll have to decide between eating or pumping, due to your work schedule and the limited times the galley is open. General Quarters and Man Overboard drills are unexpected and will require you to remain at your workplace, with no way to pump until the drill is over.

Where you will store your pumped milk is another hurdle to overcome. Some mothers have been able to store their milk in the refrigerators in Medical (per the OPNAVINST 6000.1C, the command must supply refrigeration) or down in the Supply freezers. So you'll need to talk to Medical or Supply if you choose to store your milk. Health and safety regulations and inspections may bar you from keeping the milk in your berthing or stateroom. Other mothers pump and dump while underway simply to keep their milk supply up and not have to hassle with storing the milk. If you are deployed for an extended period of time, you will need to wean, as there are no provisions to send the milk off the ship. Finally, if you plan to take an electric breast pump onboard, it will need to be certified by the ship's Electrical Safety division. Otherwise, take a battery or hand operated pump with you.

> *Stick with it and make time for it no matter how hard it is. I pumped in my rack every three to four hours for three weeks at sea, when my son was six months old. I woke up early for middle of the night watches, and I never let pumping get in the way of regular work. Get a good quality double-electric pump, so you can do it quickly and get back to work before anyone really notices. Per the OPNAVINST, ships must accommodate breastfeeding moms, too. Know your rights!* Lt., USN

> *I would go to Medical and pump four times a day, at meals times, and it worked for me. I got between four and six ounces each time. I brought extra snacks for myself because even though I was awake for all four meal times, I would have to choose between eating, sleeping, and pumping for two of them. I chose to sleep until I had to get up to pump, so I wouldn't be a total zombie on watch.* Petty Officer 2nd Class, USN

> *I went back to sea duty and had to buy a deep freezer for all the milk I've been storing up so that I can go to sea (for a few days at a time) and still have my milk at home even when ...I'm not. I keep a bunch of pictures of him near my desk/pumping station in my stateroom, so I can look at him while pumping. Breastfeeding has not suffered one bit!* Lt. Cmdr., USN

Similar to soldiers sent out on field training exercises, it is a good idea to add extra pumping sessions into your routine before you leave so that you can stockpile a good store of expressed milk. Depending on how much milk you have stored, the length of your deployment, and the age of your baby, he may or may not need to be supplemented with formula or solid foods. Keep in mind, too, that a lengthy deployment with a baby older than one year might result in weaning upon your return. You'll want to be prepared for that if it should occur, and while sad, be proud of all the milk you provided for so long (see Chapter 17 on Weaning). At first glance, it seems that pumping onboard ship would be impossible. But as the sailors above have shown, it is most certainly doable for short-term deployments.

Funny Situations

What would life as a breastfeeding mother in the military be without a few laughs? While it may not seem funny at the time, sometimes situations occur that defy explanation. Pumping in the workplace has its share of oops and blunders, with people walking in on you while pumping and other embarrassing incidents. Here are a few to remind you that we are all human, it happens to the best of us, and you will live, even if you feel like sinking through the floor at the time!

I only once had someone walk in on me. It was the detail Airman who couldn't have been more than 19 years old, and he froze when he opened the door and saw me in the midst of pumping! I had to tell the poor kid to get out! After that they left a key in the room so that I could lock the door. Captain, USAF

I was wearing my Blues (they are very light), and one morning a co-worker said, "You dropped water on yourself," and the embarrassment I felt when I said, "Oh that's not water!" I felt so horrified, but then I thought, what is he doing looking at my breasts and laughed it off. I went the rest of the day with a spot on my shirt, it was fine, I just threw my jacket on, and no one else noticed. Senior Airman, USAF

I was on a flight to Iraq to see a new base. I went with a crew that I didn't know out of a reserve unit in NY. They were very nice and happy to let me travel with them. About eight hours into our trip, I couldn't avoid it any longer; I had to pump, so I got my single pump I carried with me for quick, discreet pumping and headed to the bathroom. By this time most of the crew besides the pilot and co-pilot were sleeping, so I thought I would be safe. I got in the bathroom, locked the door, and started pumping. Half way through, the door flies open and there I am face to face with the Full Bird Colonel, with one hand holding my shirt up and boobs hanging out. Neither of us knew what to say. He apologized over and over again for the rest of the two-day trip for not knocking, but I would just laugh. He kept saying he owed me a round when we returned for embarrassing me. I learned on that trip to always keep my foot on the door, even if it appears to have a working lock. Staff Sgt., USAF

We were in the middle of three simulated emergency response drills, and I knew it would be hours before I had a chance to pump. We had a few minutes while the "victims" were being transported to us, and I realized the ambulance had outlets, so I kicked out the ambulance crew and pumped. Since this was an exercise and everyone had to know what everyone else was doing, soon all the cops and the fire department crew on scene knew the doc was in the ambulance pumping milk! Major, USAF

I had just switched from pumping every six hours to every eight hours, and my body wasn't fully adjusted to the new schedule. I was in Al Udeid, Qatar, eating at the chow hall when I felt a little cold. I looked down and one of my breasts was leaking through my shirt. Needless to say I ate quickly and crossed my arms all the way back to my room. Sometimes I feel like the only one in my situation. Captain, USAF

As is typical with those ceremonies, there was a lengthy dress rehearsal the day before. I pumped immediately before we went out there, but my immediate supervisor was rather extreme in his desire for perfection. I didn't get to pump or even a potty break for a very long time, and I wasn't the only one. Everyone out there was crossing their legs at the end of practice, after the morning's coffee had necessitated a potty break for everyone after four hours. However, I was also crossing my arms over my chest and feeling my breasts get harder and harder. By the time it was over, I was walking to my car, I could feel myself leaking pretty substantially. It was awful and unnecessary, but there were no ill effects, thankfully. Major, USA

There are far too many job specialties in the military to be able cover all of them in this book. Hopefully, this chapter has given you some ideas of how to find a place and time to pump that you can adapt for your workplace. Get creative, adapt and overcome, and don't take no for answer. And don't forget to laugh at yourself once in awhile. An embarrassing incident may not seem funny now. But looking back in a few years, it will have become a fond memory of a crazy and wonderful period in your life.

Staff Sgt. Rosemary Hernandez-Oglesby, U.S. Army, with her breastfed daughter just before a jump.

Photo courtesy Rosemary Hernandez-Oglesby. Used with permission.

Chapter 13

Deployments, Trainings, and Overseas Assignments

Temporary Duty Assignments, whether for mandatory schools or trainings, as well as deployments and overseas assignments, present their own unique challenges to maintaining breastfeeding and pumping. Here are a few guidelines and examples of how to manage breastfeeding during these challenging situations.

Temporary Duty (TAD/TDY)

Depending on the length of and distance away for your Temporary Duty Assignment for school or training, you may have a number of options for breastfeeding and pumping. For a short-term assignment of just a few weeks, you can continue to pump as you have been pumping, with the exception of deciding whether you will pump and dump or store the milk to bring back home. With an assignment located nearby, you can just go home in the evenings and bring your pumped milk with you, as you would at your regular workplace.

Advise your new supervisor of your pumping requirements when you check-in so that you can work out a pumping schedule and a place to pump. Finding time to pump while attending a school or training can be difficult. Breaks are generally only 10-15 minutes in length, which is not enough time to set-up, pump, and break-down. Furthermore, some schools require a certain number of hours of attendance in order to qualify for the certification you are seeking, and being even a little bit late returning from a pumping session can disqualify you. Finding a place to pump may require a little ingenuity. Inquire as to whether there is an unused classroom or instructor's lounge that you can use. If you find that you cannot pump while attending the training or school, you have the option to temporarily wean until you return.

I had a hard time pumping while I attended Airman Leadership School (ALS), professional military education (PME) for new supervisors. We had 10 minute breaks every hour. I talked to my teacher in the beginning, and he allowed me to come back a few minutes late twice a day during my pumping times, but the accredited institution needed to follow strict guidelines for credit hours, so I couldn't miss any class time. Our one-hour lunch break was rushed. I drove to feed the baby, tried to scarf down food if there was time, cleaned my pump, then sped back, just before class returned. Captain, USAF

Big kudos to the command I went to, which was a training command that had a rigid and very full schedule. I was still allotted time to pump at LEAST every four hours, sometimes even two to three hours. They allowed me to miss and/or be late to, or leave various activities or training if I needed to. Lt. j.g., USN

For an assignment with a longer time away, or one with a further distance, you will need to decide whether you will wean before you leave or pump and ship your milk back to your caregiver. If you choose to ship your milk home, it will require some pre-planning on your part. Thank you to SFC Rose Ryon (Soldiers' Chorus, U.S. Army Field Band) for the following information on shipping milk while TDY.

Before any TAD/TDY duty you will need to stock up on some essential supplies. In addition to your double-electric breast pump (and all the items you normally pack for pumping at work), you may want to pack some of the following items that other military mothers have found useful when "on the road" and shipping milk home (also in Appendix I):

- Hand pump or attachment–in case your pump malfunctions, pieces go missing, or you have no electricity

- Pump cleaning gear–bottle brush and dish soap or steam cleaning bags

- Hand sanitizer– you may not always have running water

- Batteries–you may not always have electricity

- Extension cord/adapter–you may not always be near a convenient outlet

- Milk storage bags–they take up less room and ship better

- Sharpie marker–to date your breastmilk

- Electric cooler–to keep your milk cold until you can ship it home (you may not have access to a refrigerator)

- Styrofoam or soft-sided coolers–for shipping milk, at least two or more, depending on how much you produce

- Shipping box–large enough to hold the cooler(s)

- Shipping labels

- Packing tape

- Larger Ziploc bags–gallon size or larger

- Newspaper and/or brown lunch bags–for wrapping frozen milk

- Gloves–if you will be using dry ice

While you are TDY, you will need to decide how many shipments you want to make, bearing in mind that they are not cheap! Choose a day when your schedule will allow you pack and ship your milk. It is time consuming to buy the dry ice (if you use it), package your milk, and ship it off. Locate, preferably ahead of time, where you can purchase dry ice. Butcher shops, bait shops, ice companies, and sometimes Wal-Mart stores carry it (it comes in five pound blocks). If you have been freezing your milk all along, you are ready to go. If not (and you've just been keeping it cold in the electric cooler), you'll need to find someplace to freeze it overnight. Finally, you'll need to arrange for transportation (if you don't have your own POV) to buy the dry ice and go to the shipping center. You can also arrange to have the carrier pick-up your package. It goes without saying that you should always have a back-up plan, since things can get FUBAR'ed in an instant.

Taking the time to package your milk carefully will ensure that it gets to your caregiver, and ultimately to your baby, in perfect shape and ready to use. Whether or not you use dry ice is your choice. Frozen breastmilk packed properly will generally stay frozen long enough to ship it overnight or second-day. The packing directions are basically the same (just omit the dry ice). Have all your supplies ready to go (shipping boxes, newspaper, labels, etc.) and go buy the dry ice. You will need one 5-pound block for each cooler, be sure not to touch it with bare hands (you can seriously injure your skin if you touch it without gloves on). Begin by putting four bags of frozen milk into a lunch bag, and then wrap with another, forming a "milk pack." Once you have them all wrapped in lunch bags, put a few of the milk packs in a Ziploc bag, creating packages of milk. Then either surround your block of dry ice with the packages of milk or line the cooler and layer the packages with newspaper. Fill any remaining space in the cooler with wadded up newspaper. Pack the coolers in the shipping box, secure it well with packing tape, and label. Be aware that it will be heavy, especially if you have used dry ice. As of this writing, the United States Post Office will not accept breastmilk for shipping, so you will have to go with FedEx©, DHL© or UPS© as your carrier, and the shipping rates are not cheap, especially for overnight or two day shipping (Ryon, 2008).

As the story below illustrates, pumping and shipping your milk while away on TDY orders is certainly possible. A Staff Sergeant in the Air Force, Mariah LeBlanc, was sent to a school in Texas for training when her daughter was six months old. She was able to pump her milk while attending school, store it in her room in the barracks, and ship it home once a week to her husband and daughter in Delaware. Her daughter was able to continue to receive her mother's milk during the duration of the four-month school, and the Staff Sergeant was able to fulfill her duties by attending a required training school.

I found out when she was about four months old that I would be going on an 18-week TDY around the time that she turned six months old. I knew I was not ready to wean my baby, and I knew that I did not want to put her on formula, so I made a snap decision that I would freeze my pumped milk and overnight it to my daughter. I'm not sure where this idea came from, but I decided that it was totally do-able! I bought an ice chest and did some research about shipping pumped milk and decided that I could do it. I pumped like crazy to build up a good stash of milk in my freezer before I left.

The morning that I was to leave, I got up, nursed my daughter one last time, put her back to bed, and then left. It wasn't until I was about an hour away that I broke down and cried. I almost had to pull my Jeep over I was crying so hard. I knew that I would have to pump and dump until I got to my destination, so at the first rest stop I came to, I pulled over to an out-of-the-way area and pumped just to walk in and dump it out. My pump had a car charger option on the pump, but for some reason, it failed to work after this first pumping. I had to resort to using a manual pump for the remainder of the two day trip...it was so hard!

As soon as I got to my TDY location, I checked into lodging and found that the fridge was one of those little mini-fridges. I tried to turn the temperature down in order to freeze everything, but it just would not get cold enough. They found another room with a fridge/freezer that I was able to move to that was only going to cost me an additional $7 a day. To me, the cost was well worth the sacrifice. A group of amazing moms that I know from an online forum got together and raised over $700 to help pay for the added expense. They also contacted several companies and were able to get me tons of milk bags in order to store and freeze my milk in. To this day, I am very grateful for the help and support that they provided. They will never know what a blessing that was to me when I opened up that envelope and saw the list of donations. I sat in my car and cried out of pure joy that there are still people in this world that care about others so much! I was and am truly awed by their generosity.

After about two weeks, my freezer could not hold any more milk. I was pumping 9-12 times a day and making more milk than I ever thought possible. I was so excited to make my first shipment of milk home to my daughter. I purchased a five-day ice chest on the advice of someone that I found on the Internet that had shipped milk to another baby. I lined the cooler with newspaper and proceeded to stack my "milk shingles" (I froze the milk laying down in milk bags in order to take up as little room in the freezer as possible) in the cooler. I placed blue ice packs on the top, lined it with more newspaper, and then sealed up the ice chest with duct tape, making sure that every crack and crevice was *totally sealed up. I brought it over to Fed-Ex and paid $175 to have it guaranteed overnight. I was so happy! Sure enough, by noon the next day, my husband had received the ice chest of milk and reported that every single milk shingle was still solidly frozen! Life was good! I knew that I could provide mama's milk for my baby no matter how long I was away from her!*

I started going to LLL meetings because it was hard not having a baby and having to pump 9-12 times a day. I needed the support of other moms and also needed to talk to a LC

There is liquid gold in these ice chests!

Photo courtesy Mariah LeBlanc.
Used with permission.

and find out tips on how to reconnect with my daughter upon my return home. The other moms were great and very supportive, and I was glad I went even though I felt out of place without having a baby there with me. I kept pumping, and at about the halfway point, my husband was able to come visit me for a few days while my parents stayed with the kids. Since he was flying out, I decided not to mail another ice chest of milk home since he had plenty for her and just to let him take the ice chest back with him on the plane. By the time he left, I had so much milk that I had to go purchase a second ice chest! While checking in his baggage at the airport, the Baggage lady asked what was in the coolers. My husband made me so proud when he looked up at the lady and said boldly, "Milk. Frozen Breastmilk! And my wife here has made it for me to take back to our daughter while she is here TDY." The lady was quite impressed and called over a man to tell him what was in the two ice chests. The man then asked me if I would like to accompany my husband back to the gate until his flight left. He said that his wife used to work in the airline industry and fly a lot and that she would pump and freeze her milk when she was flying for her twins. The man looked at my husband and said "You have quite a woman there!" to which my husband replied, "I know, she's pretty amazing"!

I had made so much milk that my husband said that he had tons of it in the freezer and probably had enough for another several months and did not need anymore any time soon. Knowing that I did not want to quit pumping and lose my supply, I contacted a milk bank and was able to donate over 300 ounces to them. I was also able to make a private milk donation to a preemie of over 1200 ounces. I cut back on my pumping to about seven times a day, which was much more manageable

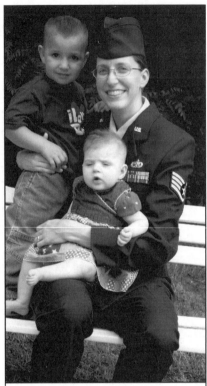

SSgt Mariah LeBlanc, USAF, with her breastfed children.

Photo courtesy Mariah LeBlanc. Used with permission.

as compared to the 9-12 times I had been pumping.

I looked forward to the time that I got to go back home and was excited about continuing my nursing relationship with my daughter, who was now almost 11 months old. Unfortunately, my daughter had no desire to continue nursing. She was so used to the bottle that she did not want to have to work for her food. I was devastated at the thought of having to continue to pump, but knew that it was what was best for her. I continued pumping and gave my daughter the fresh milk until she turned one, and I stopped pumping. We were able to continue giving her frozen breastmilk until she was well over 18 months old.

Alternatively, you can chose to temporarily wean for the time you are gone and relactate when you return, this can work if it will be for a short period of time and you cannot pump while you are training (you'll still need to express for comfort). If you know the date you'll be leaving on your TDY, then begin to wean gradually ahead of time. This will help both you and your baby make the transition easier. See the Weaning chapter for more information on Relactation and Weaning. Keep in mind that while some babies will go right back to the breast after an extended absence from you, others will not.

I am in the Navy, and when my last daughter was seven and a half months old, I was sent to a five week training command away from my family. Although I pumped the entire time, she would not nurse when I returned home, and I continued to pump for her and give her bottles. This was very upsetting for me, as the Navy implemented a policy right after I had her that no new moms can transfer until 12 months after birth. Since they called my training "temporary duty," it was a loop hole that I could not get out of no matter how much I fought it and who I talked to about it. This was definitely forced weaning for me. I was very proud that I was able to pump so much while away from her and keep my supply up. But I was very upset that she didn't return to breastfeeding. Lt. j.g., USN

Deployments and Overseas Assignments

For any type of deployment that will last longer than just a few weeks, you have a couple of choices: you may be able to pump and dump your milk and pick up nursing when you get back, you may be able to pump and ship your milk home (and may or may not pick up nursing again), or you may have to wean your baby. There are no hard-and-fast rules here, it all depends on your command, where you are being sent, the accommodations you'll have, if your family can travel to see you periodically, and other factors. There are few to no facilities available on board ship or overseas for expressing and transporting milk. Also, it is against the law in some countries to ship frozen milk due to customs regulations. However, it is not impossible to manage as the following examples show.

An Air Force medical officer, Captain Ginger Bohl, was sent to Afghanistan in support of Operation Enduring Freedom and had to leave her four-month-old son at home. She was breastfeeding at the time of her deployment, and once at her post in Afghanistan, she was able to pump five times every day. She sent her pumped, frozen milk home once a week via DHL to her husband and son in Texas. She continued to pump for her full deployment, and while she was not successful in having him return to breastfeeding, he did receive her milk until he turned one year old, her original goal for breastfeeding.

I first learned of my upcoming deployment when my son was four months old. I tried switching for a date after his first birthday, but was not successful. Three months later, I set off for Bagram Air Field, Afghanistan, leaving home on August 29, 2007. I wasn't sure what to expect, so I brought my pump along...just in case. I had heard rumors of deployed women shipping breastmilk home to their babies. Sounded pretty unrealistic and a bit crazy, but it was too hard for me to accept I may not be able to breastfeed my son again. I nursed Silas in the airport shortly before getting on the plane, appreciating the new rule that families of deploying military could accompany them through security. Thankfully, neither he nor my three-year-old daughter had any idea what was transpiring. On the way to Bagram, I pumped in airport and airplane restrooms, in tents shared with other women, anywhere semi-private and semi-clean. I dumped all the milk as I had nowhere to store it.

I arrived at Bagram to find a dirty, dusty environment, with less than desirable restrooms, and a plywood box that was partitioned off into eight rooms, one of which would be my living quarters for the next four months. I wasn't sure how this was going to work. Then I was introduced to the hospital, a fixed structure built only a few months ago. It was clean, had private exam rooms where I could pump, and had a large freezer where I could store the milk. I pumped every day at 0600, 1000, 1400, 1800, 2200 and never had any trouble with my milk supply. I froze the milk in milk storage bags and kept them in a deep freezer in Nutritional Medicine (the small kitchen where meals and snacks were served. Public Health said this was fine as long as it was on the bottom shelf of the freezer.) My mom sent me a bottle brush and bottle drying rack, and I bought dish soap and a small Tupperware to wash the pump parts in. I used bottled water and heated it up in the microwave.

Every two weeks, I put the frozen milk in an Igloo cooler (two layers of upright milk bags, separated by a layer of cardboard). I would contact DHL (shipping company) the day before shipping to get the flight time for the next day, and they would pick me and the cooler up in a van about 1.5 hours before flight time. Then I filled out all the paperwork, paid the $150-$200, and walked back to the hospital. (FYI: FedEx could not ship perishable goods out of Afghanistan and the U.S. Postal Service would take 7-10 days and couldn't guarantee refrigeration). I tracked the shipments online, and it took between 2.5 and

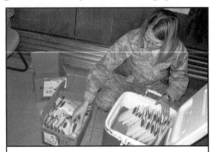

Captain Ginger Bohl, USAF, packing her breastmilk to ship home from Afghanistan

Photo courtesy Ginger Bohl. Used with permission.

5 days to arrive in Texas or Michigan. The one that took five days was held by customs for three days as they investigated this breastmilk shipment from Afghanistan!

The milk arrived mostly or completely frozen each time, except once. DHL refunded the cost of shipping for the time it had thawed, and my husband threw away all the milk. If any bags leaked, he also threw those away. (If milk can get out, you never know what might have gotten in.) I did not have access to dry ice, so we relied a lot on prayer! It took me about 5 shipments to finally find out all the paperwork I needed, since nobody had done this before from Afghanistan. My husband sent each cooler back to me after he got it (took about 7-10 days in the mail) filled with drawings from my 3-year-old daughter, pictures, things I had asked for. I had two revolving coolers, so I didn't have to worry about getting the first back in time.

Her husband, Michael Bohl, unpacks the shipped breastmilk with son, Silas, looking on.

Photo courtesy Ginger Bohl. Used with permission.

I arrived home on January 11, 2008. My son, Silas, freaked out when I tried to nurse him, screaming and pushing away. We celebrated his first birthday on January 19, 2008, with a chocolate cake facial. No signs that he would tolerate breastfeeding at that point, but I kept pumping until we transitioned him to cow's milk. I guess it was easy to wean him, but sure was a pain pumping, and then heating up a bottle in the middle of the night!

A few tips if you do plan to pump and ship your milk from overseas. You must check with any countries the milk will be transported through to be sure that it meets all customs regulations. Much like the information given in the TDY section above, you will need to freeze your milk thoroughly and wrap in newspapers (dry ice will be particularly hard to come by overseas) and place it in a cooler, preferably hard-sided. Ship your milk with the fastest shipping speed possible (overnight or two to three days) and be aware of the increased shipping charges, especially overseas. Mark the package carefully that it is fragile and perishable. Your caregiver on the receiving end should carefully check that the milk is still frozen and discard any milk that may have thawed or leaked.

If you will be sent on overseas assignment where your family can visit and you will have the ability to pump, you might be able to keep your breastfeeding relationship alive as related by the mother in the following story. Air Force Staff Sergeant, Jenny Desaulniers, was able to pump and dump her milk while on a six-month deployment overseas and resume breastfeeding her daughter upon her arrival back home in the States.

I was scheduled and left for a deployment to Spain right before my daughter was six months old. I went on a pumping frenzy. I stored milk for the months prior so my husband (also active duty) would be able to feed her. It was very hard leaving, and I wasn't sure what I was going to do about my breastfeeding, but I soon figured out. I knew that my husband was going to visit with my daughter in Spain, so I continued to pump and dump while I was deployed. I left in the beginning of July, and my husband came to visit at the end of August, beginning of September, and I re-introduced my daughter to breastfeeding. She went right back to it like I had not been gone. It was wonderful.

After they left I continued to pump. My mother, mother-in-law, and daughter came to visit me again in October. Prior to their visit, I noticed that my milk supply was getting low when I would pump, so I contacted a friend back home for advice on increasing my milk. I went on a mission to find herbal supplements to help out. It was very hard to find anything since I had trouble communicating what I needed to people at the stores. Every pharmacist I spoke with couldn't understand why I wanted something to increase my milk. They all tried to give me something to dry it up. I finally gave up on the idea of finding something on my own and went to the base hospital. It took me a few tries, but I found a great doctor who understood and helped me with a prescription to try to increase my milk. When my daughter came, I was able to re-introduce her again with no issues. Same when I returned home at the end of November.

My husband left seven days after I returned home for his own deployment, and I was sent on a short-notice deployment again in February, a month after my daughter turned one. That was when I again pumped what I could and left it for my mother-in-law since my husband was also gone. I just stopped pumping when I left and had no problems drying up. I was very lucky, more than lucky I think. To be able to go on a deployment that my family was able to visit me was a blessing. I am very happy that I pumped through my deployment and was able to feel that bond with my daughter again. It was tough at times, but all paid off to have her up against me again.

Finally, you should realize that there are going to be some situations where you simply must wean. Unaccompanied orders and shipboard deployments of six months or more are prime examples. If you opt to wean and you know your date of deployment ahead of time, wean gradually to ease the transition emotionally and physically for your baby and yourself. While you may be tempted to breastfeed your infant until the last day before departure to prolong the relationship, it is harder on you physically to do so (see the section on Weaning for more information). As tough as this time will be in your life, keep in mind that you have given your baby the gift of breastfeeding for whatever amount of time that you could. It will last his or her lifetime!

Chapter 14
What You Need to Know About Hazmat and Your Milk

HAZMAT: What's in YOUR Workplace?

Hazardous materials are a fact of life in the military. Many job specialties within the military involve working with potentially harmful chemicals, such as fuels, solvents, pesticides, heavy metals, medical drugs and gases (anesthetic and anti-neoplastic), and lead from munitions. Maintenance shops, paint shops, and weapons depots can contain volatile organic solvents, while flight line workers and fuel systems handlers are exposed to hydrocarbons in JP-8.

Military mothers are exposed to high levels of lead when they fire and handle weapons, weld, and when painting ships and vehicles. Healthcare settings pose a risk of exposure to anesthetic gases in operating rooms, when administering drugs, such as anti-neoplastics, and blood-borne pathogens, such as HIV. During training scenarios, service members are subjected to tear gas, and if stationed overseas, service members may be exposed to pathogens or biological/chemical warfare (Bell & Ritchie, 2003b; Navy Environmental Health Center, 2008). Many of these hazardous and toxic materials can potentially be passed through breastmilk to the nursing infant. This chapter aims to give you an overview of the major and most common hazardous materials and toxins normally found in the military environment. However, this is not in any way an exhaustive list or a replacement for speaking with your Occupational Health representative or Medical.

Weighing the Risks

Exposure levels at military worksites are monitored and kept within established safety limits for adults. However, military mothers in certain occupations are exposed to higher levels than the general population. We know a lot about how the various toxins affect adults. Unfortunately, there just have not been many exposure-assessment studies done to measure the levels of potentially harmful chemicals in the breastmilk of active-duty women. The problem lies with the fact that some of these chemicals do concentrate in breastmilk and may exceed safe does for infants, even though they are within safe levels for you (Giroux, Lapointe, & Baril, 1992; Navy Environmental

Health Center, 2008; Schaefer, 2007). A few studies do show that high occupational exposures can have adverse health effects on breastfed infants. However, long-term breastfeeding has been found to be beneficial and able to potentially counterbalance the impact of exposure to harmful chemicals (Condon, 2005).

This is not to say that you cannot safely breastfeed while continuing your job in the military. There is a continuum to the risk of exposure to these chemicals and substances. It is important to weigh the risk of exposure and balance it against the substantial benefits of breastfeeding and the well-known hazards associated with formula (Fisher, Mahle, Bankston, Greene, & Gearhart, 1997). Occupational exposures to toxic chemicals generally occur through inhalation, ingestion, or dermal contact. The chemicals enter and are present in the breastmilk due to maternal and chemical characteristics, such as mode and intensity of exposure, metabolism by the mother's body before transfer into milk, mother's age, number of previously breastfed children, and the pattern of breastfeeding. In addition, other factors, such as how the toxin transfers into milk (does it concentrate in fat, have high or low acidity, what is the protein binding and molecular mass?) and how long it stays in the human body before decomposing (half-life) or being flushed out, impact absorption. Unlike medications, many toxic substances stay in the body long-term and oftentimes most of it is passed on to the fetus while still pregnant. Furthermore, due to long-term accumulation, first-born breastfed children are potentially exposed to more chemicals than subsequently breast-fed children (Condon, 2005).

There are a number of questions to consider when returning to work where you may be exposed to toxic substances and chemicals. What is the probability of exposure to toxic substances in your workplace? What is the level of exposure (is it daily, once a week, once a quarter)? What is the effect of the substance on your baby? How old is your baby? How often do you pump or breastfeed? Can you be reassigned to other job duties? Is there protective gear that you can wear to reduce exposure? What is *your* comfort level of exposure before you will decide to wean versus the known benefits of breastfeeding? Except in some very unusual cases, your breastmilk, even contaminated, is still far better for your baby than the known and irreversible hazards of formula.

> *As an aircraft mechanic, my job requires me to handle hydraulic fluid, solvents, and JP-8 on a daily basis. I've weighed the pros and cons of my exposure to the HAZMAT, and I feel that my breastmilk is still better for my baby, even if it is contaminated, than giving him formula. I follow all the safety precautions of my workplace, but my baby gets my milk!* Petty Officer 3rd Class, USN

Biological/Chemical Agents

Very few breastfeeding women will be exposed to any biological or chemical agents in the course of the normal workday, and those that might be exposed while overseas in a conflict will likely not be pumping and shipping their milk home. However, all military personnel are subjected to periodic training with riot control agents, such as "tear gas," and any instructors will be exposed on a regular basis. Tear gas causes a tingling or runny nose, burning and/or pain of the eyes, blurred vision and tears, burning in the chest, difficult breathing, and nausea, as well as skin irritation, rash, or burns. It is absorbed via inhalation or ingestion and can be highly toxic in large doses. However, it is transient and disperses quickly once in fresh air. It is not known whether tear gas can pass into breastmilk. But normal precautions, such as changing out of contaminated clothing, washing exposed skin and hair with soap and water, and waiting one to two hours after exposure to breastfeed or pump should reduce any potential exposure to your baby.

Fuels and Oils

Fuel handlers, flight-line workers, mechanics, and fuel systems workers all have exposure to JP-8 and other hydrocarbons in their everyday work environment. JP-8 powers military aircraft, high performance vehicles, tanks, and generators. It is primarily composed of kerosene and contains small amounts of other additives, such as benzene and toluene. Occupational exposure occurs through breathing the raw vapors and/or exhaust, via skin contact, or swallowing food contaminated with JP-8. Known effects of JP-8 contamination include skin irritation, CNS symptoms, and possible brain damage, with high and long-term exposures. However, there is no data on the transfer into or possible effects of JP-8 in breastmilk (Ritchie et al., 2003; U.S. Army Center for Health Promotion and Preventative Medicine, 2002). Fuels and other hydrocarbons, as well as the various additives, such as benzene, are known to be fat-loving (lipophilic) substances and have been detected in breastmilk (Schaefer, 2007). It can be assumed that they would be attracted to the fat in breastmilk and might pose a potential risk of exposure to your breastfeeding baby.

Should your job specialty require that you work around JP-8 and other fuels, you can practice a few precautionary measures that might help you keep from weaning your baby. Wear protective gear, stay upwind of vapors and exhaust as much as possible, launder coveralls and uniforms, wash hands before eating, and shower before picking up your baby from daycare. You can, if you choose, delay pumping or breastfeeding by a few hours to allow any fuel to clear your system. But there is no proof that this will help or is needed.

Heavy Metals

Military mothers can be exposed to various heavy metals, such as lead, cadmium, mercury, and depleted uranium from handling and firing weapons, shrapnel, and applying or removing paint from ships and vehicles. Heavy metals (and particularly lead) can easily be transported into breastmilk due to the chemical similarity to calcium. Lead exposure occurs through inhalation and ingestion, where it enters the bloodstream and accumulates in the bones, and then is mobilized during lactation as the calcium stores are used to make milk. Studies are mixed as to the level of lead that is transferred from mother to baby via breastmilk. It is generally thought that milk levels are similar to blood levels. However, there is no known safe dose of lead that is acceptable for infants (Hale, 2008; Schaefer, 2007). Infants exposed to lead can show anemia, brain damage, and developmental delays (U.S. Army Center for Health Promotion and Preventative Medicine, 2001a).

If your MOS requires that you work with lead or other heavy metals on a daily basis, you may need to wean, as they are highly toxic. Mothers who work on firing lines and ranges or the armory on a regular basis are at increased risk of exposure to lead; from the particles that are released with every shot to the spent casings to the cleaning of the weapon. However, there are a number of precautions you can take to reduce your exposure. Wear protective equipment, change clothes and shoes before going home, and wash clothes separately from the rest of your laundry. Shower and wash your hair to remove particles, especially before handling your baby. Wash your hands thoroughly before handling your breast pump, expressed milk, or pumping. For women who have infrequent exposure for weapons qualifications, you do not need to wean. Following the precautions above should suffice (if you are in the field, use baby wipes to wash any lead dust off your hands).

Medical Gases and Drugs

Military mothers who work in hospitals and dental clinics, as pharmacists, nurses, physicians, and other healthcare workers, are potentially exposed to known chemicals that concentrate in breastmilk, such as Halothane and other anesthetic gases, anti-neoplastics drugs, and radionuclides during their preparation, administration, handling, transportation, and disposal. Many of these drugs and gases are known to be mutagens, carcinogens, or teratogens (U.S. Army Center for Health Promotion and Preventative Medicine, 2001c). In most cases, you will need to wean or be moved to another area within the hospital or clinic if your job requires that you handle or work with these types of gases or drugs.

Solvents

Aviation repair and maintenance shops, shipyards, Army depots, paint shops, and weapons cleaning areas often contain volatile organic solvents which are used in the cleaning of weapons, metal objects, and electronic parts; in pressure washers and steam cleaners; in solutions for pesticides, paints, and lubricants; and as refrigerants, degreasers, coolants, adhesives, and fire suppressants (Halon 1211 and 1301). Occupational exposure to solvents in the military mirror those found in the civilian workplace. However, less toxic solvents are often selected for use in military applications. The most common routes of exposure are through inhalation of the vapors or through the skin. Many of these solvents, such as perchlorethylene, methyl chloroform, trichloroethylene, methylene chloride, trichloro-fluoroethane, aliphatic and aromatic hydrocarbons, ketones, cellosolves, creosote, and fluorocarbons are associated with brain and kidney damage, as well as cause cancer (Leach & Metker, 1993) after chronic and long-term exposure (U.S. Army Center for Health Promotion and Preventative Medicine, 2001b). Because the breasts have a rich blood supply and human breastmilk is four percent fat, virtually all solvents are detectable in breastmilk, due in part to their lipophilic (fat-loving) nature. The levels of solvents in breastmilk range from minute quantities to well over threshold limits.

If your MOS requires that you work with or around solvents, there a few things you can do to reduce your baby's exposure and prevent the need to wean. Practice precautionary measures, such as wearing personal protective gear, washing your uniforms, and showering to remove any traces of solvents on your skin. Delay breastfeeding by a few hours to allow the solvent to pass out of the milk, or pump and dump to minimize the risk to the baby (Fisher et al., 1997). Some sources suggest not breastfeeding for three to four days after exposure (U.S. Army Center for Health Promotion and Preventative Medicine, 2010).

Your Rights and Responsibilities

See your Occupational Health Center/Medical Clinic to determine the best plan of action. They will have the resources to determine the levels of exposure for various chemicals and can give you a chit authorizing you to work in a less hazardous area if need be. See Appendix G for sample Supervisor and Worker Statements regarding Occupational Exposures of Reproductive or Developmental Concern. It is in the best interests of the military for you to minimize your exposure as much as possible, either through the use of personal protective gear, job modification, or temporary job transfer, thereby reducing as much as possible, any potential transfer to your baby.

I know many Active-Duty women have jobs that don't take place in offices and may expose them to dangerous chemicals. Request to be placed in a temporary position which will be healthy for the baby. Staff Sgt., USAF

While the military is responsible for training and protecting you about hazardous materials in your workplace, you are equally responsible for learning about the hazards in your workplace, using personal protective equipment, and following proper work practices. Since so little is known about breastfeeding hazards in the military workplace, you should also take the following steps to ensure your and your baby's safety:

- Store chemicals in sealed containers when they are not in use.

- Wash hands after contact with hazardous substances and before eating, drinking, or smoking.

- Avoid skin contact with chemicals.

- If chemicals contact the skin, follow the directions for washing in the material safety data sheet (MSDS). Military facilities are required to have copies of MSDSs for all hazardous materials used in their workplaces.

- Review all MSDSs to become familiar with any reproductive hazards used in your workplace. If you are concerned about reproductive hazards in the workplace, consult your Occupational Health department or healthcare provider.

- Participate in all safety and health education, training, and monitoring programs offered by your command.

- Learn about proper work practices and engineering controls (such as improved ventilation).

- Use personal protective equipment (gloves, respirators, and personal protective clothing) to reduce exposures to workplace hazards.

- Follow your command's safety and health work practices and procedures to prevent exposures to reproductive hazards.

- Prevent home contamination with the following steps:
    º   Change out of contaminated clothing and wash with soap and water before going home.
    º   Store street clothes in a separate area of the workplace to prevent contamination.
    º   Wash work clothing separately from other laundry (at work if possible).

°   Avoid bringing contaminated clothing or other objects home. If work clothes must be brought home, transport them in a sealed plastic bag.

This is not an easy decision to make by any stretch of the imagination. Hazardous chemicals are not to be taken lightly, nor is your baby's health. Ultimately, you will have to make a decision that you are comfortable with. If your job (evaluation or promotion) depends on you working in an environment that will put your baby in danger of exposure to hazardous materials, then certainly you have every right to decide NOT to take the unknown risk. Be sure to check out all the facts regarding the toxic chemical in question, and look at all your options before making a decision to wean.

Chapter 15

Physical Training and Breastfeeding

Maintaining physical readiness and weight standards are important for military readiness, as well as proper military appearance and bearing while in uniform. Physical fitness is essential to the health of military women during the childbearing years. While serving in the military, you are expected to participate in physical fitness training on a regular basis and pass a twice-yearly Physical Fitness Assessment and Body Composition Assessment. Not doing so can have a negative impact on your career. It is important to understand how breastfeeding can impact your postpartum physical readiness and weight standards, as well as how to manage diet and exercise while breastfeeding.

Weight Standards

All personnel in the military must adhere to body fat and weight standards, which are measured as part of your Body Composition Assessment (BCA) during the Physical Fitness Assessment (PFA) twice a year. During your pregnancy, and for 180 days after the date of delivery, the body fat and weight standards are waived. But you are required to return to proper weight standards within that time frame. Many, but not all, women find it hard to lose the weight gained during pregnancy within the six months given by the military regulations. This is due to many factors, such as fatigue, work schedules, childcare issues, and medical issues, and for some mothers, breastfeeding.

Breastfeeding can have an effect on attaining your proper weight. Research has shown that breastfeeding causes significant weight loss (one to two pounds per month) in the first six months postpartum, as the fat stores laid down in pregnancy are used up producing breastmilk. But weight loss often slows during the second six months postpartum (Dewey, Heinig, & Nommsen, 1993). Most women are back to their pre-pregnancy weight within five months of giving birth, due to the loss of body fat from the hips and thighs. For some women, however, a portion of the pregnancy weight remains until they wean completely. It is not completely understood why this happens. It may be due to increased caloric intake, or it may be the body's way of ensuring that there is an adequate supply of fat to fall back on for milk production. If you are one of those women who can't seem to shake those last few pounds, this could be a problem if you are nearing the end of your 180-day waiver.

I gained over 80 pounds during my pregnancy, and even though I worked out hard and ate a balanced diet, I owe all of my weight loss to nursing. I noticed rapid weight loss in the beginning, then it slowed down around the time my daughter was four months old. I have lost all but 10 pounds of that weight. Senior Airman, USAF

Diet

If you are finding it hard to drop your weight to within standards, you may want to consider dieting. It is safe to diet while breastfeeding provided you follow some guidelines. For the average woman, an intake of about 2500 calories a day is sufficient to promote natural, healthy weight loss of about one to two pounds a month. Follow the guidelines found at MyPyramid.com and be sure that you are eating three nutritious meals a day, as well as a few healthy snacks. Eat foods in as close to their natural state as possible (try to stay away from snack machines and processed food). Be sure that you drink enough water, especially if you are working in extreme heat or are exercising. However, don't go overboard with water intake. Too much water can actually lead to decreased milk production.

If you find that your weight loss has stalled, you can safely cut your calories to no less than 1,500 calories a day. Do not go below 1,500 calories per day, as you risk decreasing your milk supply and will find yourself becoming fatigued much easier. A safe weight-loss amount for a breastfeeding mother is no more than one to one and a half pounds a week (Institute of Medicine, 1991). Far better than cutting calories is to combine moderate exercise with a healthy diet. Mothers who diet *and* exercise have steadier and longer-lasting weight loss results than mothers who diet alone.

Exercise and Breastfeeding

All personnel in the military must do physical training (PT) in order to pass the bi-annual Physical Fitness Assessment (PFA). While pregnant, you may have been required to participate in a modified physical fitness program, depending on your branch of service. Upon your return to full duty after your convalescent leave, you are required to participate in command physical fitness. Just like the body fat and weight standards, you have 180 days to get back in shape and pass your run/swim, sit-ups, and push-ups testing as part of the PFA.

Combining command-dictated exercise with diet is a great way to lose those final few pounds. But there are a few items to keep in mind. First, there is no need to worry about your supply being affected by moderate exercise; research has not found a connection between lowered milk supply and exercise (Carey & Quinn, 2003; McCrory, 2000). However, some studies have suggested that heavy exercise changes the flavor of the milk, due to increased lactic acid (it gives milk a sour taste), and not a few mothers have commented that their babies react to their milk after heavy exercising by refusing to nurse (Wallace, Inbar, & Ernsthausen, 1992). It is not certain whether the milk is changing flavor or not, as some other, more-recent studies suggest that it is the sweat and body odor that the babies are reacting to, not a build-up of lactic acid (McCrory, 2000; Wright, Quinn, & Carey, 2002). If you feel your baby is reacting to the taste of your milk, there are a couple of things to

try: nurse your baby right before exercising since lactic acid remains elevated for about 90 minutes. Keep the intensity of your workout moderate (higher intensity increases lactic acid build-up). And of course, take a shower before nursing him. There is no need to pump and dump your milk. Some babies don't mind the taste of lactic acid, while others do.

> *I was scared to jump back into my regular workout routine because I had heard that strenuous exercise could change the flavor of your milk. I started small, but took my workouts seriously. Luckily, I work out in the morning, so I've recently nursed and don't leak much.* SSgt, USAF

Second, it is a good idea to pump or nurse right before participating in any exercise regimen, but particularly those that involve running or jumping-jack type exercises, to reduce any possible leaking and to prevent pain from heavy, milk-filled breasts while running. Vigorous jostling of the breasts can predispose you to mastitis. And many athletic women find it is most comfortable to work-out with nearly empty breasts anyway. Buy and wear a good quality, well-fitting, supportive sports bra to minimize any bouncing and damage to your breasts. Smaller breasted women can get away with compression style sports bras, while larger breasted women will want to use sports bras that separate and encapsulate each breast individually (see Resources for Sports Nursing bras). Some women find a dab of Lansinoh© on the nipples help with any chafing, and it is safe for your baby, too. If you find that you are leaking milk while exercising you can use regular pads or Lily Padz to control the leaking.

Both the American Council on Exercise (ACE) and American College of Obstetricians and Gynecologists (ACOG) statements advocate resuming exercise as soon as it is medically safe and you physically feel like it (American

College of Obstetricians and Gynecologists, 2009; American Council on Exercise, 2010). For some women that may be within a few weeks of birth, while other mothers will take the full six weeks (or longer) of convalescent leave before they feel ready.

Aim to gradually increase your exercise frequency, duration, and intensity until you can do 30-60 minutes of medium-intensity aerobic exercise, three to six times a week. In the first six weeks, be sure to watch for signs of pain, or bright red vaginal bleeding. That means you are progressing too quickly. If you had a cesarean, you will need to go slower and pay particular attention to your abdominal muscles as they heal. It bears repeating that it is important that you drink enough water while exercising. Drink before, during, and after your workouts, as dehydration can affect your milk supply.

Here are some tips for fitting exercise in when you have a (breastfeeding) infant:

- Lay your baby on the floor and do push-ups over him (this usually results in much giggling on behalf of your baby, especially if you make faces).

- Sit your baby on your belly and do sit-ups/curls.

- Alternatively do the "Flying Baby Curl" while on your back, with your knees bent at the chest. Place your baby on your shins and do curls.

- Put your baby in a front carrier or sling and do leg lunges.

- Do leg squats with your baby in a front carrier or sling.

- Holding your baby facing out and at chest level do a modified shoulder press.

- Put your baby in a sling and go for a walk.

- Invest in a jogging stroller and go running with your baby.

- Put your baby in a car seat or swing and workout on the elliptical or treadmill (the whirring noise may lull him to sleep).

- Realize that some days you'll get a good workout in and other days you simply won't.

Recently, the Army rolled out a program for their pregnant and postpartum mothers called the Pregnancy/Postpartum Physical Training (PPPT) (http://chppm-www.apgea.army.mil/dphw/readiness/PPPT.aspx), which includes exercises that are designed specifically to be safe and effective for pregnant and postpartum females, as well as health and child-rearing classes (including breastfeeding). It is being implemented throughout the Army this year (2010) after pilot testing found it to effective and successful at getting Army women back into shape and passing their APFT quicker than before. Hopefully, something similar can be implemented in the other services.

Maintaining your physical fitness and weight standards while breastfeeding doesn't have to be a problem. In fact, breastfeeding mothers who exercise have improved cardiovascular fitness, bone mineral density, and body composition. By following proper guidelines, and incorporating some dietary changes and moderate exercise, you can be sure that you'll pass your PFA with flying colors!

Chapter 16
Uniform Issues

Breastfeeding in Uniform

There may be times when you will need to breastfeed in uniform, such as at a doctor's visit or during a lunch break at the CDC. What are you to do? There are no regulations within any of the services that specifically approve or deny a breastfeeding mother from nursing her baby while in uniform. However, there are differing opinions, even from service members themselves, as to whether or not it is appropriate to do so. The question and answer lies in defining what constitutes a "proud and professional appearance that will reflect positively on the individual, the (Air Force, Army, Marine Corps, Navy), and the United States."

Does having a baby at the breast, even one that is covered, reflect positively on the Armed Forces? Do you promote a professional appearance while nursing your baby? It is a tough call to make for the nursing mother and her superiors. While some will argue that a baby needs to be fed, and as long as it is done discreetly (who defines discreet?), there should be no problem. Others will say that breastfeeding a baby in uniform is completely unprofessional and reflects poorly on the Armed Forces. As this Navy lieutenant states:

> *Given that we are instructed that holding our children while in uniform is not maintaining a professional appearance, I never thought that breastfeeding my child while in uniform would be allowed. I have, but ONLY in my home returning from work and in the doctor's office in the private room (not waiting area).* Petty Officer 2nd Class, USN

This is one area where you will need to tread carefully and realize that while your command and direct supervisor may have no problem with it, someone at Medical or over at the CDC may decide to counsel you. Until there is a written regulation about breastfeeding in uniform, it is very much on a case-by-case basis. Be prepared to hear everything from "it's OK" to "not at my command," and have another way to feed or place to go to with your baby should you be told to stop breastfeeding in uniform.

There are a few things to keep in mind if you do decide to breastfeed in uniform. Unlike in civilian clothes where you can wear a sling or be a little more revealing, while in uniform you must maintain a military appearance and remain in uniform at all times. That pretty much means no slings or fancy blankets and definitely no skin showing. Practice, practice, practice latching your baby so that you can get him latched on as quickly as possible and with as little skin showing as possible. Depending on the uniform you are wearing, this may be next to impossible or fairly easy to accomplish. For the most part, uniforms that have untucked blouses that can be pulled up from the waist or that unbutton in the front are the best for easy access without having to undress completely.

Breastfeeding in Navy NWUs

Photo courtesy Abigail Rees.
Used with permission.

Mothers in all the services agree that "cammies" (ACUs, ABUs, NWUs, etc.) are by far the easiest to breastfeed in, while any one-piece type uniform, like a flight suit or one with a blouse that remains tucked in, is either impossible to nurse in, or looks very unprofessional and out-of-uniform when untucked. If you have a uniform that comes with an over blouse or jacket worn over a t-shirt or blouse, you may find it easier to breastfeed, since the jacket hides any skin showing on the sides. Just like with civilian clothing, unbuttoning from the bottom of the shirt is less revealing than from the top down. If you would feel more comfortable, you can use a subdued, solid colored blanket, nursing cape, or burp rag to cover yourself and your baby. Bear in mind though, that a blanket or nursing cape isn't part of your uniform and doesn't exactly project a professional military appearance either. Besides, not too many babies like eating under a blanket. Ultimately, you'll have to decide what you are comfortable with and what your command will allow.

> *I feed my baby in uniform if I need to, but it depends on what uniform I'm wearing. I would never do it in my blues because I can't do it discreetly. I do in my flightsuit because I can just unzip it a bit and pull my shirt up.* Major, USAF

Pumping in Uniform

Pumping in uniform is very similar to breastfeeding in uniform, with the exception that you will be alone in a private area where you can undress further and not risk getting in trouble. While you are restricted to the uniforms prescribed by your command and the type of work you perform, uniforms that unbutton or unzip in the front or can be pulled up from the waist are the best for easy access without having to undress completely every time you need to pump. Much like breastfeeding in uniform, mothers who pump say that the cammies are the easiest to pump in, as they can unbutton the over blouse and pull up the t-shirt and pump away. Mothers who wear coveralls or flight suits generally unzip and tie the upper the part around their waist before pumping. It is a good idea to consider keeping an extra set of uniforms at work for unexpected leaks and spills.

> *I haven't had any problems pumping in uniform. Nursing is a hassle though because of the Velcro. Evidently, the uniform conceals the pumping very well, as two male coworkers walked into my office this week and took a while to realize what I was doing. One took about a minute, then he apologized and left. The other one took a bit longer, apologized, realized I wasn't bothered by it, and continued what he needed me to do. Go ACUs!!!* Captain, USA

To control leaking while in uniform, invest in some nursing pads. You will probably only need them for the first few weeks back at work (although a few lucky women need them throughout their nursing career). There are various types of pads available: cotton and wool pads are very absorbent and reusable but bulky; while disposable nursing pads are thinner, but may have a plastic backing and cost money over the long haul. Both types of pads will need to be changed frequently to prevent sore nipples or thrush. There is another type of pad, Lily Padz©, that is made of thin silicone that prevents leaking by applying pressure to the nipple. They are reusable and are suitable for times when you know you won't be able to pump for an extended period of time and cannot have any leaking or bulky pads show through, such as during a ceremony, uniform inspection, or a long flight (see Appendix B for resources). They are also good for swimming and will keep your nipples from showing through a thin shirt or blouse if you have particularly perky nipples. They are not meant for everyday wear, however, and you should remain vigilant about plugged ducts and mastitis while using them, and if you will be going for an extended period of time without nursing or pumping.

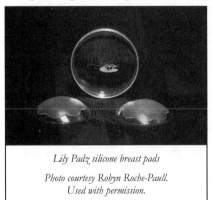

Lily Padz silicone breast pads

Photo courtesy Robyn Roche-Paull.
Used with permission.

Chapter 17
Career, Co-Worker, and Rank Issues

This book would not be complete without mentioning a few of the downsides that you may encounter while combining breastfeeding and active-duty service. The reality of breastfeeding in the military is that rank does sometimes play a role in how easily you can secure a place to pump and time to do so. Your career may suffer because you took a tour of duty that would keep you from deploying, and that doesn't look so good for promotion. And sometimes, bringing something as feminine as breasts into the warrior culture of the military can cause uncomfortable feelings and possible problems amongst your co-workers.

RHIP (Rank Has its Privileges)

Rank often plays a role in how difficult or easy you may find it to pump at work. Enlisted personnel, especially junior enlisted (E-1 to E-3), have the hardest time with pumping at work, as you are at the mercy of the work schedule and your supervisor's needs. As this prior enlisted Army officer says, *"My daily timeline was unpredictable at best and fully under someone else's control."* There are other factors, unique to enlisted personnel, that are out of your control and that can affect pumping at work: not having a private office in which to pump, feeling intimidated or uncomfortable approaching authority figures in the chain-of-command to discuss breastfeeding and pumping, and concerns about peer pressure or how your supervisor perceives you in the workplace (Stevens & Janke, 2003; Sykora, 1995; Uriell, et al., 2009). This is especially true if you must request permission or check-in/out for a break every time you need to pump.

Some mothers feel it is more competitive at the lower ranks, and since you are not yet well established, it is better to not rock the boat by requesting time for pumping. It is also harder to balance the demands of work and home, especially for first-time, young, often single moms on small paychecks. Unfortunately, too, there is a stigma surrounding junior enlisted, unfairly or not, that many get pregnant or breastfeed to get out work or deployment.

I worried more about peer pressure and how I was perceived by my superiors as a young Marine. By the time I was an E-5, I was established and had learned to balance the demands of work and home in a more healthy way. Sgt, USMC

I personally feel the stigma for enlisted starts before the baby is born. How many times have you heard complaints about these women getting out of their obligations, both ship and shore, by getting pregnant. Then to continue that with having to pump unlike the other women who "actually help" since they formula feed. Petty Officer 3rd Class, USN

Higher ranking individuals, senior NCOs, and officers generally have an easier time pumping at work due to more flexible schedules, private office spaces, and the ability to dictate their own time and space to pump. There is no need to request permission for time to pump, as this Air Force officer states, *"The higher in rank, the more control you have over your schedule."* However, with higher rank often comes more responsibility, and you may find you have more work to do in a supervisory position and less time to actually pump (Stevens & Janke, 2003; Sykora, 1995; Uriell et al., 2009).

One of the most important things you can do as a breastfeeding officer is to make use of the wonderful opportunity you have to make your command breastfeeding friendly for the lower-ranking individuals. As a leader, you are in a position to make changes, if not at this command and level of seniority, then maybe at the next one (see Chapter 19 on Command Support).

I will be honest in saying that it helped that I was an officer and accustomed to asserting my opinions given my career field. I don't envy junior enlisted women who may feel pressure to not disrupt the workplace by pumping. Captain, USAF

I worked in an F-15 squadron while breastfeeding both of my daughters: eight years difference between births! I was able to breastfeed my first child for a year and was only able to nurse for about six months with my second daughter. I definitely feel it was harder to pump as a TSgt than it was as an Airman. I had more responsibilities when I was an NCO and felt pulled between my responsibilities to the Air Force and my responsibilities to my child. There are also fewer women in the upper ranks which made it interesting to explain why I had to have a break at certain times of the day. Tech. Sgt., USAF

I helped a few Soldiers from other, stricter units by giving them some tips about how to approach a supervisor. It always made me smile to have a Soldier thank me for the small tips I would give them about getting maximum output while pumping or maintaining their pumps or using a cooler for TDY. I couldn't take them all under my wing and supervise them, but I could help them educate their respective bosses about why pumping milk was actually good for the unit. Major, USA

Children and Your Career

Much like the corporate world, the "Mommy Track" in the military can lead to lowered evaluations and possible pass-over for promotion (Hochhausen, 2001; Krueger, 2002). Your supervisor might feel that you take too much time for pumping or aren't reliable and give you a lowered evaluation. You might decide to forgo a prime tour of duty that would assure you the next promotion, but not if it means being away from your baby for six months. Lowered evaluations and not being promoted due to becoming a mother and insisting on your right to continue breastfeeding is not supposed to happen, nor does it always, but it is something to consider. Unintended pregnancies, and those that occur during sea duty tours or when a unit is getting ready to deploy, garner the most resentment and least support from co-workers and supervisors (Evans & Rosen, 1997).

Planning your childbearing around your tours-of-duty to minimize the "damage" to your career and maximize the time you can spend with your little one and continue to breastfeed is one option. Conflicting loyalties between your career and your children are nothing new for working women, civilian and military alike. But unlike the civilian world, you cannot just give notice and quit. Most mothers in the military feel that the sacrifice is worth it for their baby's health and well-being.

Co-Worker and Supervisor Problems

It is not uncommon for breastfeeding mothers in the military to face harassment, rude comments, and a general air of disapproval from co-workers and supervisors--some subtle and others not-so-subtle--regarding breastfeeding and pumping in the workplace. This can stem from a number of reasons. One of the most challenging to overcome is the collision between the masculine, warrior culture of the military and the feminine, nurturing act of breastfeeding (Hochhausen, 2001). For both men and women, there is a mental shift to make from the everyday reality of being a soldier/sailor/airman to the obviously nurturing act of providing breastmilk for your infant. There is a conflict between the roles of soldier and mother that must be overcome. Some women find that they can (and must) separate their roles as warrior and mother in order to function while on duty, while other mothers find that having that daily reminder that they are a mother when pumping helps to keep them grounded and in tune with their baby. As this Air Force mother says:

> *The fact that you're in the military...you're not a woman, you're unisex, and once you've had the baby, you're no longer a woman, but back to being unisex. I think the nursing keeps you thinking-I am a mother, I am a woman, and I'm taking care of this child. That in itself keeps you sane. You don't lose your identity (Stevens & Janke, 2003).*

For the women who work in the more untraditional jobs in the military, this can be an especially hard transition to make. It is still an unfortunate reality that women in the military fight against gender stereotypes and must work harder, longer, and faster to be considered an equal. Toss breastfeeding into the mix and now there is a conflict between the military and motherhood.

You may face some awkward or uncomfortable moments upon your return to work when you announce your need to pump. This can stem from a variety of reasons, depending on whether your co-workers are male or female. If your co-workers or supervisor are male, they may be embarrassed or "grossed out" by even the mere thought that pumping or breastfeeding might be going on by you, their coworker (Hochhausen, 2001). This can be especially apparent if they "see" you as just another soldier and have forgotten that you are a woman under your uniform. If you've always been "one-of the guys," and now suddenly you are a mother and need to go pump, it is a wake-up call to the guys that "oh yeah, she is a woman."

Other females in your command who don't have children, or who chose not to breastfeed, or weaned earlier than they planned, may have anger or guilt over their decision that is directed at you, particularly if you are successful (Bristow, 1999). As one Petty Officer notes, *"Ironically, it was the women in my command who gave me the hardest time about supporting my breastfeeding."*

Another reason lies with the fact that our society is not comfortable with breasts being used for their intended purpose, and, therefore, they are usually thought of as sexual, particularly when "exposed" in the public workplace due to pumping. Unfortunately, due to the military environment where sexual harassment is always a concern, even talking about breasts and breastfeeding can create uncomfortable and awkward scenarios for everyone involved (Stuart-Macadam & Dettwyler, 1995).

Finally, there are plenty of co-workers, male and female, that simply don't even know that a policy on breastfeeding exists and, therefore, don't understand why you should get "special" time off. They may feel that you are receiving preferential treatment or abusing your break time by getting time off to go pump (Krueger, 2002). Others may feel that by breastfeeding you are being selfish, whereas mothers who formula feed can go right back to work and are helpful because they don't need to take time off. Uncomfortable feelings surrounding all of these issues may come from your co-workers in the form of jokes and nervous laughter to outright disgust and rude comments.

Harassment and feeling like I was a slacker was big after my first baby. I was told all the time that I was letting my coworkers down because they would have to catch my jets or they would have to help me with my load if I had to run off and go pump. In the eight months I was in the line shack after that, I only missed four jets because they came early. During the down time between flights, the plane captains would sit and talk or have a snack since there really wasn't anything to do. I would pump because that was the only time to do it. Somehow they were never called lazy or never told they were exploiting their "free" time. Petty Officer 2nd Class, USN

If they asked where I was I simply said "I had to pump my breasts so my son could eat." Men would blush...women would get angry... it meant nothing either way. I was willing to take a counseling if need be....it wasn't going to be the first and definitely not my last, LOL. Sgt., USA

Although I informed all of my people in the need to know that I would be breastfeeding/pumping after my baby was born, and although they complied as they were capable, I got lots of grief for not pulling my weight because I had to break once every two hours to keep my supply up. It didn't help that all but one of them fed their babies formula, so they didn't understand. I wish there were more resources for the higher ups, so that there was less friction from lack of knowledge. Petty Officer 3rd Class, USN

You may also find that you are not supported in your efforts to pump, while not being outright denied the opportunity either. Trips to the snack bar and smoking breaks can be another obstacle. Many active-duty women complain of how their co-workers can take as many or more smoke or snack breaks as they wish throughout the day (an unhealthy behavior), while the breastfeeding mother is denied time for two or three pumping breaks (a healthy behavior).

I've always believed that a unit that has enough time to let its soldiers go out and smoke from time to time, has enough time to let a woman pump from time to time. There is no way you can tell a new mother that a smokers "right" to slowly kill themselves is more important than a mother's right to gather food for her infant. I always suggest taking that line of attack when it comes to resistant supervisors. Major, USA

If anyone gave us a hard time, we kindly pointed out how many smoke breaks everyone went on and that even with four or five pumping sessions, we still worked longer than they did!!! Captain, USMC

They were surprised to hear my suggestion of considering pumping as the same as a smoke break. So many Soldiers smoke and since smoking is prohibited inside, they must take a break to go outside. Heavier smokers spend a lot of time out there and nobody questions it much. When all that is added up, it is no less than what would be required for a pumping mom to go to the bathroom and pump, then return to her desk, and her productivity would be no different than that of the smokers in the unit. Major, USA

Non-supportive supervisors are another problem. Some supervisor's don't agree with allowing pumping breaks or feel they are not warranted after a certain age of the baby. One active-duty Navy mother found that her command wasn't supportive at all.

> *...I breastfed until she was four months old, after that my chain of command told me that they could not afford me taking so many breaks. Even my female Chiefs were very "the job comes first."*

Unfortunately, there are some supervisors that also do not put a stop to the harassment or inappropriate comments made by co-workers, leaving you to deal with it on your own. If your command is one that does not value breastfeeding, and is one in which the supervisors do not follow the policy and regulations, or who turn a blind eye to harassment, it can have a detrimental effect. Not only is it stressful to deal with the comments and lack of support, but many a breastfeeding mother has stopped pumping at work, suffered from lowered milk supply, or stopped breastfeeding altogether due to lack of support or outright harassment. As hard as it may seem to you at the time, it is vital that you take your complaints to a higher level. All of the services support breastfeeding and none tolerate harassment and neither should you.

> *I found that although my command was "supportive" by the book, it was frustrating hearing comments from co-workers that no one in the command (LPOs would be right there when comments either about breastfeeding moms or me in particular were made) felt necessary to address. I wish the upper chain of command at any level would have been mature enough to say something positive instead of turning their heads.* Petty Officer 3rd Class, USN

> *It is in the instruction that no harassment would be tolerated and that a private room would be supplied where available. My friend and I hopped onto that and went straight to the CMC. She went to the DIVO and all the harassment stopped, and a month later, we had a clean, private room available to all the women who were breastfeeding (which turned out to be about eight women).* Airman, USN

> *Ideally, the OPNAVINST was written to advocate for breastfeeding rights in the Navy, so all women should be waving that thing around to anyone who gives them a problem. If a woman is doing her job well and still able to balance pumping, then there really shouldn't be a problem.* Lt., USN

There are no easy answers here. This is just a brief overview of what you may face in combining breastfeeding while on active duty. Oftentimes, these problems are left unspoken and new military mothers are blind-sided by them. It is important that you not allow the harassment to continue, but instead use the policies and regulations to your advantage. Find a supervisor or another person within your chain of command who will take your issues seriously and put a stop to the mistreatment. Not being allowed to pump (when there is time and a place for it) or having to endure comments is not a reason to give up on breastfeeding your baby. Some mothers have found that getting out of the military is the best choice for themselves and their families, whether it is due to the return to deployable status or problems pumping in the workplace. Ultimately, you will have to decide for yourself if you can put up with the downsides of breastfeeding on active duty. But overall, many mothers feel the benefits far outweigh the negatives.

Chapter 18
Weaning

Weaning is the transition from exclusive breastfeeding to receiving food from another source completely. In the broadest sense, weaning begins with the first bottle of formula given or the first bites of solid food and ends when your baby no longer feeds at the breast. There is no magic age at which weaning must occur. However, the AAP and World Health Organization does recommend that all babies be exclusively breastfed for *at least* six months, and then supplemented with solid foods in addition to breastfeeding until *at least* the baby's first birthday, and thereafter for as long as both mother and baby desire (Gartner et al., 2005).

Weaning can be a very abrupt process that happens at an early age or a long, gradual process that stretches into the second or third year of your baby's life. There are many valid reasons for weaning, and more than one way to wean your baby. As a mother in the military you may have to wean abruptly if called up for an unexpected deployment, or you may have the luxury to wean when your baby is ready. Depending on the age of your baby and reasons for weaning, there are various methods of weaning that will be easier or harder on you and your baby, both emotionally and physically. But no matter the age or reason, weaning is a significant transition and milestone in your baby's life, as well as yours.

The following guidelines will explain the different types of weaning and how to do so properly to cause the least amount of pain (emotionally and physically). You can always contact your local La Leche League Leader or IBCLC for more information on weaning. Please consult with your healthcare provider if you encounter any health problems related to weaning.

Abrupt Weaning

Abrupt weaning is the least desired, and most difficult, form of weaning for both you and your baby. Abrupt weaning may be unavoidable in the case of an emergency deployment or call-up. However, if it is at all possible, it is best to avoid waiting until the last minute to wean your baby. Physical discomfort and potential health problems can arise when weaning is done too quickly. For starters, your body will continue to produce milk for a period of time after the last nursing session. If the milk is not removed, you can become painfully engorged, which may lead to mastitis or a breast abscess.

The abrupt withdrawal of the hormones associated with breastfeeding can also lead to feelings of sadness and depression. An abrupt weaning can be traumatic for your baby, too, as breastfeeding is more than just food. It is a comfort tool and a security object as well. If this weaning will be followed by your immediate departure, be sure that other family members and caregivers give your baby plenty of physical affection and attention to offer reassurance and to compensate for the emotional distress he may be feeling.

- Plan to tailor your weaning timetable to both your expected departure date and your baby's nursing pattern. If you will be leaving in two days, and your four-month-old nurses 10 times a day, you might eliminate every other nursing the first day, and eliminate the remainder of the nursing sessions the next day. With a week's (seven days) notice you might drop two breastfeeding sessions per day.

- Replace the nursing sessions with pumping sessions, but only pump to comfort.

- Gradually increase the amount of time between pumpings and do not completely drain your breasts. The frequency at which you should express your milk should be determined by your comfort level. As you express less, your breasts will make less milk and your supply will dwindle.

- Be prepared to hand express or take a small battery or hand-pump along with you and pump as above.

- Wear a firm bra, such as a sports bra for support, and use nursing pads to absorb any leaking. Some women find ice packs to be helpful to provide some relief from any swelling. Cabbage leaves in your bra can help with engorgement as well (see engorgement section, Chapter 4).

- Take a pain reliever as needed to relieve breast discomfort.

Gradual Weaning

Gradual weaning is the best way to wean your baby and can be done at any age. It is also much easier, emotionally and physically, for both of you. Weaning gradually is a much slower process, one that can take weeks to months, even years to complete, depending on what type of weaning you prefer. There are two types of gradual weaning: baby-led and mother-led. With baby-led weaning, you follow your baby's developmental needs and readiness signs for the next stage in the process. Often your baby will continue to nurse well into his second or even third year of life. This is normal for babies in most countries. In fact, the normal age of weaning across cultures is between two and a half and seven years old (Stuart-Macadam & Dettwyler, 1995).

In baby-led weaning, your baby will drop a nursing here and there over time, usually leaving his favorite nursing session as the last to let go of. Days may go by without him asking to nurse, and soon you will look back and realize it has been weeks since he last asked. With baby-led weaning, breastfeeding your baby moves from being a method of feeding to a method of providing comfort and security. This method of weaning is certainly do-able, even for a military mother. In fact, once you get over the hard part of pumping in the early months, and your baby is older and really only nursing in the mornings, evenings, and weekends, you can continue to breastfeed until you are both ready to wean. This style of weaning allows for a wonderful closeness and bond to develop that really makes the daily separation so much easier to deal with for both you and your baby.

> *Weaning was gradual for me and pretty mutual. As he got more mobile, he preferred a sippy cup (I introduced cow's milk at one year), so he basically nursed for comfort and at night. When I found out that I was pregnant with my second child (my son was 16 months old), I decided to wean him completely. I let it happen over the period of a month, so he was 17 months when we stopped. It was a wonderful and perfect experience for both of us.* Staff Sgt., USAF

> *I was fortunate that my daughter slowly self-weaned. At a year old, she usually nursed four times a day (luckily none of those feedings were during duty hours), and it seems that each month she dropped a feeding. At 15 months, she was down to just nursing before bedtime and eventually stopped asking. I'm proud that I was able to breastfeed her until she was ready to stop.* Senior Airman, USAF

Mother-led weaning is the way most babies are weaned in our society and is often done to suit your desires, needs, or plans. There are many reasons why you might choose to initiate weaning, such as an upcoming deployment, a predetermined goal (six, nine or 12 months) or health issues. This style of weaning can take anywhere from weeks to months and is best for mothers who have a set goal or have a date in mind for weaning and plenty of time to plan for it.

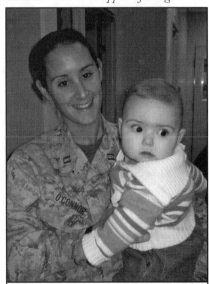

Gradual weaning is easiest on mom and baby

Photo courtesy Kelly O'Connor.
Used with permission.

In mother-led, gradual weaning, you begin by dropping the least favorite nursing session and substituting it with a bottle of expressed breastmilk, formula, or solids, depending on the age of your baby. After a week to a few weeks, you can drop another nursing session, and continue in this fashion until your baby is receiving all his nutrition by another source. Another option is to "use" a TDY as an excuse to wean. You'll be away from your baby, and if you don't pump while gone, your milk supply will decrease significantly. Other mothers have taken advantage of their baby's natural distractible stage near the nine-month age to not offer the breast and substitute solids and a sippy cup instead. There are many gentle, yet effective ways to wean if that is what you decide to do.

> *Weaning was very gradual for us. He was 28 months when we finally quit, and I was four months pregnant. I'm not even sure I had any milk left. It was more just going through the bedtime routine and nursing was part of it. We had a three-week period apart, and I decided that would be a good time to stop.* Major, USAF

Either form of gradual weaning allows your milk supply to decrease slowly, without causing fullness, discomfort, and possible mastitis. However, you may need to pump, depending on how fast your gradual weaning proceeds, just to remain comfortable. If your baby is older than seven or eight months, he can be weaned to a cup. And over one year of age, you can wean him to cow's milk. Babies under a year old should be given formula or you can use expressed breastmilk if you have a large stockpile.

Gradual weaning allows your baby to adjust to the change over time. However, it is important to watch your baby and proceed slowly. Provide your baby with extra attention and cuddles to help compensate for the loss of breastfeeding. Some babies take better to weaning than others, with some adjusting easily, while others are very reluctant to stop breastfeeding. Be flexible in your weaning schedule and enlist the help of other caregivers if at all possible. If your baby is older, you may need to wear clothes that do not allow for easy nursing and stay away from a "favorite" nursing spot or chair.

> *The decision to wean Joey was partially made by me and partially by the Air Force. I ended up going TDY for one week to a conference when Joey was eight months old. I had enough milk stockpiled in the freezer to get him through that week without me, and I took my pump with me. I pumped first thing in the morning, again at lunch, again in the afternoon/early evening, and finally one more time before bed. After the time away and exclusive pumping; however, my supply was slightly diminished, and I wasn't able to keep up with Joey's demands. We started introducing formula to replace one bottle a week until he was fully weaned at nine months. It was sad, but I think that by taking three weeks to make the full transition, I had time to emotionally "let go" of the attachment that I had.* Captain, USAF

Partial Weaning

Partial weaning is an alternative to total weaning. This is an option if you wish to continue breastfeeding when you are at home, but cannot pump while at work. Depending on the storage capacity of your breasts, your milk supply will down-regulate to match the needs of your new nursing pattern. Mothers with a larger storage capacity have far better luck with this method, as they *can* go longer periods without pumping and still maintain their milk supply. Mothers with a smaller storage capacity, however, *must* pump or breastfeed often to keep their supply up.

Depending on the age of your baby, you may need to replace the pumped breastmilk with formula during the workday. Or if your baby has started on solids, you may be able to replace your breastmilk with those instead. See your baby's doctor about what to substitute for your breastmilk. It is very important, if you do a partial weaning, to breastfeed as often as possible when you are home to maintain a milk supply, especially at night. A nice benefit to partial weaning is that you can always go back to breastfeeding or pumping more frequently if your work situation changes. Partial weaning, like gradual weaning, can go on for months or until you and your baby are ready to move to the next stage. Many working mothers continue to nurse their babies well into their second year or beyond by nursing only in the morning and evenings. It is not so much about the nutrition, although that is still important, but more about the comfort and closeness that breastfeeding brings to both mother and child after daily separation.

> *By four months I ended up breastfeeding only at night and supplementing during the day with formula. I was lucky that I had enough of a supply to continue to do this.* Petty Officer 2nd Class, USN

Temporary Weaning

Temporary weaning is an option if you will be away for a short amount of time, such as a training exercise or deployment of only one to four weeks, and plan to resume breastfeeding upon your return. Much like abrupt weaning, temporary weaning can be emotionally and physically stressful for you and your baby. Many of the same rules apply here, except that you will be expressing to keep up your milk supply while you are gone. Breastmilk is produced on a supply and demand basis, so it will be important to express regularly, day and night, while you are gone.

Upon your return, you may find that your milk supply has decreased. But depending upon the length of your absence, you may find that frequent, unrestricted breastfeeding will bring back a full supply. Even with pumping while separated, some mothers find that their milk supply has decreased to a point that they do not regain a full supply, even with increased and regular pumping once back home. Some mothers have had luck with herbal preparations or prescription medications to boost their supply. See your HCP or IBCLC for more information (also see Chapter 10-Milk Supply Issues).

Keep in mind that after about a month, without any stimulation via pumping or breastfeeding, your breast tissue will begin to return to its pre-pregnant state, and the weaning may be permanent. If you have a frozen stockpile of expressed milk, your baby can be fed that while you are gone, and even for awhile after your return, while you boost your supply back up. It is also important for you to realize that not all babies will go back to the breast after a temporary weaning, especially if they are older. Be prepared for this possible outcome. It can be heart-wrenching to deal with the rejection of your baby for the breast, especially after you have spent countless hours pumping your milk in the hopes of having him back at the breast upon your return. See an IBCLC or La Leche League Leader for information on boosting your milk supply or for help if your baby is reluctant to go back to breastfeeding upon your return.

> *I went on a two week TDY overseas when my son was eight months old--it was the first time I'd been away from him for more than a couple of days. I intended to resume nursing when I returned, but he really wasn't interested AT ALL. I guess bottles were easier. I was gutted at first, but then decided it made weaning pretty painless, so I decided to be thankful.* Major, USAF

Relactating

If you had to wean abruptly or before you were ready, and have a willing baby, you might be able to relactate upon your return. Relactation is the process of bringing your milk supply back and enticing your baby to return to the breast. Some women are successful in bringing in a full supply, while others can only bring in a partial supply. Either way, it is difficult to predict how much you will be able to produce.

Relactation is generally more successful if you only recently weaned within a few months. Ways to increase your milk supply include frequent pumping with a hospital-grade breast pump, putting your baby to the breast (with a supplemental nursing system to simulate milk flow), and taking milk-enhancing herbs or drugs. You will need to monitor your baby's weight gain and track how much supplementation he needs as your milk supply increases. Because it is difficult to know how much your baby will be receiving from your breasts, it is important that you have an IBCLC or other breastfeeding helper monitor your efforts.

If you are trying to woo a reluctant baby back to the breast, especially after an absence, there are a number of things you can try. Lots of skin-to-skin contact with your baby between your breasts is one of the best methods. Wearing your baby in a sling is another way to entice your baby back to the breast. Co-bathing together, offering the breast at night or when he is drowsy, and starting with the bottle and switching part way through the feeding to your breast have all been shown to be helpful. The main thing to remember is to remain patient and try not to feel rejected. Time and lots of love can go a long ways towards convincing your baby that the breast is a good place to be again.

What to Expect

Whether weaning is abrupt or gradual, there are some common physical processes that occur that you should be aware of. As your milk supply decreases, your milk will become more salty and colostrum-like. Babies generally don't like the salty taste and ask to nurse less. Many women are able to express drops of milk for several months, and even up to a year after weaning, especially if you check often or do any nipple-play during sex (which stimulates the breasts to continue milk production). It is also common for your areola and nipples to remain darker after weaning. Your breasts may be soft at first, but should revert to their pre-pregnancy size and firmness within a few months. If your menstrual cycles have not yet returned, you can expect them to start again soon after weaning. Finally, some mothers lose those few extra pounds of pregnancy weight, while others gain weight upon weaning.

Ideally, weaning will occur when both you and your baby are ready. For some mothers though, weaning happens much too soon, before you or your baby are ready. When this occurs, it is not a trivial matter. It is a very real and sad time for you both. Those who have not breastfed a child cannot understand or appreciate the sense of disappointment and loss that can accompany an undesired weaning, or the longing for a breastfeeding relationship that was cut short. Take the time to mourn what was lost, talk with a trusted friend or an LLL Leader who can appreciate what breastfeeding meant to you. Hopefully, with time, you can remember the sweet memories of the brief time you did spend breastfeeding your baby and enjoy new milestone in your baby's and your life together.

Even if weaning is by your choice and what you desire, it is still an often bittersweet time in your life. Mothers who choose to wean and do not feel coerced or pressured into weaning, often feel better about the decision (and find it easier to do as well). No matter the reason, the length of breastfeeding, or the way in which you wean your baby, know that you gave your baby the very best start in life that you could. See "What If I Want to Wean" in Appendix N for a listing of all the wonderful benefits you and your baby will receive by breastfeeding, broken down by the age at weaning.

SECTION FIVE

Abby's Story

At first, I only planned on breastfeeding during the six weeks of convalescent leave prior to returning to work. But I was able to successfully breastfeed my son until he was one year old.

When I was still pregnant, I made the decision to breastfeed after my sister, who was currently in nursing school, explained to me how vital the milk was to the baby. I ended up reading as much material on the subject as I could, including an old copy of The Womanly Art of Breastfeeding from the library. I read that you should have a support group. Well, being stationed overseas and knowing no one else who was breastfeeding, my only support was my siblings and mother over the phone, and my husband who was by my side. I told him that the book says he should get me a glass of water and pillow while I'm nursing the baby. I was very adamant about him not making fun of me or discouraging my breastfeeding. He agreed to help me emotionally and physically. I had my breast pump ready, along with the milk storage bags and breast pads, sitting on a shelf at home when I went to the hospital.

At the hospital, I underwent a slow labor process, and I was pushing for almost three hours until Mason was finally born! I had read before that it's important to breastfeed during the first one to two hours after birth to stimulate the milk supply. After I finally gave birth to Mason, I laid down on the bed and told the nurses that I would like to take a quick nap, then feed him. "Well," they said, "he's hungry now. If you don't feed him, we'll feed him formula!" I was so tired, but the nurses told me to lay on my side and that they would help me. I was very nervous at how this would happen, and I did as the books said by taking my breast and stroking my nipple downward against his bottom lip. He immediately started nursing!! I was so excited! Since he was hungry, it was so easy. I didn't realize that there would be a lactation consultant who would help me in the hospital or that the nurses would help us when we needed it.

When we came home from the hospital, it seemed like I was nursing Mason all the time. I didn't feel like I ever had a break. My husband said, "You wanted to breastfeed, and we're going to do this." He was my motivation. He encouraged me and helped me whenever I needed it. After about three and a half days, my milk came in. I knew because I noticed white on the end of my nipple after a feeding. My routine was to nurse 15 minutes on one side, change the baby's diaper, then nurse 15 minutes on the other side. I would then play with him, and he'd take a nap after about an hour. About two and a half to three hours after the previous feeding, he'd be ready to nurse again. I would start him off on the opposite side from where I started last time, like if I nursed him from the left breast first last feeding, then I'd nurse him on the right breast first next time.

Going back to work was tough. It was the first time being away from my baby for so long, and I worried about him. On my first day back at work, I got up early, got myself ready, and then fed and dressed the baby as my last thing before I left for work. While at work, I pumped mid-morning, during lunch, and mid-afternoon. I cleaned out an old, unused office for a pumping room, and I'd sneak into my private room to pump, and then clean the parts in the bathroom. My advice would also be to not be afraid like I was. Be proud that you want to provide healthy milk to your child. Notify your supervisor of your intentions to breastfeed, and ask for help finding a private place to pump, and work out a schedule while you're allowed extra time to pump when you need to. I know that people say, go to a private office, dim the lights, set up pictures of your child, play soft music, and take your time to pump. Some of us military girls aren't that lucky! My tiny secret office soon turned into storage, and there was no room for me when it was filled with computers and a refrigerator. My boss's office was in the back of my office, and I was only allowed to use that during the few times it was available. When I was in there, everyone could hear the "reeh-raw" of the pump moving, and it embarrassed me that I couldn't have any REAL privacy. Most of my pumping was done in the BATHROOM. I know that shouldn't even be an option, but it was the only one that I saw. There wasn't too much traffic in the bathroom, and I was near the sinks to use my bottle brushes and soap to clean the parts and put them back in my book bag when I was done. It was very embarrassing and uncomfortable when someone would come in to pee in the stall next to mine! They never said anything like, "Hey, what's that noise? Who's over there?" But I felt that's what everyone was always thinking.

I did not pump as much at work as I would at home, probably because of my lack of comfort. I would usually stand in the stall while I pumped. After I realized how much time it took to get set up, collect the milk, clean the pump parts, then get back to work, I started feeding Mason during lunch at daycare. Since I was already on base while he was at the CDC, it actually took less time to drive there, feed him, and drive back. The teachers in the room allowed me to feed Mason in their room while sitting in a glider they had. I kept a nursing cover in his diaper bag, so it was always there and ready for use. Eventually, I'd only pump mid-morning and mid-afternoon with lunchtime feedings, and my day was easier. Sometimes, I was on a mission and too busy to pump. My breasts just grew bigger and fuller (thank God I always wore my pads), and I pumped as soon as I was able. I ended up keeping my supply pretty well.

At about six months, we introduced baby cereal, and it was so much fun to finally feed Mason solids. At that time, I decided to "give in" and introduce formula as well. I still fed him during lunchtime. I also fed him (no bottles) on the weekends for every meal. In retrospect, that is probably what kept my milk supply up, even though we were supplementing with formula during the week. Once I had a routine down, my baby got a bit older to where he could find the nipple without my help, and I had support on my side, the following months went by smoothly. I was determined to breastfeed my son for his whole first year of life. Towards the end of the year, I got down to just feeding him four times a day, and then just three: when he woke up at 5 a.m., no lunch feeding or pumping, after school at 5 p.m., and before bed around 8 p.m. After he turned one, my husband and I were able to wean him. I am so happy that my child was able to receive breastmilk during his first year of life. I feel a real sense of accomplishment that I did not give up.

Chapter 19
Family, Friends, and Partner

Your partner is your biggest support in this endeavor besides yourself. Research has proven time and again that the father's support for breastfeeding is the biggest factor in whether or not you will succeed at breastfeeding (Arora, McJunkin, Wehrer, & Kuhn, 2000; Bar-Yam & Darby, 1997; Pisacane, Continisio, Aldinucci, D'Amora, & Continisio, 2005; Tohotoa et al., 2009; Wolfberg et al., 2004). He can be there to cheer you up on a rough day, wash the pump parts when you come home from work dead tired, and help with the baby care. He should tell you what a good job you are doing and offer to help in any way possible. After all, he has got the easy part of the parenting right now! Oftentimes, military husbands have a better understanding of the rigors of combining breastfeeding and active-duty service, as they are on active duty themselves. Get him on your side. Tell him the benefits of breastfeeding for you, the baby, and for him, too. As this mom in the Air Force attests:

> *It takes a whole family to undertake the mission of breastfeeding. I couldn't have done it without the support of my husband.*

He'll be a believer and your biggest supporter when he sees how happy and healthy your children are, and how much more sleep he'll get if you breastfeed. Please have him read the following section, written specifically for fathers by a Certified Nurse Midwife, IBCLC, and the father of eight breastfed children, who also happens to be a Major in the U.S. Army.

Dads and Breastfeeding

With Thanks to Major Jarold "Tom" Johnston, CNM, IBCLC (Ft. Drum, NY) for writing this section.

This section is dedicated to the father of your baby. Please feel free to read it (you will find a lot of the information helpful as well), but it is written specifically for the father of your baby.

The evidence is clear that a helpful and supportive father is the key to breastfeeding success. Studies have repeatedly shown that new mothers value the support of their husbands more than any other form of support available.

Believe it or not, your husband is more helpful than midwives, nurses, lactation consultants, even your own mother. Unfortunately, men are rarely completely welcomed into the breastfeeding relationship. Most books written about men in breastfeeding limit the father's role to preparing and passing the baby to mom. Fathers are capable of much, much more. Pass this section to your husband and invite him to help and support your desires to breastfeed.

Dad, if you are reading this section, you and your wife are expecting a beautiful baby, I say congratulations! You are already well on your way down the path of parenthood. Make no mistake; you become a parent long before your baby is born, just as your child knows both mom and dad long before he or she is born. The road that you are on will be tough. It will lead you through countless trials and conquests, ups and downs, and twists and turns. I am very fond of saying that parenting is a contact sport, but the rewards are tremendous. Each new skill, each new word, every new step you experience as your child grows is an exciting and miraculous journey down the road of life. Enjoy the journey, the hard times, and the easy times. Nothing in life compares.

Dads are integral to mom's success

Photo courtesy Julie Hansen.
Used with permission.

As a midwife, a lactation consultant, and a father of eight beautiful breastfed babies, I'm often asked to share my perspectives with new parents. I have found through personal and professional practice that almost everything is hard the first few days or weeks with a new baby. And breastfeeding is no different. I encourage you to talk to your healthcare provider, your lactation consultant, and especially friends who have successfully breastfed for more than six months. You will do well to learn as much as you can about breastfeeding before the baby is born. Learn from the women and men in your life who have successfully breastfed for more than six months, and ignore the advice of couples who failed at breastfeeding. If they knew what they were talking about, they would not have failed in the first place.

The breastfeeding family is a lot like a cohesive military unit. No unit can succeed if its members are not all working together toward a common goal. And likewise, breastfeeding families must all work together to achieve their goals in breastfeeding. Each member of your unit has a specialized task that only they can do. Mom will offer the baby the breast. The baby will feed himself. And Dad will serve as a coach or guide to help make sure everything goes well.

The Mother's job is to put the baby "in the kitchen." That means that mom has to offer the baby the breast. Breastfeeding is easiest, at least for the first few days or weeks, when the mother removes the baby's clothes and puts his naked chest right up against her bare chest, then covers the two with a blanket. When the mother and baby are in direct skin-to-skin contact and covered with a blanket, the baby stays warm, and the mother stays modest. Once the baby is "in the kitchen," all you really have to do is wait for him to do his job. When the time is right, he will feed himself. If you really feel the need, you can coax him to nurse, you can talk to him, pet him, stroke his face and mouth, and encourage him to feed. But ultimately the baby knows what he's doing and all you really have to do is wait. You will notice that I didn't tell you that a mother feeds her baby because she doesn't. The baby will feed himself.

The Baby's job is demanding, but the healthy newborn is well prepared at birth. The baby has to identify the breast, he will wrap his cute little hands around it, put it where he needs it to be, open his mouth VERY wide ,and take the entire areola deep into his mouth, down his throat, and suck and swallow until satisfied. I usually encourage baby to take mom's breast all the way back to her elbow. The more breast a baby takes in, the easier and more effective feeding will be. Remember, it is the baby's job to feed himself. He is bright, energetic, and ready to feed within an hour of being born. Some babies will wait for a while, but all babies will eat when they are ready, usually within the first 48 hours. Don't rush him. Being born is hard work, and he is very tired after the adrenalin of birth wears off. If he sleeps from four hours of life until 24 hours of life, he is a normal newborn. Mom, all you really have to do is hold him close, keep him "in the kitchen," and allow him to do what he needs to do. Your healthy newborn will surprise you, I promise.

The Father, oh yes, the father; you, my friend, have the hardest job in the family. I hate to say it, but it is true. Have no fear; I know that you are man enough to breastfeed for your family. Dad, your job is to do my job when you take your lovely new family home. When your bride wakes up at 3:00 in the morning and needs help getting your progeny to the breast, she won't ask me to help get the baby on. When you go home, the spotlight will be on you. You are a powerful team member, and your team will have a much better chance to succeed if you are actively involved. So get in there, roll up your sleeves, and breastfeed. Don't worry. I'll show you how.

First, why would anyone want to breastfeed? In the old days, we used to talk about the benefits of breastfeeding, and you will still hear some people mention it. But not me. Believe it or not, breastfeeding doesn't make your baby bigger, stronger, faster, or smarter. Breastfeeding doesn't make him super human; it just makes him human. The problem is that formula is incomplete nutrition. It is missing several essential nutrients that a growing baby needs. Formula feeding makes your baby weaker, slower, and dumber than his breastfeeding colleagues. There are indeed risks to formula feeding, just like there are risks to eating fast food every day. If you eat Burger King three meals a day for two years, you would be weaker, slower, and dumber, too. Breastfeeding is perfect nutrition, and as a human mammal, your child is designed to drink human milk made especially for him by his mother. If you don't believe me, there are more than 9,000 clinical trials, and hundreds of other sources to prove my point. Honestly, if you don't think that formula is substandard nutrition, you have been purposely hiding from the truth, and nothing I say here will help change your mind.

So, if you've come this far, you're still with me, and it's time to learn how to breastfeed. I break it down into three simple steps.

1. When does the baby need to eat?

2. How does the baby eat?

3. When is the baby done eating?

It really is that simple, so let's dive in.

When does the Baby need to eat? First thing you have to understand is that in all my years working with families, I've never met a baby that read the rulebook before birth. Contrary to traditional teaching, a baby does not eat for 10 minutes on each breast, every two to three hours. That is nonsense. Babies are not born with watches. And even if you give him one, he can't read it anyway. When a baby has stress (hunger, cold, wet or dirty diapers, pain, or loneliness), he will show you some very predictable signs. He'll curl up his hands and feet and bring them to the center. He'll bend at the knees and cross his feet or put his heels together (that's called centering behavior). He'll start to turn his head and may suck on his hands. Eventually, he'll start to fuss, and finally cry. All of these are stress signs. Sometimes he'll be hungry, sometimes lonely; but when he does those things he is asking for you to pick him up and tend to his needs. Since you won't know what he wants by looking at him, I always recommend you start in the kitchen. If he's hungry, he'll take the breast when you offer it. But never insist that a baby "has to be hungry" just because it's been a while since he's had the breast. And the opposite is true as well. Don't automatically assume he can't be hungry just because he only ate an hour ago. Babies are unpredictable. When you offer the breast, he'll eat if he's hungry. As a general rule, newborns eat 8-12 times a day, usually in clustered groups of three to four times in a four-hour period, they then take a three to four hour nap, and start over again. Don't count on it. But know that while no two babies eat on the same schedule, very rarely will a baby actually eat for 10 minutes on each breast every two to three hours, as most books would suggest.

How does the baby eat? This is a tough one. Every baby is different, just like every person is different. But there are a few simple principles that you can follow. When baby is ready to eat and he's in the kitchen, he will stretch out his hands, move the breast to where he wants it, open his mouth VERY wide, and take the breast deep into his mouth. He'll latch on well, he'll suckle in bursts of 10-15 rapid sucks followed by a short pause, you may hear a soft, quiet, swallowing sound, and then he'll do it again. Sometimes he'll appear to be sleeping, as he lies peacefully on the breast, while holding the breast in his mouth. Don't be fooled, babies don't really sleep on the breast. They rest and wait for their drinks to settle in their stomach. Only college students and Army privates like to chug. Everyone else takes a few sips and puts their drink down, and then they start again. Don't expect him to chug his milk and eat non-stop, no one does that, he wouldn't expect the same from you.

When your baby is on the breast, you need to make sure he is latched on well and that he is transferring milk well from mom to baby. Every time your baby latches on, you will need to look for signs of a good latch, and here they are.

1. **Nose and chin touching the breast.** He should bury his face deep in the breast. Never try to pull the breast away from his face because that will pull the nipple away from his mouth, or change the shape of the breast in his mouth. Never fear that he will suffocate on the breast. First, remember, he isn't stupid. He won't suffocate for one more drink of breastmilk. If he can't breathe, he'll just turn his head or pull away. Second, have you ever noticed the creases on the side of your nose and how they tend to run up to your eyes? Have you ever noticed that there is a dimple on the side of your head where your eye sockets are? That is a continuous channel from the nose to the side of the head that I call, "The Baby Snorkel System." Air moves from his mouth, to his eyes, under his eyes, and out the side of his head. If you don't believe me, put your face underwater, cover your face with your hands and blow air out of your nose, you'll see the air move out of the side of your head.

2. **Full round cheeks without dimples.** If his mouth is full of breast, his cheeks are full of breasts. If you see dimples on his cheeks or creases around his mouth, he does not have the breast deep in his mouth. He is creating a vacuum of empty space, and he is hurting your lovely bride.

3. **Wide open jaw.** The infant has a small mouth, and he has to open that mouth VERY wide to get all that breast tissue deep into his mouth. Measure the angle of his jaw, (Oh yeah! Finally, something you can measure.) The angle from his nose to his ear to his chin should be greater than 60 degrees, but 90 degrees is even better. I use my fingers. Put your index finger on the chin, your palm on his

ear, and your middle finger on his nose, and measure that angle: 45 degrees is a closed and empty mouth.

4. **No Pain.** NO PAIN! NO PAIN! NO PAIN! Did I mention it shouldn't hurt to breastfeed? Traditionally, nipple pain in early breastfeeding was considered normal and unavoidable. That is a beast whose time is long past. New understanding of the anatomy of breastmilk structures in the nipple and areola shows that there is no fat or cushion in the nipple and that all cushion is held back on the areola. When the infant pinches the nipple with his mouth or tongue, your wife will get pain, which is exactly the same thing that will happen if you pinch the nipple with your thumb and forefinger. Pinching the nipple is always a bad thing, and mom wouldn't let *you* do it either! If you can't get away with it, neither should the baby. Not only will the baby hurt his mother, he will also not be able to effectively bring milk out. When you pinch the nipple, you bend the tubes that bring down breastmilk. If you bend a straw, you can't drink from it. Don't let the baby bend those tubes or pinch the nipple. If your wife has nipple pain, you need to help fix the latch immediately. And if you can't, you need to get in to see a lactation consultant as soon as possible.

5. **Flared Lips, Up and Down.** In order for a baby to take the breast deep in his mouth, he will have to flare his lips as he opens his mouth widely. His tongue will extend and push out his lower lip, and he will wrap his lips around the areola. If there is a latching problem, it is often failure to flare the bottom lip. All that being said, when he is properly buried into the breast, you can't see his lips. Know that if everything else is OK, the lips are probably OK. But if there is pain, dimples in the cheeks, or a narrow jaw, you will need to help your baby open his mouth and push his bottom lip and tongue out.

"How do I do that?" one may ask. Don't worry. They taught you how to solve the problem when you were in basic training. Corrective action for the breastfeeding baby is the same as corrective action for the M-16 (or M-4). When a baby has a bad latch, it is almost always a double feed. You have two rounds in the chamber at the same time (in this case, breast and lower lip). Just like any other double feed, you'll have to pull **SPORTS** (slap, pull, observe, release, tap, and shoot). If you remember your basic rifle marksmanship, you will know what to do without even asking.

SPORTS

S – Slap – Put your hand on the baby's back and push him toward the breast.

P – Pull – Reach one finger between the chin and the breast and pull down on the baby's chin to elicit a rooting reflex.

O – Observe – Does the jaw open, do the cheeks fill and round out, do the lips flare, and does the pain go away?

R – Release – let go of the chin and let the baby suckle and test the new latch.

T – Tap/Try again – Repeat the first four steps two or three times to see if you can correct the bad latch.

S – Shoot – Darn it! We have to take him off the breast and try again.

From *Major Jarold "Tom" Johnston, CNM, IBCLC.* Used with permission.

If you can't fix the latch with the basics of **SPORTS,** you are going to need remedial action. You're going to have to drop the magazine (take the baby off the breast), clear the chamber (calm the child, then elicit a rooting reflex off the breast to encourage a VERY wide open mouth), and reload (put him back to the breast).

Eventually these steps will almost always help solve a bad latch. Very rarely you may find that even though you do everything right, your baby will not latch correctly. He may have chosen to sleep rather than eat. He may be over stimulated. Or he may just need an experienced hand to help him out. Give him a break, let him rest for an hour or so, and try again. If he ever goes 24 hours without eating, get in to see a lactation consultant right away.

When is my baby finished eating? When baby is finished eating, he will relax his hands, release the breast, pull away from the breast, and fall into a deep sleep that I call "The milk coma." Remember, your baby can't tell time. Some babies will finish the breast in 10-15 minutes; some will finish the breast in 45-60 minutes. Both babies will have taken the same amount of milk, and that amount is "ENOUGH." There is no easy way for you to measure how much a baby eats when he is on the breast. But know that the actual amount of ounces he drinks is immaterial. What is important is that he goes to breast interested in feeding, and that he pulls away content, relaxed, and sleeping. A baby that is satisfied after feeding, steadily growing, healthy looking, and generally happy is getting "enough" to eat. The number-one concern of new mothers is that they do not make enough milk. Dad, your job is to reassure her with your actions, your knowledge, and your confidence that your baby is, in fact, getting plenty to eat. Try not to worry about it. Keep offering the breast to the baby, and he will always get enough to eat.

So there you have it: breastfeeding from a man's perspective. Fathers are powerful allies contributing to breastfeeding success. Do not allow yourself to be excluded from this time in your child's life. Study and learn, roll up your sleeves and get in

It takes a family to make breastfeeding in the military a success.

Photo courtesy Courtney Power. Used with permission.

the game. Your family stands a much better chance of succeeding when you actively support breastfeeding and actively help your wife breastfeed.

Other Family Members

The second most important members in your support team are your family–especially your own mother. Military members travel all over the world and often do not stay near their families, so you may or may not have any family near where you live. For new mothers, this can be especially difficult, as a new mother's mother can often be a great support in the early days and weeks of parenting a new baby. Research has shown that the support of the baby's grandmother for breastfeeding plays a huge role in whether or not you will be successful (Ekström, Widström, & Nissen, 2003; Grassley & Eschiti, 2008). If your mother is supportive in your efforts to breastfeed your baby, even if she did not breastfeed you, you are much more likely to continue breastfeeding, even through problems and a return to work. Her support can be as simple as telling you you're doing a good job to finding you the help you need if a problem arises. If you do not live near your mother, you will have to get your support from her through increased phone calls, Skype, and more visits if at all possible.

> *My sisters and mother supported me from the U.S. over the phone. My mother breastfed her four children, and she was a huge inspiration to me.* Captain, USAF

On the other hand, if your mother is not supportive of breastfeeding, living far away may be a blessing in disguise, as you will not have to listen to and deal with questions about whether your milk is enough nutrition for your baby or that you are spoiling the baby. Unsupportive grandmothers can be a very real detriment to breastfeeding success due to misinformation and a quick offer to give the baby formula if a breastfeeding problem arises (Grassley & Eschiti, 2008).

> *My mom, who owned a baby boutique, brought a bunch of videos about "how to give your baby a bath" and "baby's first night at home," things like that. One of the videos that she brought was a Breastfeeding video by LLL, complete with a little booklet. As she handed it to me, she said something to the effect that I would not need that video because I was not BF (not that this was something that she and I had ever talked about) and that I could just give it to someone else if I wanted. She was very negative about breastfeeding.* Staff Sgt., USAF

> *My mother-in-law never breastfed because she heard it makes breasts sag, and she was not supportive. I think she was actually offended by my choosing to breastfeed since she didn't and her children turned out okay. Maybe she thought I was trying to be a better mother than her? I still stuck to my decision, even when she tried to talk me out of it. After a few of those conversations, I just told her that my mind was made up, and I didn't need to hear her trying to change it.* Captain, USAF

★ How Grandmothers Can Help ★

If you are a new grandmother, congratulations! This is an exciting period in your life as you watch your daughter or daughter-in-law step into parenthood. As a grandmother, you can do a lot to help smooth the way for her, especially if she is breastfeeding. It can be particularly hard to see your daughter struggling with breastfeeding, especially if you also had difficulties. You may not know how to help--or if you even should. But you can be a great help to her by offering your unconditional support, an empathetic ear, and some practical help around the house, so she can concentrate on learning how to breastfeed your new grandchild. Be aware that many of the things you learned as a new mother regarding breastfeeding (and parenting in general) have changed. Her way of breastfeeding and parenting may be different than what you did. But it is not a reflection on you. Rather, it is based on what we have learned is good for babies. Here are some tips that mothers say are the most helpful:

- **LISTEN, LISTEN, LISTEN**. If you do nothing else, be an ear to listen to her as she learns how to be a mother and how to breastfeed.

- **Offer emotional and morale support**. Be there to give her a hug or rub her shoulders. Tell her what a wonderful job she is doing and that it will get better.

- **Ask what you can do to help**. And then do it, no questions asked.

- **Answer her questions**. But don't tell her what to do, remember be a listening ear while she vents and sorts out her emotions.

- **Offer to call for professional help**. If it seems she is really in need of breastfeeding help, ask if she wants you to call LLL or an IBCLC.

- **Read about breastfeeding.** If you know what is normal for a breastfed baby, you can better help her meet her baby's needs (and spot a problem brewing).

- **Attend a support group meeting with her.** You'll see what normal breastfeeding looks like and meet other mothers parenting like your daughter.

- **Help with household chores.** One of the best things you can do is start a load of laundry or wash the dishes while your daughter sits on the couch and learns how to breastfeed her baby.

- **Don't hog the baby.** Hold the baby when your daughter needs a shower or eats lunch. Otherwise Mom gets the baby.

- **Don't offer a bottle**. If she is having trouble, get her some HELP!

Friends

Having a close friend (or friends) who is or has breastfed, successfully, can be a great help when you are starting out, particularly if your friend's child is a few months older than yours. You can compare notes and understand that many of the concerns and questions you have about breastfeeding and pumping are perfectly normal. Your friend can give you tips regarding what worked for her and much needed support when you are just having a rough day. Research has found that after your partner's and mother's support, having a friend's support is also very important to the success of breastfeeding (Raj & Plichta, 1998). This support is even more important for the military mother who may be stationed far from home, or even overseas, and is without her own mother's support.

> *A best friend of mine, Jen, was also a great support. Her son is about five months older than mine, and it's great to know that she's been where I am headed in breastfeeding and our child's development.* Captain, USAF

If you don't have anyone in your immediate command or circle of friends that is breastfeeding, you'll have to go searching. Don't be afraid to attend a breastfeeding class or support group, either on or off base, as they are a great way to meet other moms with babies close in age to yours. Oftentimes, friendships forged during the crazy-baby stage last long after your kids have graduated high school! And with the advent of Facebook and Skype, it is easy to stay in touch, even if you all get orders to opposite ends of the continent or world.

★ How Friends Can Help ★

As a friend, you have a lot to offer a new mother. Your support is especially important because you are her confidante and compatriot in this adventure. With children close in age, you'll be going through the same things together and can compare notes and swap tips and techniques. You can be a huge support in the early weeks, as your friend navigates the hormone-ridden roller-coaster of new mommyhood. But even more important, you can be there as she returns to active duty and learns the ropes of working and pumping in the military.

- **LISTEN, LISTEN, LISTEN.** If you do nothing else, be an ear to listen to her as she sorts through her feelings about being a mother, breastfeeding, working, etc.

- **Ask what you can do to help.** And then do it, no questions asked.

- **Help with household chores.** One of the best things you can do is run a load of laundry or wash the dishes for her. Bringing a meal by is always needed and welcomed, too.

- **Read about breastfeeding.** If you haven't breastfed a baby, read up on the basics, so you'll know what she is going through. You can then better help her meet her baby's needs (and spot a problem brewing).

- **Offer to call for professional help.** If it seems she is really in need of breastfeeding help, ask if she wants you to call LLL or an IBCLC.

- **Take her to a support group meeting.** Seeing other moms breastfeeding and getting information and support is very helpful to a new mother. Your morale support is always welcome--especially if it's the first time she's left the house since her baby was born.

- **Swap tips and techniques.** Be honest about what worked for you and what didn't. But don't tell her what to do. She needs to find what works for her.

- **Offer emotional and morale support.** Be there to give her a hug or take her out for coffee and let her vent. Remind her of what a wonderful job she is doing, and that this too shall pass.

Chapter 20
Command Support

Support from your command can make or break your ability to breastfeed successfully in the military. A successful and supportive breastfeeding environment flows from the top down in the military. The attitude of the leaders is key. If your Commanding Officer is supportive of breastfeeding, then his or her opinion will affect the climate of the entire command (Bell & Ritchie, 2003b). Having a Commanding Officer that supports breastfeeding means that a command-wide policy may be written, a lactation room might be created, and training is more likely to be given to all hands. Even if none of the above happens, you are more likely to receive individual support when you go to ask for a place and time to pump and are less likely to endure any harassment from co-workers.

At commands where supportive policies have been implemented, the concerns regarding increased cost, time, and mission conflicts have not been realized. Instead, the changes in policy and education of personnel results in increased morale and productivity, reduced maternal-child healthcare costs, and retention of their personnel who feel supported in their quest to breastfeed on active duty. Oftentimes, the commands that are breastfeeding-friendly have had a high-ranking individual in charge who either breastfed children herself or whose wife did and understands just what a difference breastfeeding makes in the lives of babies and their mothers.

Thankfully I have a boss with two kids and a CO with five...all of which were breastfed for a year, so ... they were very supportive. Sgt., USMC

I had a very competent and supportive supervisor at work that made it very possible for me to continue to nurse my daughter until it became absolutely necessary to wean her. Otherwise, he supported me even when I elected to defer mandatory NCO schools in order to continue to nurse my daughter until she weaned. The work environment is essential to successful breastfeeding in the military. Sgt., USA

I will say that, in my experience, the Navy has definitely improved. I am glad that the policy for deterring sea duty for postpartum women was changed from four months to one year, and feel it is a giant leap forward for women in the Navy. I also think that adding the extra instructions about breastfeeding and pumping in the work place made for another step forward. I have encountered no harassment, and this command does supply us with a private room. I am ecstatic about the changes, and it is one of the bigger reasons I am reenlisting for one more term. Petty Officer 2nd Class, USN

Unfortunately, unsupportive commands do exist, and no manner of policy changes will make a difference. When a new mother sees that other women in the command have not been successful at breastfeeding, she may choose not to breastfeed at all, or she may not pump upon her return to work. Or she may stop pumping while at work due to the harassment and unsupportive environment, and then find that her milk supply has dropped too far, and ends up quitting after only a few weeks. This has far-reaching effects beyond that of herself and her baby, as the service member may chose not to reenlist or remain on active duty, and then the command and the military loses out on a qualified and trained professional.

> *I'm a former Army nurse who had a horrible experience with nursing while in uniform….my treatment during nursing was one of the reasons I got out of the Army.* Captain, USA

> *It is possible (to breastfeed), but not all of the Navy is supportive… it's part of the reason I am now separated from active duty.* Petty Officer 2nd Class, USN

> *Even with the 6000.1c, there are still the excuses and delays to pumping. Many just give up or don't try.* Lt., USN

In order to have a successful breastfeeding program at a command, there needs to be gatekeepers. Gatekeepers are the various personnel within a command who control the time, place, and support necessary for a breastfeeding mother to pump (Bar-Yam, 1998; Bell & Ritchie, 2003b). Within a command, the commander is the first and foremost gatekeeper, as he or she is responsible for overall command climate and policy change. Other gatekeepers may include the training officer who schedules educational training on breastfeeding in the workplace and the logistics officer who may order supplies and equipment for a lactation room.

Senior non-commissioned officers play a vital role as gatekeepers by establishing a breastfeeding-friendly climate for enlisted mothers through scheduling breaks and providing a place to pump, as well as monitoring and taking action if any harassment surfaces from co-workers. Oftentimes, it takes a higher-ranking officer who is currently breastfeeding to bring the need for breastfeeding support to the attention of her command and institute the changes needed.

> *As for breastfeeding support, just like with any organization, it needs leadership support. At my command, I was the primary breastfeeding advocate. I created the first-ever pump room that followed all the codes laid out in the OPNAVINST. I also made it inviting and comfortable with plants, pictures, a comfy chair, and a picture board*

for all the women to post baby pictures. I also provided mentoring and counseling to other women at my command. So for my command, an enlisted woman was treated no differently when it came to needing to pump because I made sure of it. My advice is for shore commands that have pregnant and nursing woman present, they need a khaki (E-7 or above/Officer) to advocate for each of them. In some cases, a command's medical officer or medical LCPO can fill that role if no one steps up. Lt., USN

Very often, a command does not have any sort of breastfeeding policy in place. Your supervisors may not be aware that they are required to provide any sort of accommodation for breastfeeding because it has never come up before. Just because there is a service-wide policy in existence doesn't mean that it has ever needed to be implemented at the command level up until your arrival. If you are at a command that is not supportive, and has no one in charge, it may be up to you to be that agent of change. This can be very difficult, especially if you are lower-ranking. But it is not impossible. Try to seek out a senior enlisted Chief/NCO or officer that is amenable to breastfeeding and work out the changes needed, no matter how minor. What you start may snowball and be the start of a great program for future breastfeeding mothers at your command.

Below are some examples of programs that have been implemented in the past at various military commands for breastfeeding mothers. These are given here to show what can be done to promote breastfeeding at the command level for future reference.

Joint Base Lewis McChord and Madigan Army Medical Center

In 2000, a unique program was started at the former Ft. Lewis (now Joint Base Lewis McChord) in Washington State, in conjunction with Madigan Army Medical Center, as part of the *Policy on Support for Soldiers with Nursing Infants*. This program provided pre-deployment education to lactating soldiers preparing to engage in field-training exercises (FTX) lasting from 24 hours to one to four weeks, and also provided daily courier runs to transport expressed breastmilk in coolers back to headquarters, where caregivers could pick up the milk (Kellogg & Jones, 2004). At Madigan Army Medical Center, a lactation room was created with hospital-grade breast pumps, a sink, and educational resources. While this hasn't been adopted Army-wide, it does offer ideas and a policy in place at one post for future reference.

NAS Jacksonville

A program was begun at NAS Jacksonville's largest hangar: AIMD Hangar 100. It was coordinated with the CO and the Senior Chief to turn a former locker room/shower into a pump station for the moms. One of the female chiefs and the Officer's Wives Club decorated the space and provided the comfy chair and table. The pump had been obtained through a fund raiser by the helicopter squadron's Officer's Wives Club. The pump station was used by the junior enlisted moms. Sometime later, the Admiral's wife called for information and set up the same program at AIMD Mayport Naval Station.

NAS Sigonella

U.S. Naval Hospital Sigonella established a breastfeeding space within the Aircraft Intermediate Maintenance Department (AIMD) on Naval Air Station Sigonella. The female bunkroom within the command had a hospital-grade electric breast pump for use by women at AIMD, Helicopter Support Squadron HC-4, and any other women authorized to enter the AIMD buildings. Another breastfeeding room was set up in the hospital's pediatric clinic. The All Officer's Spouses Club and the Chaplain's Department via the MOMS Club of Sigonella donated funding for the breast pump in AIMD.

★ How Commands Can Support Breastfeeding Mothers ★

With women making up nearly 15% of the active duty force, and with 17% of all active-duty women becoming mothers of newborns every year, it is vital to support their efforts to breastfeed. It is well-known that support for breastfeeding affects recruiting and retention of qualified women by improving their quality of life. It also improves unit readiness by improving both mother and child health, resulting in fewer illnesses and decreased healthcare costs (Bell & Ritchie, 2003a). Given these factors, commands should have a policy in place that supports breastfeeding and is in line with the parent service policy (if there is one). In fact, the current U.S. Navy policy indicates that each commanding officer "shall develop written policies to delineate support of servicewomen with breastfeeding infants" (Chief of Naval Operations, 2007). The vast majority of commands can create a policy that supports breastfeeding with minimal disruption to missions and workflow, and little in the way of cost or time expenditures.

- Set command-level policy. A policy that provides guidance for both commanders and breastfeeding military personnel must be developed and enforced. The policy should cover topics such as: place/time to pump, breastfeeding education, scheduling, supplies, HAZMAT, PT, and deployability. The Policy on Support for Soldiers with Nursing Infants is an example of such a command-level policy.

- Appoint gatekeepers. An Officer or Senior Enlisted personnel can be appointed to delegate the tasks needed to enforce the command policy. One or more personnel need to provide training, locate and maintain a suitable pumping location, schedule pumping breaks, and obtain supplies.

- Education and training at all levels. Breastfeeding education for pregnant personnel by a qualified breastfeeding professional on overcoming difficulties related to expressing milk at work and recognizing exposure risks to hazardous materials should be mandatory. Training for all hands on the benefits of breastfeeding for the command and how to support a breastfeeding co-worker should be provided by a trained breastfeeding expert.

- Provide place and time. A suitable location with a locking door, an outlet, and running water nearby are the bare minimums required. A restroom or toilet stall is not appropriate. Breastfeeding mothers need two to four breaks, depending on work hours, of at least 15-30 minutes to express their milk.

- Provide supplies (if needed). If possible, a hospital-grade pump, refrigeration, a sink with soap and water, and a table and chairs are useful. Coolers, dry ice, and transportation from the field back to headquarters can be implemented for mothers in field situations.

- Make information available. Women in the command need to know where they can go for further information if they are having difficulties. Make clear who in the command they can go to for help and what resources are available both on base, at the local MTF, or in the civilian sector.

- Encourage Workplace Support Groups. Where possible, create workplace support groups for AD breastfeeding mothers.

Chapter 21
Medical Support

There are many different types of breastfeeding help available to new mothers, and knowing which ones are right for your situation can be tricky. It may seem that a doctor would know more about breastfeeding than say a speech therapist. But you might be surprised. Having a medical degree does not always mean that the individual has had any training in breastfeeding. But knowing what the different initials after a person's name means can help you find the information you need in your situation. The following chapter highlights what kind of help you can expect from various medical personnel that you may encounter at the base clinic or MTF (links to all of these resources can also be found in the Appendices at the back of this book).

IBCLC

Most of the major military hospitals have a "lactation consultant" on staff. She/he may be a civilian or a military member, and may work full- or part-time. Usually, their lactation duties are secondary to their regular job on the floor. Most base clinics do not have a lactation consultant on staff. When requesting help for a breastfeeding problem, it is important that you ask whether your breastfeeding helper is an IBCLC or not, as there is a big difference in the quality of care, experience, and training. International Board Certified Lactation Consultants are the gold standard of breastfeeding care. An IBCLC, also known as a lactation consultant, is a professional who has received the highest level of education and training, and possesses the knowledge and skill to help mothers with even the most difficult breastfeeding situations. To use the letters IBCLC after her name (there are a few male lactation consultants), she must pass a rigorous international credentialing exam. To be eligible to even sit for the exam, she must have extensive education (usually a four-year degree) and many years of experience working with breastfeeding mothers. To retain the IBCLC credential, she must attend conferences and earn continuing education credits.

An IBCLC does **not** have to be a doctor or a nurse to practice, although many lactation consultants are nurses, midwives, dieticians, or speech therapists. Most IBCLCs work in hospitals, clinics, or in private practice. An International Board Certified Lactation Consultant is there to provide clinical help, breastfeeding information, and strategies for combining work and breastfeeding. Oftentimes, IBCLCs will carry breastfeeding supplies, such as pumps and other items you may find necessary to return to work.

An IBCLC knows the ins and outs of how breast pumps work, the advantages and disadvantages of each, and can help you choose the proper model for your circumstances. She can help you with any breastfeeding problems you may encounter (sore nipples, engorgement, mastitis, thrush, milk supply issues) and refer you for the necessary medical attention, if need be. IBCLCs often have an area of expertise, such as working mothers, low milk supply, or babies with cleft palates. So you should look around for one that fits your needs. An IBCLC's sole job is to help you achieve your breastfeeding goals. Generally, lactation consultants charge for their services (TRICARE does not cover lactation consultations). You can visit www.ilca.org to find a lactation consultant near you.

There are many lactation educators, lactation counselors, and lactation specialists that work in healthcare settings who often help new mothers with breastfeeding. They are also known as a CLCs or CLEs, and these individuals have generally taken one or more short-term breastfeeding courses and may have received a local or national certification. They are capable of teaching mothers about breastfeeding and helping with normal problems, but may or may not have the experience or expertise to help with difficult breastfeeding problems. They generally work in hospitals and clinics and may also be nurses, dieticians, or other allied healthcare workers. See Appendix C for more information.

★ How IBCLCs Can Support Active-Duty Breastfeeding Mothers ★

As an IBCLC, you have a wonderful opportunity to make a difference in the lives of the active-duty mothers you come into contact with. Research has shown that IBCLCs have a positive effect in increasing the rates of initiation and duration for military mothers (Haas et al., 2006; Rishel & Sweeney, 2005). Further, lactation consultants are a key resource for accurate breastfeeding information and support for mothers, due to the lack of training received by medical personnel. However, much of the information and support provided by IBCLCs is focused on general prenatal breastfeeding education and the early postpartum period, rather than military-specific return to work information and support (Bell & Ritchie, 2003a). In addition, the active-duty population needs services after hours to accommodate their work schedules, as well as breast pump loan programs. Finally, there exists a great need for command-level training and education (Bell & Ritchie, 2003b). If you work on or near a military base, you can implement some of following steps below to provide much needed breastfeeding support.

- **Provide education.** Offer education and training to commands (to include commanders, supervisors, and troops) on the importance of breastfeeding, common concerns, setting up lactation programs, and writing policy.

- **Learn.** Educate yourself on the many unique challenges faced by active-duty breastfeeding mothers (read this book!), so you can better help them. Become familiar with Military Policies, Hazardous Materials, etc.

- **Provide classes.** Offer military-specific breastfeeding education on return-to- work concerns.

- **Setup** a Lactation Support Program on your base.

- **Provide** breast pump loans or discounted rentals for AD moms (especially junior enlisted).

- **Host** an Active-Duty Breastfeeding Support Group.

- **Be available** at odd hours by phone, e-mail, text, Skype, or in-person. Many active-duty moms work 12-hour days, work nights, or have duty on the weekends.

- **THINK OUTSIDE THE BOX!**

RNs/MDs/CNMs

Medical doctors and Registered Nurses may or may not have any breastfeeding training. Both nurses and doctors have a few hours to a day or two of breastfeeding education during their formal schooling. It has been shown repeatedly that even residency-trained pediatricians, obstetricians, nurse practitioners, and nurses do not have the knowledge needed to manage common clinical problems related to breastfeeding, nor do they understand the hazards of formula in relation to the normalcy of breastfeeding (Anderson & Geden, 1991; Hellings & Howe, 2004; Klitsch, 1995; Szucs, Miracle, & Rosenman, 2009). Certified Nurse Midwives (CNMs) may receive more breastfeeding education during their specialized training, due to the focus on normal healthcare during the childbearing year. But it is not guaranteed.

Very often the breastfeeding information given by MDs, RNs, and CNMs is based on their own personal breastfeeding experience or that of their spouse, rather than being evidence-based. Of course, there are fabulous doctors, midwives, and nurses who have gone on to take extra training in breastfeeding management and who attend lactation conferences to stay up-to-date on the latest evidence-based information. Some become IBCLCs. But overall, they are still few and far between, especially within the military healthcare system.

Corpsman and Medics

Do not expect corpsman and medics to be familiar with breastfeeding or to be able to offer any type of information or support. Breastfeeding information is simply not taught at this level of training. Any breastfeeding knowledge that a corpsman or medic might have on breastfeeding is generally self-taught via personal breastfeeding experience or through a volunteer breastfeeding program or class.

★ How Medical Personnel Can Support Active-Duty Breastfeeding Mothers ★

Medical personnel are in the position of being on the frontlines of breastfeeding support for active-duty women. As a healthcare professional, you bear the responsibility of having patients look to you first for accurate information regarding breastfeeding. You have an opportunity to make it clear to military mothers that breastfeeding on active duty is normal, desirable, and achievable. Helping active-duty mothers begins with updating your own breastfeeding education, so you can better handle common breastfeeding concerns.

Implementing the Ten Steps to Successful Breastfeeding at your MTF and reducing the amount of formula given at discharge, or when breastfeeding problems arise, also supports the active-duty breastfeeding mother (Grizzard, Bartick, Nikolov, Griffin, & Lee, 2006; Rosenberg, Stull, Adler, Kasehagen, & Crivelli-Kovach, 2008). In addition, offering classes on breastfeeding and return to work, as well as creating a breast pump loan program through the MTF are all important ways medical providers can offer support for the active-duty mother who wishes to breastfeed (Bell & Ritchie, 2003b). As you work with active-duty mothers at your local MTF, you can implement some of following steps to provide much needed breastfeeding support.

- **Understand** the importance of breastfeeding and the differences between breastfed and formula-fed infants.

- **Education.** Learn how to manage common lactation concerns and help AD mothers get breastfeeding off to a good start.

- **Implement.** Start instituting the Ten Steps at your hospital.

- **Offer programs** to train commands, supervisors, peers, and breastfeeding mothers.

- **Create** a loan program for hospital-grade pumps for AD mothers.

- **Offer** military-specific breastfeeding educational materials and classes.

- **Do NOT hand out formula or formula-sponsored materials to your AD mothers.**

Chapter 22
Resources

There are many resources available to you within the civilian, military, and online communities. Check out these resources while you are still pregnant for information and classes you can sign up for. Know your resources, so you are not caught in a bind when you need them after the baby is born. Please visit my website (www.breastfeedingincombatboots.com) for an up-to-date and more extensive listing of breastfeeding-friendly resources.

Military Resources

The military community takes care of its own and has a large number of parenting-related resources available to you at low cost or no charge. Some of these resources may be more breastfeeding-friendly than others, and may or may not have up-to-date breastfeeding information. However, they should know of breastfeeding resources in the community and how put you in touch with the services you are seeking. Be sure to also ask around at your command and among your co-workers.

Active-Duty Mother Groups

Active-Duty Mother Groups are found on many bases worldwide. They offer active-duty mothers the chance to provide support and encouragement to one another while navigating the difficult path of combining motherhood and the military. You may or may not find other breastfeeding mothers at these group meetings, and you should be aware that there likely will not be any trained breastfeeding personnel in attendance. Any breastfeeding information given out should be verified with a LLL Leader or IBCLC.

MTF/Hospital Breastfeeding Support Groups

Many military treatment facilities offer breastfeeding classes, as well as support groups. Most have some kind of breastfeeding or lactation support program in place. However, the classes and support group meetings very often are held during the day and are usually attended by spouses, many of whom stay at home with their babies. Most military hospitals offer support for employed mothers in the way of classes and support groups. Be sure to ask during your OB appointment or at your six-week check-up.

Mom-2-Mom Breastfeeding Support Groups

Mom-2-Mom Breastfeeding Support Groups are part of a volunteer breastfeeding support program that was begun by the Army to encourage new mothers to breastfeed during at least the first two months of a baby's life. The Mom-2-Mom program uses peer support in the form of volunteers who have breastfed their own baby for at least three months. Volunteers have been given basic breastfeeding training to offer support and information to new breastfeeding mothers. Education is provided by local community lactation consultants, pediatricians, and community health nurses. Mom-2-Mom Breastfeeding Support Groups are found on various Army installations worldwide.

Finding support is crucial to your breastfeeding success.

Photo courtesy Amanda Ferguson.
Used with permission.

NPSP/NPST

New Parent Support Program or Team is a military-wide program run by the Family Advocacy Program. The NPSP is a home-based program to provide military families with the skills needed for a happy and healthy childrearing experience. Families receive visits from a Registered Nurse and/ or Social Worker who help with maternal, prenatal, breastfeeding, postpartum, and parenting issues. The NPSP Team also provides education on newborn, infant, and toddler and child behavior, childcare, growth and development, and more.

Support can be provided for other family, health-related, or stress problems. New Parent Support Programs often offer information specifically for active-duty mothers returning to work as well. Be aware that any breastfeeding information given through NPSP may or may not be accurate, as the Home Visitors are given little to no training in breastfeeding and the educational materials they use are often formula-company sponsored (some New Parent Support Programs hand out formula samples to all pregnant and new mothers regardless of feeding choice). However, there are NPS programs that have IBCLCs on staff, with up-to-date educational materials and classes. If the breastfeeding information doesn't sound right, check with your own IBCLC.

Branch-Specific Resources

Each branch of the military has their own support centers and Aid Societies that exist to help service-members and their family members. They are found both stateside and overseas and are often free. Breastfeeding information and support varies widely from installation to installation.

- **Air Force**
  - The Air Force offers services through the Air Force Family Support Centers found on every base worldwide. Included are parenting and family classes, as well as the New Parent Support Program. The Air Force Aid Society offers financial assistance and counseling. Assistance for a breast pump may be available on a case-by-case basis.

- **Army**
  - The Army offers services through the Army Community Services (ACS) program, including the New Parent Support Program at every base worldwide. Many ACSs offer Breastfeeding Basics classes free of charge. The Army Emergency Relief Society offers financial aid and counseling and may be able to assist with a loan for a breast pump.

- **Coast Guard**
  - The Coast Guard offers services through the Human Resources and in conjunction with the Navy. The Coast Guard Mutual Assistance offers financial aid and counseling. Assistance in the form of a loan or grant may be available for a breast pump. Coast Guard personnel are eligible for New Parent Support Program services through the Fleet and Family Service Centers found near naval bases.

- **Marine Corps/Navy**
  - The Marine Corps and the Navy offer very similar, and in some cases overlapping, programs for pregnant and new mothers. The Navy and Marine Corps Relief Society (NMCRS) offers financial assistance and counseling, as well as a "Budgeting for Baby" class that includes "Baby's First Seabag" filled with layette items. Assistance for a breast pump may be available on a case-by-case basis. Breastfeeding Basics classes are offered through a few NMCRS offices. Some NMCRS centers have a Visiting

Nurse program staffed with nurses who are specifically trained to come to your home after the birth of your baby. Whether or not their breastfeeding information is accurate is as individual as the program and the person who visits you. Few, if any, IBCLCs are employed by the NMCRS.

º   Fleet and Family Service Centers (FFSC) are also found on every base and offer a variety of classes for parents and parents-to-be. The New Parent Support Teams are also available through the FFSC.

Civilian Resources

Outside the gates, there are various civilian resources for breastfeeding support available to you. Each will offer a different perspective on breastfeeding, but all have the same goal in mind, to offer support and encouragement.

La Leche League International

La Leche League International (LLLI) is probably the most well-known breastfeeding support group in the world. LLLI was founded in 1956 by seven women to provide mother-to-mother support, and it is still offering monthly support group meetings today in locations all across the world. There are Groups on or nearby nearly every major military base in the United States and overseas. LLLI is a breastfeeding support group where you will receive up-to-date breastfeeding information from an Accredited Leader and be able to share your experiences with other breastfeeding mothers. An Accredited Leader is a mother who started out as a La Leche League member and has successfully breastfed for at least nine months and completed a lengthy accreditation process with extensive coursework to become a La Leche League Leader.

LLL Leaders are volunteers who provide peer support by facilitating monthly support group meetings and offering breastfeeding counseling via telephone and e-mail support. Some Leaders also offer home visits. One of the nice things about LLLI is that you'll get a taste of home if you are stationed overseas. Many Groups offer nighttime meetings or specialty meetings for employed mothers, most Groups offer a lending library of books, and members receive a bi-monthly magazine filled with tips on breastfeeding. A 1-800-LA-LECHE phone call will put you in touch with a Leader if you have a breastfeeding question or concern. La Leche League publishes the book *The Womanly Art of Breastfeeding,* and offers online support (including online meetings), information, and a Group locater at www.llli.org.

WIC

The Women, Infants, and Children Program is run by the Department of Agriculture to provide nutritional counseling and services to pregnant and breastfeeding mothers and children under the age of 5 who meet certain income and nutritional guidelines. WIC is available on or near every military base worldwide. Breastfeeding mothers receive extra vouchers for healthy food and counseling on breastfeeding issues. Under the new WIC guidelines, breastfeeding mothers are given different food packages, depending on whether they are fully or partially breastfeeding. Some WIC programs also have fully electric, double-breast pumps available for mothers who are working full-time or attending school.

All WIC offices employ Peer Counselors who are mothers who are or have been on the WIC Program and have successfully breastfed their infants. They receive extensive training, provide peer counseling and teaching to new moms, and can often help with normal breastfeeding problems. WIC Peer Counselors generally work in WIC offices, although a few will do home or hospital visits.

★ How Volunteers Can Support Active-Duty Breastfeeding Mothers ★

Volunteers have a wonderful opportunity to make a difference in the lives of the active-duty mothers. Research has shown that peer support has a positive effect in increasing the rates of breastfeeding duration (Dennis, 2002). Further, volunteer breastfeeding counselors may be the only source of accurate breastfeeding information and support available for active-duty mothers stationed overseas. You may be the only piece of home that seems familiar, and the only breastfeeding support available in English. If you work on or near a military base, you can implement some of following steps to provide much needed breastfeeding support.

- **Offer education** to both AD breastfeeding mothers and commands on the importance of breastfeeding and common concerns.

- **Learn.** Educate yourself on the many unique challenges faced by active-duty breastfeeding mothers (read this book!), so you can better help them. Familiarize yourself with Military Policies, Hazardous Materials, etc.

- **Help.** Make sure mothers get off to a good start with breastfeeding during their convalescent leave.

- **Offer.** Support Group meetings on or near bases when AD mothers can attend (evenings, weekends). Be available by phone (Warmline) or e-mail for help.

- **Resources.** Know the various breastfeeding resources, pump rentals, and IBCLCs to refer AD moms to in your area.

Online Resources

The Internet can be a boon to the military mother who is far away from family (and maybe friends) and in need of support to continue breastfeeding. You can log on at any time day or night to find information and read messages of support from virtual friends across the globe. The Internet offers everything from newsy blogs to chock-full-of-information websites, as well as online forums and discussion boards. Most of these websites are aimed towards breastfeeding mothers, in general, while a few are for more select groups, such as those moms who work and breastfeed. While there may not be any specific to the military mother, many of the issues talked about on these websites and discussion boards are similar and the support is wonderful.

Blogs

Blogs are a fabulous way to stay up-to-date on breastfeeding news, as they are usually updated more frequently than websites. Blogs can be one person's thoughts on a particular subject or a part of a larger website. There are a few blogs that are well researched and up-to-date (see Appendix B).

Facebook

You may not think of Facebook as the first place to go for breastfeeding information or support. However, you might be surprised at the amount of virtual support that can be found on Facebook. A growing number of breastfeeding Groups and Fan Pages (including *Breastfeeding in Combat Boots*) have sprung up in recent years, and many of the Groups have discussion boards and links to resources that are helpful. Fan Pages often link back to products and websites that you might find useful. Posting a status update on your Profile regarding a concern you have about breastfeeding can provide you with an outpouring of virtual support, if not a few suggestions to try. Another nice benefit of Facebook is the ability to stay in touch with friends and co-workers made at one command after you receive orders to a new command.

Skype

While most people think of Skype, or any of the web-based video chat clients that are available, as a wonderful way to stay in touch with friends and family, there is another less-well-known use for Skype and that is its usefulness for long-distance breastfeeding help. Some Lactation Consultants offer breastfeeding help via Skype, as they can speak and see you in real-time as they work with you to solve your breastfeeding issue. Much like phone consults, a Skype consult is not the same as being seen in person. And it should not take the place of a regular LC visit. But in a pinch, it might just be the bit of help you need to get you over the hump and onto successful breastfeeding. Payment is usually by PayPal or credit card.

YouTube

YouTube, along with many crazy clips on subjects ranging from asteroids to zebras, has a large number of how-to videos on breastfeeding. Many women find reading about latching a newborn baby not at all helpful, but a well-done video showing a mother latching her baby is the next best thing to being in the same room. Just be sure to check who is sponsoring the video clip; anything posted by a formula company is likely to be full of misinformation. There are a number of clips posted by Dr. Jack Newman and La Leche League.

Websites

There are numerous websites devoted exclusively to breastfeeding. Some are very general in nature and cover a wide range of subjects, while others are devoted to just one aspect of breastfeeding. Some websites also have breastfeeding discussion boards or forums where you can find other women facing the same issues and share tips and receive support from the comfort of your own home.

Websites vary in the quality of information presented, so it is wise to check out anything you read with a qualified breastfeeding helper. While using a website to get information can be helpful at 0300 when you don't want to wake your LC, you shouldn't rely on diagnosing low milk supply or thrush via a website alone. Appendix B has a more extensive list of websites, covering everything from birth to medications, which are available to you 24 hours a day, seven days a week.

Support is critical to making breastfeeding successful, especially while on active duty. As was mentioned in the introduction to this book, breastfeeding on active duty takes commitment. But it takes commitment from more than just you-it requires commitment from your family, friends, spouse, and your command, as well as support from a Lactation Consultant, support groups in the community, and the military resources on base. Even the virtual community online can, and should, be committed to providing you with support. You can't and shouldn't do this alone. You need to pull together a team to help you manage your commitments to the military and make breastfeeding successful for you and your baby.

Epilogue

As a woman in the military, you understand the responsibility you owe to your co-workers, your chain of command, and your country. Breastfeeding a baby is no different. You are responsible to your baby for his health and well-being. Your co-worker in this endeavor is your baby. Working together, you will learn what is needed to make breastfeeding and employment in the military work for you both.

You will find that it is at times harder than you could ever imagine, and you may wonder why you are doing this when it would just be "easier" to give some formula and go back to sleep. Instead, you'll put the pump flanges to your breasts one more time to pump a few more ounces of your precious breastmilk. Or you'll lose a few more minutes of sleep, so you can breastfeed your baby in the middle of the night because it is the one time you get to snuggle and gaze at one another (and it boosts your milk supply to boot). You'll continue to express your milk at work, even if your co-workers make jokes or you have to find an empty stall in the latrines, because you know how important your milk is to your baby and to you as well.

Breastfeeding in the military may well be one of toughest things you will ever do. And yet in the end, for however long you manage to breastfeed while on active duty, you will find that it was worth it. To see your child grow and thrive on the milk you produce and pump day after day is a wonderful feeling. To come home after a long, 12-hour shift or FTX and sit in your favorite chair and snuggle with your sweet baby, while he pats your cheek and contentedly nurses, is a feeling of bliss like no other.

My desire and hope, as one (former) active-duty breastfeeding mother to another, is that you will find the joy and love and pride that comes with breastfeeding your baby while on active-duty. That you will find breastfeeding in the military IS

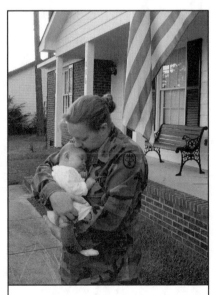

Thank you for your service to our country while breastfeeding your baby!

*Photo courtesy Judy Hany Federigan.
Used with permission.*

doable and IS worth it. Because it is. It is the best thing you will ever do for yourself and your baby.

And one more thing. I care about my sisters in uniform, so don't hesitate to drop me a line and let me know how breastfeeding in the military goes for you. I can be reached at bfincb@icloud.com. I look forward to hearing about your journey as a breastfeeding mother in combat boots.

References

Academy of Breastfeeding Medicine. (2004). *Clinical Protocol Number #8: Human Milk Storage for Home Use for Healthy Full Term Infants.* Retrieved June 22, 2010 from http://www.bfmed.org/Resources/Protocols.aspx.

American College of Obstetricians and Gynecologists. (2009). *Getting in shape after your baby is born.* Retrieved May 13, 2010 from http://www.acog.org/publications/patient_education/bp131.cfm.

American Council on Exercise. (2010). *Fit facts: Postpartum health.* Retrieved 01/13/2010, 2010, from http://www.acefitness.org/fitfacts/fitfacts_display.aspx?itemid=2602

Anderson, E., & Geden, E. (1991). Nurses' knowledge of breastfeeding. *JOGNN: Journal of Obstetric, Gynecologic & Neonatal Nursing, 20*(1), 58-64.

Appolonio, K. K., & Fingerhut, R. (2008). Postpartum depression in a military sample. *Military Medicine, 173*(11), 1085-1091.

Arora, S., McJunkin, C., Wehrer, J., & Kuhn, P. (2000). Major factors influencing breastfeeding rates: Mother's perception of father's attitude and milk supply. *Pediatrics, 106*(5), E67.

Baby-Friendly USA, B. (2010). U.S. *Baby-Friendly Hospitals and birth centers as of December 2009.* Retrieved Jan 30, 2010, from http://www.babyfriendlyusa.org/eng/03.html.

Ball, T. M., & Bennett, D. M. (2001). The economic impact of breastfeeding. *Pediatric Clinics of North America, 48*(1), 253-262.

Bar-Yam, N. B. (1998). Workplace lactation support, Part II: Working with the workplace. *Journal of Human Lactation, 14*(4), 321-325.

Bar-Yam, N. B., & Darby, L. (1997). Fathers and breastfeeding: A review of the literature. *Journal of Human Lactation, 13*(1), 45-50.

Bartick, M., & Reinhold, A. (2010). The burden of suboptimal breastfeeding in the United States: A pediatric cost analysis. *Pediatrics, 125*(5), e1048-1056.

Bell, M., & Ritchie, E. (2003a). Breastfeeding in the military: part I. Information and resources provided to service women. *Military Medicine, 168*(10), 807-812.

Bell, M., & Ritchie, E. (2003b). Breastfeeding in the military: Part II. Resource and policy considerations. *Military Medicine, 168*(10), 813-816.

BFUSA. (2009). *Baby-friendly hospitals and birth centers.* Retrieved December 18, 2009, from http://www.babyfriendlyusa.org/eng/03.html.

Biagioli, F. (2003). Returning to work while breastfeeding. *American Family Physician, 68*(11), 2201-2222.

Bostock, D. (2001). *Breastfeeding issues in the military population*. Washington, DC: Uniformed Services University of Health Sciences.

Bristow, K. M. (1999). *Barriers and facilitators of breastfeeding for primiparous active duty military mothers: A qualitative study*. Bethesda, MD: Uniformed Services University of Health Sciences.

Carey, G. B., & Quinn, T. J. (2003). Effects of exercise on lactation in women. *International SportMed Journal, 4*(6), 1-9.

Centers for Disease Control. (2009, October 20, 2009). *Breastfeeding FAQs*. Retrieved March 25, 2010, from http://www.cdc.gov/breastfeeding/faq/index.htm

Chief of Naval Operations. (2007). *Management of pregnant women, naval instruction 6001.1C*. Washington DC: U.S. Department of the Navy.

Cohen, R., Mrtek, M. B., & Mrtek, R. G. (1995). Comparison of maternal absenteeism and infant illness rates among breast-feeding and formula-feeding women in two corporations. *American Journal of Health Promotion, 10*(2), 148-153.

Condon, M. (2005). Breast is best, but it could be better: What is in breastmilk that should not be? *Pediatric Nursing, 31*(4), 333.

Cotterman, K. (2004). Reverse pressure softening: A simple tool to prepare areola for easier latching during engorgement. *Journal of Human Lactation, 20*(2), 227.

Dennis, C. (2002). Breastfeeding peer support: Maternal and volunteer perceptions from a randomized controlled trial. *Birth: Issues in Perinatal Care, 29*(3), 169-176.

Dennis, C., & McQueen, K. (2009). The relationship between infant-feeding outcomes and postpartum depression: A qualitative systematic review. *Pediatrics, 123*(4), e736.

Department of Defense. (2003). 1010.10 *Health Promotion and Disease/Injury Prevention*. Retrieved on May 13, 2010 from http://www.dtic.mil/whs/directives/corres/pdf/101010p.pdf.

Dewey, K., Heinig, M., & Nommsen, L. (1993). Maternal weight-loss patterns during prolonged lactation. *American Journal of Clinical Nutrition, 58*(2), 162-166.

DiGirolamo, A., Manninen, D., Cohen, J., Shealy, K., Murphy, P., MacGowan, C., et al. (2008). Breastfeeding-related maternity practices at hospitals and birth centers—United States, 2007. *MMWR, 57*, 621-625.

Divers Alert Network. (2010). *Diving and breastfeeding FAQ*. Retrieved Jan 23, 2010, from http://www.diversalertnetwork.org/medical/faq/faq.aspx?faqid=105

Dòrea, J. (2009). Breastfeeding is an essential complement to vaccination. *Acta Pædiatrica, 98*(8), 1244-1250.

Ekström, A., Widström, A-M., & Nissen, E. (2003). Breastfeeding support from partners and grandmothers: Perceptions of Swedish women. *Birth, 30*(4), 261.

Evans, M. A., & Rosen, L. (1997). Pregnancy planning and the impact on work climate, psychological well-being, and work effort in the military. *Journal of Occupational Health Psychology, 2*(4), 353-361.

Evans, M. A., & Rosen, L. N. (2000). Demographic and psychosocial risk factors for preterm delivery in an active duty pregnant population. *Military Medicine, 165*(1), 49-53.

FDA. (2008). *Tattooing & permanent makeup.* Retrieved September 10, 2009, from http://www.fda.gov/Cosmetics/ProductandIngredientSafety/ProductInformation/ucm108530.htm.

Federal Aviation Administration. (2010). *Altitude decompression sickness.* Retrieved May 18, 2010, from http://www.faa.gov/pilots/safety/pilotsafetybrochures/media/dcs.pdf

Fisher, J., Mahle, D., Bankston, L., Greene, R., & Gearhart, J. (1997). Lactational transfer of volatile chemicals in breast milk. *American Industrial Hygiene Association Journal, 58*(6), 425.

Forbes, J., Weiss, D., & Folen, R. (1992). The cosleeping habits of military children. *Military Medicine, 157*(4), 196.

Frederick, I., & Auerbach, K. (1985). Maternal-infant separation and breast-feeding. The return to work or school. *The Journal of Reproductive Medicine, 30*(7), 523.

Gartner, L. M., Morton, J., Lawrence, R. A., Naylor, A. J., O'Hare, D., Schanler, R. J., et al. (2005). Breastfeeding and the use of human milk. *Pediatrics, 115*(2), 496-506.

Geddes, D. (2009). The use of ultrasound to identify milk ejection in women: tips and pitfalls. *International Breastfeeding Journal, 4*(1), 5.

Giroux, D., Lapointe, G., & Baril, M. (1992). Toxicological index and the presence in the workplace of chemical hazards for workers who breast-feed infants. *American Industrial Hygiene Association Journal, 53*(7), 471-474.

Grassley, J., & Eschiti, V. (2008). Grandmother breastfeeding support: What do mothers need and want? *Birth: Issues in Perinatal Care, 35*(4), 329-335.

Grizzard, T. A., Bartick, M., Nikolov, M., Griffin, B. A., & Lee, K. G. (2006). Policies and practices related to breastfeeding in Massachusetts: Hospital implementation of the Ten Steps to Successful Breastfeeding. *Maternal & Child Health Journal, 10*(3), 247-263.

Groer, M., & Davis, M. (2006). Cytokines, infections, stress, and dysphoric moods in breastfeeders and formula feeders. *JOGNN, 35*(5), 599.

Groer, M. W., Davis, M. W., & Hemphill, J. (2002). Postpartum stress: Current concepts and the possible protective role of breastfeeding. *Journal of Obstetric, Gynecologic, and Neonatal Nursing, 31*(4), 411-417.

Guendelman, S., Kosa, J. L., Pearl, M., Graham, S., Goodman, J., & Kharrazi, M. (2009). Juggling work and breastfeeding: Effects of maternity leave and occupational characteristics. *Pediatrics, 123*(1), e38-46.

Haas, D. M., Howard, C. S., Christopher, M., Rowan, K., Broga, M. C., & Corey, T. (2006). Assessment of breastfeeding practices and reasons for success in a military community hospital. *Journal of Human Lactation, 22*(4), 439-445.

Hale, T. W. (2008). *Medications and mothers' milk.* Amarillo, TX: Hale Publishing.

Hanna, N., Ahmed, K., Anwar, M., Petrova, A., Hiatt, M., & Hegyi, T. (2004). Effect of storage on breastmilk antioxidant activity. *Archives of Disease in Childhood Fetal and Neonatal Edition, 89*(6), F518.

Hellings, P., & Howe, C. (2004). Breastfeeding knowledge and practice of pediatric nurse practitioners. *Journal Of Pediatric Health Care: Official Publication of National Association of Pediatric Nurse Associates & Practitioners, 18*(1), 8-14.

Hills-Bonczyk, S. G., Avery, M. D., Savik, K., Potter, S., & Duckett, L. J. (1993). Women's experiences with combining breast-feeding and employment. *Journal of Nurse-Midwifery, 38*(5), 257-266.

Hochhausen, A. K. (2001). *The lived experiences of military women who discontinued breastfeeding before planned: A Heideggerian hermenutic analysis.* TriServices Nursing Research Initiative.

Horta, B., Bahl, R., Martines, J., & Victora, C. (2007). *Evidence on the long-term effects of breastfeeding.* Geneva: World Health Organization.

Hudson, K. L. (2009). *Living canvas : Your total guide to tattoos, piercing, and body modification.* Berkeley, CA: Seal Press: Distributed by Publishers Group West.

Hunziker, U. A., & Barr, R. G. (1986). Increased carrying reduces infant crying: A randomized controlled trial. *Pediatrics, 77*(5), 641-648.

Institute of Medicine. (1991). *Nutrition during lactation.* Washington, D.C.: National Academy Press.

Ip, S., Chung, M., Raman, G., Chew, P., Magula, N., DeVine, D., et al. (2007). Breastfeeding and maternal and infant health outcomes in developed countries. *Evidence Report/ Technology Assessment, 153*, 1.

Jones, E., Dimmock, P., & Spencer, S. (2001). A randomised controlled trial to compare methods of milk expression after preterm delivery. *British Medical Journal, 85*(2), F91.

Jones, N., McFall, B., & Diego, M. (2004). Patterns of brain electrical activity in infants of depressed mothers who breastfeed and bottle feed: The mediating role of infant temperament. *Biological psychology, 67*(1-2), 103-124.

Kellogg, J., & Jones, L. (2004, Spring). Merging motherhood with the military. *Breastfeeding Best for Baby and Mother.* Retrieved September 20, 2005, from http://www.aap.org/advocacy/bf/newsletter3104.pdf

Kendall-Tackett, K. (2007). A new paradigm for depression in new mothers: The central role of inflammation and how breastfeeding and anti-inflammatory treatments protect maternal mental health. *International Breastfeeding Journal, 2*(1), 6.

Kendall-Tackett, K., & Hale, T. W. (2009). Survey of mothers' sleep and fatigue: Preliminary findings. Department of Pediatrics, Texas Tech University School of Medicine.

Kendall-Tackett, K. A. (2010). *Depression in new mothers: Causes, consequences, and treatment alternatives* (2nd ed.). London: Routledge.

Kent, J., Mitoulas, L., Cox, D., Owens, R., & Hartmann, P. (1999). Breast volume and milk production during extended lactation in women. *Experimental Physiology, 84*(2), 435-447.

Kent, J. C., Mitoulas, L.R., Cregan, M.D., Ramsay, D.T., Doherty, D.A., & Hartmann, P.E. (2006). Volume and frequency of breastfeedings and fat content of breast milk throughout the day. *Pediatrics, 117,* e387-3395.

Kent, J., Ramsay, D., Doherty, D., Larsson, M., & Hartmann, P. (2003). Response of breasts to different stimulation patterns of an electric breast pump. *Journal of Human Lactation, 19*(2), 179.

Klitsch, M. (1995). MDs lack lactation knowledge. *Family Planning Perspectives, 27*(2), 53.

Kramer, M., Aboud, F., Mironova, E., Vanilovich, I., Platt, R., Matush, L., et al. (2008). Promotion of Breastfeeding Intervention Trial (PROBIT) Study Group. Breastfeeding and child cognitive development: New evidence from a large randomized trial. *Archives of General Psychiatry, 65*(5), 578-584.

Krueger, M. V. (2002). *Barriers to breastfeeding experienced by active duty soldiers.* Seattle, WA: University of Washington.

La Leche League International, L. (2008). *Storing human milk.* Schaumburg, IL: La Leche League International.

Lawrence, R. A., & Lawrence, R. M. (2005). *Breastfeeding: A guide for the medical profession* (6th ed.). St. Louis: Mosby.

Leach, G. J., & Metker, L. W. (1993). Occupational health: The soldier and the industrial base. In D. P. Deeter & J. C. Gaydos (Eds.), *Textbook of military medicine. Part III, Military preventive medicine and the environment v. 2* (pp. xv, 637 p.). Aberdeen Proving Grounds, Md.

Madlon-Kay, D. J., & Carr, R. J. (1988). The effect of decreasing maternity leave on breast-feeding patterns. *Family Medicine, 20*(3), 220-221.

Manning, L. (2005). *Women in the military: Where they stand* (5th ed.). Washington, DC: Women's Research and Education Institute.

Martin, J., Hamilton, B., Sutton, P., Ventura, S., Menacker, F., Kirmeyer, S., et al. (2009). National vital statistics reports. *National Vital Statistics Reports, 57*(7).

McCrory, M. A. (2000). Aerobic exercise during lactation: Safe, healthful, and compatible. *Journal of Human Lactation, 16*(2), 95-98.

McGrath, S., & Kennell, J. (2008). A randomized controlled trial of continuous labor support for middle-class couples: Effect on cesarean delivery rates. *Obstetrical & Gynecological Survey, 63*(10), 620.

McKenna, J., & McDade, T. (2005). Why babies should never sleep alone: A review of the co-sleeping controversy in relation to SIDS, bedsharing and breast feeding. *Paediatric Respiratory Reviews, 6*(2), 134-152.

McNeary, A. M., & Lomenick, T. S. (2000). Military duty: Risk factor for preterm labor? A review. *Military Medicine, 165*(8), 612-615.

Mennella, J., Jagnow, C., & Beauchamp, G. (2001). Prenatal and postnatal flavor learning by human infants. *Pediatrics, 107*(6), e88.

Mitoulas, L., Lai, C., Gurrin, L., Larsson, M., & Hartmann, P. (2002). Efficacy of breastmilk expression using an electric breast pump. *Journal of Human Lactation, 18*(4), 344.

Mohrbacher, N., & Stock, J. (2003). *The breastfeeding answer book* (3rd rev. ed.). Schaumburg, IL.: La Leche League International.

Nathavitharana, K. A., Catty, D., & McNeish, A. S. (1994). IgA antibodies in human milk: Epidemiological markers of previous infections? *Archives of Disease in Childhood. Fetal and Neonatal Edition, 71*(3), F192-197.

Navy Environmental Health Center. (2008). *Reproductive and developmental hazards: A guide for occupational health professionals.* Norfolk, VA: Navy Environmental Health Center.

Newcomb, P., Storer, B., Longnecker, M., Mittendorf, R., Greenberg, E., Clapp, R., et al. (1994). Lactation and a reduced risk of premenopausal breast cancer. *New England Journal of Medicine, 330*(2), 81.

O'Boyle, A. L., Magann, E. F., Ricks Jr, R. E., Doyle, M., & Morrison, J. C. (2005). Depression screening in the Pregnant Soldier Wellness Program. *Southern Medical Journal, 98*(4), 416-418.

Occupational Health & Safety Administration. (1992). *Breastmilk does not constitute occupational exposure as defined by standard.* Retrieved March 25, 2010, from http://www.osha.gov/pls/oshaweb/owadisp.show_document?p_table=INTERPRETATIONS&p_id=20952

Palmer, B. (1998). The influence of breastfeeding on the development of the oral cavity: A commentary. *Journal of Human Lactation, 14*(2), 93-98.

Palmer, G. (2009). *The politics of breastfeeding: When breasts are bad for business* (3rd updated and rev. ed.). London: Pinter & Martin.

Peterson, A. & Harmer, M. (2010). *Balancing breast and bottle: Reaching your breastfeeding goals.* Amarillo, TX: Hale Publishing, L.P.

Pisacane, A., Continisio, G. I., Aldinucci, M., D'Amora, S., & Continisio, P. (2005). A controlled trial of the father's role in breastfeeding promotion. *Pediatrics, 116*(4), e494-498.

Quillin, S., & Glenn, L. (2004). Interaction between feeding method and co-sleeping on maternal-newborn sleep. *Journal of Obstetric, Gynecologic, and Neonatal Nursing, 33*, 580-588.

Raj, V., & Plichta, S. (1998). The role of social support in breastfeeding promotion: A literature review. *Journal of Human Lactation, 14*(1), 41.

Ransjo-Arvidson, A., Matthiesen, A., Lilja, G., Nissen, E., Widstrom, A., & Uvnas-Moberg, K. (2001). Maternal analgesia during labor disturbs newborn behavior: Effects on breastfeeding, temperature, and crying. *Birth, 28*(1), 5-12.

Reardon, J. (2008). *The complete idiot's guide to getting a tattoo.* New York: Penguin.

Rishel, P. E., & Sweeney, P. (2005). Comparison of breastfeeding rates among women delivering infants in military treatment facilities with and without lactation consultants. *Military Medicine, 170*(5), 435-438.

Ritchie, G., Still, K., Rossi Iii, J., Bekkedal, M., Bobb, A., & Arfsten, D. (2003). Biological and health effects of exposure to kerosene-based jet fuels and performance additives. *Journal of Toxicology & Environmental Health: Part B, 6*(4), 357.

Roche-Paull, R. (2009). Body modifications and breasfeeding. *New Beginnings, 29*(4), 4-8.

Roche-Paull, R. (2010). *Breastfeeding in combat boots fan page.* Retrieved Febuary 20, 2010, from http://www.facebook.com/BreastfeedinginCombatBoots

Rosenberg, K. D., Stull, J. D., Adler, M. R., Kasehagen, L. J., & Crivelli-Kovach, A. (2008). Impact of hospital policies on breastfeeding outcomes. *Breastfeeding Medicine: The Official Journal Of The Academy Of Breastfeeding Medicine, 3*(2), 110-116.

Rychnovsky, J., & Beck, C. T. (2006). Screening for postpartum depression in military women with the Postpartum Depression Screening Scale. *Military Medicine, 171*(11), 1100-1104.

Rychnovsky, J. D. (2007). Postpartum fatigue in the active-duty military woman. *JOGNN: Journal of Obstetric, Gynecologic & Neonatal Nursing, 36*(1), 38-46.

Ryon, R. S. (2008). *A touring mom's survival guide.* Unpublished manuscript.

Schaefer, C. (2007). *Drugs during pregnancy and lactation: Treatment options and risk assessment* (2nd Ed.). Amsterdam: Elsevier.

Schumer, C. E., & Maloney, C. (2007). *Helping military moms balance family and longer deployments.* Retrieved from http://jec.senate.gov/archive/Documents/Reports/MilitaryMoms05.11.07Final.pdf.

Simkin, P., & O'Hara, M. (2002). Nonpharmacologic relief of pain during labor: Systematic reviews of five methods. *American Journal of Obstetrics and Gynecology, 186*(5), S131-S159.

Simmer, K., Patole, S. K., & Rao, S. C. (2008). Longchain polyunsaturated fatty acid supplementation in infants born at term. *Cochrane Database Syst Rev*(1), CD000376.

Smillie, C. M. (2008). How infants learn to feed: A neurobehavioral model. In C. W. Genna (Ed.), *Supporting sucking skills in breastfeeding infants* (pp. 79-95). Sudbury, MA.: Jones and Bartlett Publishers.

Smith, L. J. (1998). *Don't shake the milk.* Retrieved March 25, 2010, from http://www.bflrc.com/ljs/breastfeeding/shakenot.htm

Smith, L. J. (2010). *Impact of birthing practices on breastfeeding* (2nd Ed.). Sudbury, MA: Jones and Bartlett.

Stevens, K. V., & Janke, J. (2003). Breastfeeding experiences of active duty military women. *Military Medicine, 168*(5), 380-384.

Stuart-Macadam, P., & Dettwyler, K. A. (1995). *Breastfeeding: Biocultural perspectives.* New York: Aldine De Gruyter.

Stuebe, A. (2009). The risks of not breastfeeding for mothers and infants. *Reviews in Obstetrics and Gynecology, 2*(4), 222-231.

Stuebe, A., Rich-Edwards, J., Willett, W., Manson, J., & Michels, K. (2005). Duration of lactation and incidence of type-2 diabetes. *JAMA, 294*(20), 2601.

Sykora, W. S. (1995). *Barriers to breastfeeding among active-duty military personnel: A qualitative study.* Unpublished faculty development fellowship presentation, University of North Carolina, Chapel Hill.

Szucs, K. A., Miracle, D. J., & Rosenman, M. B. (2009). Breastfeeding knowledge, attitudes, and practices among providers in a medical home. *Breastfeeding Medicine: The Official Journal Of The Academy Of Breastfeeding Medicine, 4*(1), 31-42.

Taveras, E. M., Li, R., Grummer-Strawn, L., Richardson, M., Marshall, R., Rego, V. H., et al. (2004). Opinions and practices of clinicians associated with continuation of exclusive breastfeeding. *Pediatrics, 113*(4), e283-290.

Tohotoa, J., Maycock, B., Hauck, Y., Howat, P., Burns, S., & Binns, C. (2009). Dads make a difference: An exploratory study of paternal support for breastfeeding in Perth, Western Australia. *International Breastfeeding Journal, 4*(1), 15.

Tully, M. (2000). Recommendations for handling of mother's own milk. *Journal of Human Lactation, 16*(2), 149.

U.S. Army Center for Health Promotion and Preventative Medicine. (March 1, 2010) *Reproductive and Developmental Hazards.* Power Point retrieved from http://chppm-www.apgea.army.mil/dhpw/Readiness/ReproductiveAndDevelopmentalHazards.PPT

U.S. Army Center for Health Promotion and Preventative Medicine. (2001a). *FAQ-Lead Exposure.* http://chppm-www.apgea.army.mil/documents/FACT/65-015-0503.pdf

U.S. Army Center for Health Promotion and Preventative Medicine, C. (2001b). *Just the Facts-Solvents.* Retrieved from http://chppm-www.apgea.army.mil/documents/FACT/65-018-0503.pdf.

U.S. Army Center for Health Promotion and Preventative Medicine, C. (2001c). *Just the Facts: Guidelines for Controlling Occupational Exposure to Hazardous Drugs.* http://chppm-www.apgea.army.mil/documents/FACT/56-033.pdf.

U.S. Army Center for Health Promotion and Preventative Medicine, C. (2002). *Fact Sheet JP-8*. Retrieved from http://chppm-www.apgea.army.mil/documents/FACT/65-028-0503.pdf.

UNICEF, W. (2003). *Global strategy for infant and young child feeding*. WHO: Geneva: World Health Organization.

United States Breastfeeding Committee. (2002). *Economic benefits of breastfeeding*. Retrieved July 28, 2006 from http://www.usbreastfeeding.org/LinkClick.aspx?link=publication s%2FEconomic-Benefits-2002-USBC.pdf&tabid=70&mid=388.

Uriell, Z., Perry, A., Kee, A., & Burress, L. (2009). Breastfeeding in the Navy: Estimates of rate, duration, and perceived support. *Military Medicine, 174*(3), 290-296.

Vanderlaan, J. (1990). *The breast feeding experiances of military women*. Seattle: University of Washington.

Vennemann, M., Bajanowski, T., Brinkmann, B., Jorch, G., Yucesan, K., Sauerland, C., et al. (2009). Does breastfeeding reduce the risk of sudden infant death syndrome? *Pediatrics, 123*(3), e406.

Wallace, J. P., Inbar, G., & Ernsthausen, K. (1992). Infant acceptance of postexercise breastmilk. *Pediatrics, 89*(6 Pt 2), 1245-1247.

Williamson, M. T., & Murti, P. K. (1996). Effects of storage, time, temperature, and composition of containers on biologic components of human milk. *Journal of Human Lactation, 12*(1), 31-35.

Wolfberg, A. J., Michels, K. B., Shields, W., O'Campo, P., Bronner, Y., & Bienstock, J. (2004). Dads as breastfeeding advocates: Results from a randomized controlled trial of an educational intervention. *American Journal of Obstetrics and Gynecology, 191*(3), 708-712.

World Health Organization. (2009). *Infant and young child feeding: Model chapter for textbooks for medical students and allied health professionals*. Geneva: World Health Organization.

Wright, K. S., Quinn, T. J., & Carey, G. B. (2002). Infant acceptance of breastmilk after maternal exercise. *Pediatrics, 109*(4), 585.

Zoppou, C., Barry, S., & Mercer, G. (1997). Comparing breastfeeding and breast pumps using a computer model. *Journal of Human Lactation, 13*(3), 195.

Appendix A
Books

Pregnancy & Birth

Your Best Birth by Rikki Lake and Abby Epstein

Doula's Guide to Birthing Your Way by Jan S. Mallak, 2LAS, ICCE-CD-CPD, IAT, CD-PCD (DONA), CPD (CAPPA) and Teresa F Bailey, J.D., M.L.S., CD (DONA), LLLL

Breastfeeding

The Womanly Art of Breastfeeding by La Leche League International

Breastfeeding Made Simple: Seven Natural Laws for Nursing Mothers, 2nd Edition. by Nancy Mohrbacher, IBCLC and Kathleen Kendall-Tackett, PhD., IBCLC

The Ultimate Breastfeeding Book of Answers by Jack Newman, MD, IBCLC & Teresa Pitman

Balancing Breast and Bottle: Reaching Your Breastfeeding Goals by Amy Peterson, IBCLC and Mindy Harmon, MA, CCC-SLP

The Breastfeeding Mothers Guide to Making More Milk by Diana West, IBCLC and Lisa Marasco, MA, IBCLC

Working & Breastfeeding

Hirkani's Daughters: Women Who Scale Modern Mountain to Combine Breastfeeding and Working by Jennifer Hicks

Nursing Mother, Working Mother: The Essential Guide for Breastfeeding and Staying Close To Your Baby After You Return to Work by Gale Pryor

Working Without Weaning: A Working Mother's Guide to Breastfeeding by Kirsten Berggren

Sleeping

Good Nights by Jay Gordon, MD

The Baby Sleep Book by William Sears, Martha Sears, Robert Sears, and James Sears

The No Cry Sleep Solution by Elizabeth Pantley

PPD

Depression in New Mothers, 2nd Ed. by Kathleen Kendall-Tackett, PhD, IBCLC

Appendix B
Website Resources

Breastfeeding Information and Support

Breastfeeding in Combat Boots – My own website that is devoted completely to breastfeeding in the military. Site offers FAQs, links to helpful sites, a blog, and forums for discussing breastfeeding concerns with other breastfeeding military mothers. www.breastfeedingincombatboots.com

Balancing Breast and Bottle – This is the companion website to the book, *Balancing Breast and Bottle: Reaching Your Breastfeeding Goals*, and has information about how best to manage bottle-feeding while preserving breastfeeding. www.breastandbottlefeeding.com

Breastfeeding.com – This is a very popular site for breastfeeding information, Q&A with an Expert, discussion boards, videos, chat rooms, fun stuff, and a LC directory. www.breastfeeding.com

Breastfeeding Made Simple – Just as the title implies, this site (and book) present breastfeeding as the biological norm and that breastfeeding is much simpler if mothers follow the "Seven Natural Laws" of breastfeeding. This site has a wealth of links to breastfeeding information. www. breastfeedingmadesimple.com

International Lactation Consultants Association – ILCA is the professional organization for IBCLCs. If you need to find an IBCLC in your area, go to this website and click on "Find a LC" link. From there you will be given a listing of the IBCLC's in your area. A Board Certified Lactation Consultant is worth her weight in gold. www.ilca.org

Kellymom.com – This is the clearinghouse of breastfeeding information on the web. Kelly is an IBCLC. She thoroughly researches all of the breastfeeding information she posts and keeps it up-to-date. If you can't find it here, it probably hasn't been written about yet! www.kellymom.com

La Leche League International – LLL is the "Mother" of all breastfeeding sites. LLL offers a wide range of information for mothers who work outside the home. Many LLL Groups can be found around the globe, and those overseas are often found on or near military bases. You can find a listing of

Groups, Leaders, Warmlines in your area, chat boards, and lots of information at this great website. www.llli.org

Nursing Mothers Counsel – NMC is a nonprofit organization that helps mothers to have a normal breastfeeding relationship by providing information and support. www.nursingmothers.org

Promom – If you are looking for down and dirty reasons why you should breastfeed, this is your site. Promom offers 101 reasons to breastfeed, many breastfeeding articles and related links, as well as a plethora of other advocacy resources. www.promom.org

Work and Pump – This is an older site, but still very relevant for the working mother. While not military specific, many of the tips and tricks still apply or can be modified to suit the military mother going back to work at six weeks. www.workandpump.com

Childbirth

DONA – DONA International provides information and research about birth and postpartum doulas, childbirth, and the postpartum experience, as well as training for those interested in becoming a doula. www.dona.org

Mother's Advocate – Handouts and videos covering evidence-based childbirth practices so that you can have the healthiest, safest and most satisfying birth possible. www.injoyvideos.com/mothersadvocate/

My Best Birth – Companion website to the book, Your Best Birth, with numerous resources to help you have the birth you want. www.mybestbirth. com

Government

CDC – Centers for Disease Control provides information about national and state rates of breastfeeding, FAQs, and link to other breastfeeding resources. www.cdc.gov

DHHS OWH – Department of Health and Human Services, Office of Women's Health offers breastfeeding information, a helpline, and FAQ's in English and Spanish. www.4women.gov

WIC – Special Supplemental Nutrition Program for Women, Infants, and Children provides food, health-care referrals and nutrition education for low-income pregnant and breastfeeding mothers and children up to age five.

The website has breastfeeding information, as well as how to apply for WIC services. www.fns.usda.gov/wic

Medical and Health Organizations

AAP – American Academy of Pediatrics website offers information on a variety of parenting topics, including breastfeeding and human milk. www.aap.org

BFHI – Baby Friendly Hospital Initiative website offers information on the global program to encourage and recognize those hospitals that provide optimal care for breastfeeding mothers and babies. www.babyfriendlyusa.org

HMBANA – Human Milk Banking Association of North America website provides information on how to contact a milk bank to either donate milk or order screened and processed breastmilk. www.hmbana.org

WHO – World Health Organization website offers breastfeeding information, as well as growth charts based solely on breastfed babies reflecting a more accurate measurement. www.who.int/childgrowth/

Other

Attachment Parenting International – Organization whose mission is to educate and support parents in raising attached, empathetic children. www.attachmentparenting.org/

Babywearing International – International organization dedicated to providing accurate and evidence-based information on the benefits and proper way to wear your baby. www.babywearinginternational.org/

LACTMED – A free online database of information regarding drugs and medications and lactation run by the National Library of Medicine's Toxicological Data Network. www.toxnet.nlm.nih.gov

Mothering Multiples – Website devoted to successfully breastfeeding twins, with information, resources, and support. www.karengromada.com/karengromada/faq.htm

Postpartum Support International – Organization devoted to increasing awareness of pre and postnatal depression. Provides information, resources, and support. www.postpartum.net

Mother-Baby Behavioral Sleep Laboratory – Home of Dr. McKenna's research and articles on safe co-sleeping with your baby. www.nd.edu/~jmckenn1/lab/safe.html

Blogs

Motherwear Breastfeeding Blog – One of the oldest and best-run breastfeeding blogs. http://breastfeeding.blog.motherwear.com/

Blacktating – A breastfeeding blog for women of color. www.blacktating.com

Best for Babes – An advocacy and informative blog detailing the need to make breastfeeding normal and how to find help and support for breastfeeding. www.bestforbabes.org

Product Websites

Ameda – Manufactures quality hospital-grade and personal use breast pumps, as well as personal breastfeeding accessories. Order online or through local LC's and retailers. www.ameda.com

Medela – Manufactures quality hospital-grade and personal use breast pumps, as well as personal breastfeeding accessories. Order online or through local LC's and retailers. www.medela.com

Hygeia – New pump company that carries "green" recyclable personal use and hospital-grade pumps. www.hygeiababy.com

PJ's Limerick – Carries lightweight, portable hospital-grade pumps that double as personal use pumps. www.limerickinc.com

Freemie – A new system for hands-free pumping, using the pump you already own. www.freemie.com

Bravado Bras – The leader in nursing bras, these bras are stylish, supportive, and will last for years. www.bravadodesigns.com

Easy Expression Bustier – Hands-free pumping bras to make pumping easier. www.easyexpressionproducts.com

Lily Padz – Invisible, reusable, silicone breast pads to wear under your uniform, prevents leaking. www.lilypadz.com

MilkMate – Bottle rack system that always keeps milk in order of pumping date. www.mothersmilkmate.com

Pumping Pals – Angled breastpump flanges and hands-free strap system for more comfortable pumping. www.pumpinpal.com

Sensible Lines Milk Trays – Neither a bottle nor a bag, these are trays to freeze your milk in one ounce servings. The frozen "milk sticks" drop right into a bottle. www.sensiblelines.com

Military Websites

Air Force Aid Society – Emergency funds and Budgeting for Baby classes available. www.afas.org

Army Emergency Relief – Emergency funds and resources. www.aerhq.org/

Coast Guard Mutual Assistance – Emergency funds and resources, including a baby layette. www.cgmahq.org/

Military One Source – One stop resource for military information and support, including parenting resources. www.militaryonesource.com

Mom2Mom – Army breastfeeding support group, available at some installations. http://chppm-www.apgea.army.mil/dhpw/population/M2MWebPage. aspx

New Parent Support Program/Team –DOD-mandated parenting program available to all services, offering parenting information and skills from prenatal through age 5. http://www.militaryhomefront.dod.mil/tf/newparentsupport

NMCRS – The Navy and Marine Corps Relief Society has a Budgeting for Baby class and a Visiting Nurse program. http://www.nmcrs.org/index.html

Appendix C
Choosing Your Breastfeeding Support Person

You and your baby deserve the best care when it comes to breastfeeding help. There are many different levels of breastfeeding support available to you as a consumer. Of the many "Breastfeeding Helpers" to choose from, each will have varying levels of expertise and training. The different titles reflect the type of training she (or he) has received; however, correct titles are often misused, making choosing the proper breastfeeding support person very confusing and difficult.

IBCLC. International Board Certified Lactation Consultant. This is the gold standard of breastfeeding care. An IBCLC, also known as a lactation consultant, is a professional who has received the highest level of education and training and possesses the knowledge and skill to help mothers with even the most difficult breastfeeding situations. To use the letters IBCLC after their name, she/he must pass a rigorous international credentialing exam. To be eligible to even sit for the exam, she/he must have extensive education (usually a four-year degree) and many years of experience working with breastfeeding mothers. To retain the IBCLC credential, she/he must attend conferences and earn continuing education credits. Lactation consultants can also be doctors, nurses, midwives, dieticians, or speech therapists, and they work in hospitals, clinics, or in private practice. IBCLCs often have an area of expertise (such as working mothers or cleft palate babies), so you should look around for one that fits your needs. Generally, lactation consultants charge for their services (TRICARE does not cover lactation consultations). Visit www.ilca.org to find a lactation consultant near you.

Lactation Educator/Counselor/Specialist. Also known as a CLC or CLE, this individual has generally taken one or more short-term breastfeeding courses and may have received a local or national certification. She/he is capable of teaching mothers about breastfeeding and helping with normal problems, but may or may not have the experience or expertise to help with difficult breastfeeding problems. They generally work in hospitals and clinics and may also be nurses, dieticians, or other allied healthcare workers.

La Leche League Leader. This individual is a mother who started out as a La Leche League member and has successfully breastfed for at least nine months and completed a lengthy accreditation process with extensive coursework to become a La Leche League Leader. LLL Leaders are volunteers who provide peer support by facilitating monthly support group meetings and offer breastfeeding counseling via telephone and e-mail support. Some Leaders also offer home visits. Visit www.llli.org to find a Group or Leader near you.

WIC Peer Counselor. Peer Counselors are mothers who are or have been on the WIC Program and have successfully breastfed their infants. They receive extensive training, provide peer counseling and teaching to new moms, and can often help with normal breastfeeding problems. WIC Peer Counselors generally work in WIC offices, although a few will do home or hospital visits.

No matter who you chose to help you with your breastfeeding, if you are not comfortable, or your situation does not improve within a few days, seek out another more knowledgeable expert. Here is a short checklist of questions to ask any potential breastfeeding support person, so you can better determine if she will be able to assist you properly with your situation.

- What are your qualifications?

- How long have you been practicing?

- Do you attend breastfeeding conferences and maintain your continuing education credits for recertification?

- What kind of experience do you have (hospital, private practice, newborns, older babies, working and/or military mothers)?

- Did you nurse your own children?

- Do you have an area of expertise?

- Do you follow the WHO recommendations for weaning (two years)?

- What are your hours?

- Do you offer home visits, can/will you come on base/post?

- Can mothers bring support people to the consultation?

- How long do consults generally last?

- Do you take a complete history and offer a written care plan?

- Do you offer follow-up visits or telephone support?

- How much do you charge?

- Do you offer special packages or a military discount?

Appendix D
Military Policy Resources

AIR FORCE

Air Force Instruction 44-102 (Section 4.15)
http://www.af.mil/shared/media/epubs/AFI44-102.pdf

ARMY

Guide to Female Soldier Readiness (Section X)
http://chppm-www.apgea.army.mil/documents/TG/TECHGUID/
TG281January2007-1.pdf

Breastfeeding Support Plan, Sample Memo
http://usachppm.amedd.army.mil/dhpw/population/samplebreastfeeding
memocommanderfinal0807.pdf

COAST GUARD

COMDINST M1000.6A (Chapter 9.A.4)
http://www.uscg.mil/directives/cim/1000-1999/CIM_1000_6A.pdf

MARINE CORPS

MARINE CORPS ORDER 5000.12E
Marine Corps Policy on Pregnancy and Parenthood (Section 15)
http://www.awhonn-af.org/resources/MCO5000.12E.pdf

NAVY
BUMEDINST 6000.14 Support for Service Women with Nursing Infants
http://www.med.navy.mil/directives/ExternalDirectives/6000.14.pdf

OPNAVINST 6000.1 Guidelines Concerning Pregnant Servicewomen
(Ch. 2 Section 209)
http://doni.daps.dla.mil/Directives/06000%20Medical%20and%20Dental
%20Services/06-00%20General%20Medical%20and%20Dental%20Support
%20Services/6000.1C.PDF

Policy to Support Breastfeeding and Human Lactation
http://www.awhonn-af.org/resources/6450_2.pdf

Appendix E
Military Lactation Policies

(See table, next page.)

Military Breastfeeding Policies

Branch	Deployment	Supervisors	Private Area	Time	Breast Pump Equipment	Education	Other
Air Force	• 12-month deferment from deployment after birth of child. • Remain eligible for field training and mobility exercises. BF encouraged.	Supervisors should work with AF members on a plan to continue breastfeeding.	Provide private, clean area for milk expression; restrooms are not appropriate.	• Attempt to arrange schedules to allow 15-30 minutes every 3-4 hours to express milk. • BF is not a reason for granting "excessive" time away from work.	AF members supply their own equipment and handle storage of milk. Airmen in the field may need to discard milk collected.		Contact MTF or community hospital to ask for a lactation consultant. Airmen may be exposed to environmental contaminants and should discuss with HCP or Occupational Health.
Army	• 6-month deferment from deployment after birth of the child. • Remain eligible for field training and mobility exercises. BF encouraged.	Discuss needs with supervisor or commander. *sample letter available*	Soldiers will need access to a private space.	• Mothers will need 2-3 20-minute breaks during 8-hour workday. • BF is not a reason for granting "excessive" time away from work.	Army members supply their own equipment and handle storage of milk. Soldier in the field may need to discard milk collected.	Information provided on collecting and storing human milk, using a breast pump, frequency.	Contact MTF or community hospital to ask for a lactation consultant. Soldiers may be exposed to environmental contaminants and should discuss with HCP or Occupational Health.
Coast Guard	Direct access to baby handled on a case-by-case basis.	Communicate with Commanding Officer to address concerns or issues.	Commanding Officer will ensure availability of a private, clean room for expressing milk.	BF is not a reason for granting "excessive" time away from work.	Coast Guard members supply their own equipment and handle storage of milk. Guardsman onboard ship may need to discard milk collected.		
Marine Corps	• 6-month deferment from deployment after birth of child. • Remain eligible for field training and mobility exercises. BF encouraged.	Report to chain of command as soon as possible to allow for evaluation of the workplace.	Servicewomen must be provided, at a minimum, a clean, secluded space (not a toilet space) with ready access to water source.	• Mothers will need 2-3 20-minute breaks during 8-hour workday. • BF is not a reason for granting "excessive" time away from work.	Marine members supply their own equipment and handle storage of milk. Marines in the field or onboard ship may need to discard milk collected.		Contact MTF or community hospital to ask for a lactation consultant. Marines may be exposed to environmental contaminants and should discuss with HCP or Occupational Health.

| Navy | • 12-month deferment from deployment after birth of child.
• Remain eligible for field training and mobility exercises. BF encouraged. | MTF and clinic personnel encouraged to develop plans to educate supervisors, Cos, and OICs, including child development centers. | Must provide private accommodations for breast milk expression with door that can be secured, running water accessible. | • Mothers will need 2-3 20-minute breaks during 8-hour workday.
• BF is not a reason for granting "excessive" time away from work. | Navy members supply their own equipment and handle storage of milk.

Sailors onboard ship may need to discard milk collected. | Breastfeeding education should begin at first prenatal visit.

Health care staff should be trained in breastfeeding management and counseling. | Navy strongly endorses BF for the first year of the infant's life. Free formula discouraged, and if given, must be accounted for, controlled, and issued with standard medical supply procedures.

Sailors may be exposed to environmental contaminants and should discuss with HCP or Occupational Health. |

*Note: MTF = "Medical Treatment Facility"

This is NOT an official DOD document and is neither endorsed nor approved by the DOD.

Appendix F
Memo for Breastfeeding Support Plan on Return to Duty

(See next page.)

DEPARTMENT OF THE ARMY
[COMPANY]
[UNIT]
[LOCATION]

[ATTN LINE]   [DATE]

MEMORANDUM FOR Commander,
[UNIT, AND OFFICIAL MILITARY ADDRESS]

SUBJECT: Breastfeeding work plan

1. Purpose: Provide a breastfeeding work plan to gain permission/support for
    the Soldier to breastfeed her baby upon return to duty.

    a. Meeting with supervisor to discuss breastfeeding work plan on return to
        work is scheduled for [date].

    b. Occupational Health workplace hazards consultation is scheduled for
        [date].

    c. Work schedule with the following times to pump is as follows: [insert
        specific times of day below as appropriate]

        1)   Before PT time
        2)   Morning break
        3)   Lunch
        4)   Afternoon break

    d. Use of a room [indicate location] that allows for privacy, adequate space,
        electrical outlet, and access to nearby sink.

    e. In emergencies or unusual situations, such as during field-training
        exercises or long duty days, the following processes will be implemented
        for pumping/storing/transporting. [insert what will be done, i.e., pump
        prior to FTX and freeze milk, pump during FTX and dispose of milk,
        bottle feed].

    f. Breast milk will be safely stored [explain where and how, and what has
        been done to demonstrate that the infant has adapted to feeding from an
        alternative source (i.e., nipple feeding or alternate feeding methods)].

Encl

[NAME AND SIGNATURE BLOCK]

Appendix G
OSHA Regulations

Occupational Exposures of Reproductive or Developmental Concern - Supervisor's Statement

To be completed by the supervisor for any worker with concerns regarding workplace reproductive or developmental hazards. This form should then be forwarded to appropriate medical personnel such as Occupational Medicine, OB/GYN, etc. Please attach material safety data sheets (MSDS) for any substances to which this worker is exposed. Revised 8-2008

PLEASE PRINT.

Worker's Name _____ *Last* _____ *First* _____ *m.i.*   SSN ___ — ___ — _____

Rank/Rate/Job Code _____   Date ___ ___ ___ *Day* *Month* *Year*

Supervisor _____

Command/Shop _____   Supervisor's Telephone _____   Worker's Telephone _____

Job Duties (not job title) _____

Check all boxes that apply

Workplace: ☐ Shipboard ☐ Shop ☐ Office ☐ Outdoors

☐ Other (describe): _____

Is the worker exposed to:

Chemical Agents
☐ Inorganic chemicals
☐ Organic solvents and fuels
☐ Metals - lead, cadmium, mercury, etc. (specify below)
☐ Pesticides (specify below)
☐ Pharmaceuticals/drugs (specify below)
☐ Other hazards (specify below)

Physical Agents
☐ Ionizing radiation
☐ "Noise" (intense sound)
☐ Thermal stress (heat or cold)
☐ Vibration
☐ Other hazards (specify below)

Biological Agents
☐ Bacteria ☐ Protozoa
☐ Endotoxins (aflatoxin) ☐ Viruses
☐ Other hazards (specify below)

Physical Conditions
☐ Irregular or shift work
☐ Strenuous work
☐ Other hazards (specify below)

Specify agents or conditions here

Personal Protective Equipment required:
☐ None ☐ Hearing protection ☐ Gloves
☐ Protective clothing ☐ Respirator

Is the worker required to work shifts? ☐ No ☐ Yes
If yes, which one(s)? _____

Is the worker in a medical surveillance program?
☐ No ☐ Yes ☐ Don't know

Has the worksite had an Industrial Hygiene survey in the last two years? ☐ No ☐ Yes ___ ___ ___ *Day* *Month* *Year*

Are there Industrial Hygiene sampling data for the involved worker? ☐ No ☐ Yes

Did the Industrial Hygiene survey reveal reproductive or developmental hazards? ☐ No ☐ Yes Specify

Has the worker reported an occupational illness or injury in the last year? ☐ No ☐ Yes Specify

Has a detailed evaluation of the worksite(s) and/or process(s) with which the worker is involved been performed? ☐ No ☐ Yes

Supervisor's Signature _____

Occupational Exposures of Reproductive or Developmental Concern - Worker's Statement ^{Revised 8-2008}

After your supervisor has completed the other side, please fill this out and have it with you when you see the health care professional who will help with your evaluation. **PLEASE PRINT.**

Worker's Name _____ | SSN ___ - __ - ____
Last.   First   M.I.

Rank/Rate/Job Code _____ | Today's Date | Day | Month | Year

Age ___ Sex ___ Phone (work) ( ) - Phone (home) ( ) -

Females only

Are you pregnant? Yes ___ No ___   Number of previous pregnancies ___

Date last menstrual period began _____
Day   Month   Year

Males only

How many children have you fathered (ever)? ___

All workers

How many years have you had your current job? ___

What did you do at your previous job? _____

What does your spouse or mate do at work? _____

How many were: Live births ___   Stillbirths ___   Miscarriages ___   Abortions ___

Have you ever gotten sick or injured because of your job? No ___ Yes ___

Have any of your children had birth defects? No ___ Yes ___

Do you have any illnesses you see the doctor for regularly? No ___ Yes ___

Do you take medications regularly? No ___ Yes ___

Do you use any other drugs, including tobacco? No ___ Yes ___

Give details of any "yes" answers here

How much alcohol do you usually drink per week? ___ < 6 drinks ___ 6 to 14 ___ 15 to 21 ___ 22 or more ___

Reason for consultation _____

What reproductive or developmental hazards are you most concerned about? _____

In your activities at home, recreation, hobbies, second job, etc., are you exposed to any of the following? (check all that apply)

Chemical Agents
- [ ] Inorganic chemicals
- [ ] Organic solvents and fuels
- [ ] Metals (lead, cadmium, etc.)
- [ ] Pesticides
- [ ] Pharmaceuticals/drugs
- [ ] Other hazards (specify) _____

Physical Agents
- [ ] Ionizing radiation
- [ ] "Noise" (intense sound)
- [ ] Thermal stress (heat or cold)
- [ ] Vibration

Biological Agents
- [ ] Bacteria
- [ ] Endotoxins (aflatoxin)
- [ ] Protozoa
- [ ] Viruses

Physical Conditions
- [ ] Irregular or shift work
- [ ] Strenuous work

- [ ] None of the above

Worker's Signature _____

Appendix H
Childcare Provider Checklist and Journal

(The following two forms were excerpted from *Balancing Breast and Bottle: Reaching Your Breastfeeding Goals* by Amy Peterson and Mindy Harmer. Reprinted with permission.)

How to Feed My Baby

My Baby: _____   Age:_____

1. Brand of nipple and/or feeding system my baby uses:_____

2. Counting from the beginning of a feeding, my baby usually eats every _____ hours. When s/he roots and eats his hands, feel free to feed him if s/he is hungry.

3. Gently swirl the bottle of milk before feeding the baby to redistribute fat in the milk. <u>Do not shake the breastmilk.</u>

4. If I have time to pump before bringing my baby, you will find my baby's first bottle stored in the diaper bag at room temperature. Please do not refrigerate this first bottle.

5. Other bottles need to be refrigerated or frozen until feeding time.

6. To defrost a bottle of milk, please
   - ☐ hold the bottle under warm (not hot) water
   - ☐ place in a dish of warm water 30 minutes before a feeding
   - ☐ use the bottle warmer I provided

7. It is / is not necessary to warm my baby's bottle.

8. My baby eats about _____ ounces for daytime feedings. If my baby would like more, please pour 1 additional ounce of breastmilk into the bottle to offer.

9. If my baby does not finish a feeding, please:
   - ☐ discard
   - ☐ put the bottle in the refrigerator and offer it again within four hours; discard if the next feeding is after four hours.

10. If my baby would like a bottle within one hour of being picked up, please offer a smaller quantity "end-of-the-day" bottle.

My Baby Ate Journal

Please fill in this journal on the days circled because it will help me send the right amount of milk, and also let me know when it is time to adjust my baby's nipple size.

Baby's name:_____

Monday	Time offered	How long feeding lasted	Amount eaten	Leftovers	Amount added
1st feeding					
2nd feeding					
3rd feeding					
4th feeding					

Comments:

Tuesday	Time offered	How long feeding lasted	Amount eaten	Leftovers	Amount added
1st feeding					
2nd feeding					
3rd feeding					
4th feeding					

Comments:

Wednesday	Time offered	How long feeding lasted	Amount eaten	Leftovers	Amount added
1st feeding					
2nd feeding					
3rd feeding					
4th feeding					

Comments:

Thursday	Time offered	How long feeding lasted	Amount eaten	Leftovers	Amount added
1st feeding					
2nd feeding					
3rd feeding					
4th feeding					

Comments:

Friday	Time offered	How long feeding lasted	Amount eaten	Leftovers	Amount added
1st feeding					
2nd feeding					
3rd feeding					
4th feeding					

Comments:

Appendix I
Checklist for Work

Items for Work/Duty

- Breast pump with all parts and tubing
    - ° Extra set of flanges, tubing, membranes
- Two bottles or collection bags for *each* pumping session
    - ° Extra set of bottles/collection bags
- Power supply, extension cord, batteries
    - ° Adapter if overseas
- Hand pump
- Ice packs and tote or cooler
- Breast pads or Lily Padz©
- Cleaning supplies
    - ° Steam bags
    - ° Ziploc bag with water & dish soap
- Extra set of uniforms
- Hands-free bra or bustier (optional)
- Baby pictures
- MP3 player or iPod with music/photos/baby's sounds

Items for TDY/FTX

- Breastpump – double electric if you will be staying in hotel/barracks
    - ° Extra valves, tubing, membranes, flanges
- Hand pump or attachment, in case your pump malfunctions, pieces go missing, or you have no electricity, or you are on FTX or maneuvers
- Pump cleaning gear–bottle brush and dish soap or steam cleaning bags
- Hand sanitizer/wipes–you may not always have running water
- Batteries–you may not always have electricity
- Extension cord/adapter–you may not always be near a convenient outlet
- Milk storage bags–they take up less room and ship better

- Sharpie marker–to date your breastmilk
- Blanket–for comfort and concealment (if needed)
- Breast pads–always a good idea
- Laptop, MP3 player, or iPod with music/photos/baby's sounds

Items for Shipping Breastmilk

- Electric cooler–to keep your milk cold until you can ship it home (you may not have access to a refrigerator)
- Styrofoam or soft-sided coolers–for shipping milk, at least two or more depending on how much you produce
- Shipping box–large enough to hold the cooler(s)
- Shipping labels
- Packing tape
- Larger Ziploc bags–gallon size or larger
- Newspaper and/or brown lunch bags–for wrapping frozen milk
- Gloves–if you will be using dry ice
- List–FedEx info, dry ice suppliers, etc.

Appendix J
Breast Pump Types

(See table, next page.)

Types of Breast Pumps

Type of Pump	Description	Suction & Cycles	Advantages	Disadvantages	Cost Range	Examples
Manual Pump	Hand powered	Variable	Small, portable, quiet, inexpensive	Labor intensive Single-pumping May not be able to achieve proper cycling or suction *Not for maintaining supply*	$15-50	Ameda One-Hand Avent Isis Lansinoh Hand Pump Medela Harmony Simplisse
Battery-Operated Pump	Battery-operated motor	Variable	Small, portable, inexpensive Can double pump with two units	Goes through batteries quickly May provide inadequate cycling and suction Most models offer manual cycling only *Not for maintaining supply*	$50-150	Avent Isis iQ Uno Medela Swing

Pump Type	Description	Cycles/Suction	Features	Disadvantages	Price	Brands
Occasional-Use Electric Pump	Small electric pump	Variable	Small and quiet Double or single pumping	Semi-automatic cycling, Some models only offer manual cycling Difficult to achieve adequate cycling and suction Requires electricity or car adapter *Not for maintaining supply*	$50-200	Avent Isis iQ Duo Bailey Nurture III Evenflo Comfort Select First Years MiPump Lansinoh Double Electric Medela FreeStyle Playtex Embrace
Personal-Use Electric Pump	Medium electric pump	40-60 cycles per min 50-220 mmHg suction	Double or single pumping Automatic cycling Efficient and compact (carrying case or backpack)	Expensive Requires electricity or a car adapter	$150-400	Ameda Purely Yours Hygeia EnJoye Medela Pump in Style
Hospital-Grade Electric Piston Pump	Large piston driven electric pump	40-60 cycles per min 50-250 mmHg suction	Double or single pumping Automatic cycling Highly efficient Mimics baby's suction pressure and cycling rate	Large and heavy Very expensive, usually rented Requires electricity	Rental: $30-80 / month plus personal kit Purchase: $700-1500	Ameda Elite or Lact-E Medela Symphony, Lactina or Classic Hygeia EnDeare PJ's Limerick

Adapted from: (Biagioli, 2003), www.breastpumps.com, www.ameda.com, www.hygieababy.com, www.medela.com, www.nursingmothersupplies.com, www.amazon.com, www.babiesrus.com

Appendix K
Military Pumping Scenarios

Military Pumping Scenarios			
	Morning	**Lunch**	**Afternoon**
Scenario One *Best (Unlikely)*	Breastfeed at CDC	Breastfeed at CDC	Breastfeed at CDC
Scenario Two *Very Good (Possible)*	Pump 10-15 minutes	Breastfeed at CDC	Pump 10-15 minutes
Scenario Three *Good (Most Common)*	Pump 10-15 minutes	Pump 20 minutes	Pump 10-15 minutes
Scenario Four *Good (Common)*	Pump 5 minutes to relieve engorgement	Pump 10-20 minutes	Pump 5 minutes to relieve engorgement
Scenario Five *OK (Common)*	? Pump ?	Pump 10-20 minutes	? Pump ?
Scenario Six *Not Good (Likely)*	No Pumping	Pump 10-20 minutes	No Pumping
Scenario Seven *Worst (Likely)*	No Pumping Breastfeed at Home, Supplement on Duty		

Appendix L
Milk Storage Guidelines

Human Milk Storage			
Type of Milk and Storage Area	Temperature	Storage Time	Comments
Freshly Expressed Milk			
Countertop or table	Room temperature Up to 77°F or 25°C	4 hours (ideal) 6 hours (acceptable) 8 hours (maximum)	Keep containers covered and as cool as possible
Insulated cooler & frozen gel packs	5-39°F or -15-4°C	24 hours	Keep ice packs in contact with milk; limit opening the cooler bag
Refrigerated Milk			
Fresh	32-39°F / 0-4°C	3 days (ideal) 5 days (acceptable) 8 days (maximum)	Store milk towards back of main part of refrigerator
Thawed	32-39°F / 0-4°C	24 hours	
Frozen Milk			
Freezer compartment inside refrigerator	5°F or -15°C	2 weeks	
Freezer compartment with separate door	0°F or -18°C	3-6 months	Store milk towards back of freezer
Separate deep freeze	-4°F or -20°C	6-12 months	
Adapted From: (Academy of Breastfeeding Medicine, 2004; La Leche League International, 2008)			

Appendix M
Hand Expression

How to hand express

1. Massage breasts gently to encourage let-down.

2. Place thumb and index finger on either side of your areola, about one to two inches back from the nipple. Your hand should form a "C" shape.

3. Press back towards the chest wall.

4. Compress your fingers together towards the nipple (like making fingerprints, do not slide or squeeze).

5. Relax.

6. Repeat around the breast to empty all the ducts.

7. Repeats steps on other breast.

Most mothers express from each breast for three to five minutes or until the milk flow changes from a stream to a trickle. Express from each breast two to three times. The entire process should take about 20-30 minutes.

Appendix N
What If I Want To Wean
My Baby?

*Breastfeeding your baby for even a day is the best baby gift you can give. Breastfeeding is almost **always** the best choice for your baby. If it doesn't seem like the best choice for **you** right now, these guidelines may help.*

IF YOU NURSE YOUR BABY FOR JUST A FEW DAYS, he will have received your colostrum, or early milk. By providing antibodies and the food his brand-new body expects, nursing gives your baby his first–and easiest–"immunization" and helps get his digestive system going smoothly. Breastfeeding is how your baby expects to start, and helps your own body recover from the birth. Given how little it takes to offer it, and how very much your baby stands to gain, it just makes good sense to breastfeed for at least a day or two, even if you plan to bottle-feed after that.

IF YOU NURSE YOUR BABY FOR FOUR TO SIX WEEKS, you will have eased him through the most critical part of his infancy. Newborns who are not breastfed are much more likely to get sick or be hospitalized, and have many more digestive problems than breastfed babies. After 4 to 6 weeks, you'll probably have worked through any early nursing concerns, too. Make a serious goal of nursing for a month, call La Leche League or a certified lactation consultant (IBCLC) if you have any questions, and you'll be in a better position to decide whether continued breastfeeding is for you.

IF YOU START WEANING AT 3 OR 4 MONTHS, her digestive system will have matured a great deal, and she will be much better able to tolerate the foreign substances in commercial formulas. Giving nothing but your milk for the first four months gives strong protection against ear infections for a whole year. If there is a family history of allergies, though, you will greatly reduce her risk by waiting a few more months before adding anything at all to her diet of breastmilk.

IF YOU NURSE YOUR BABY FOR 6 MONTHS without adding any other food or drink, she will be much less likely to suffer an allergic reaction to formula or other foods. The American Academy of Pediatrics and the World Health Organization recommend waiting until 6 months to start solids. Nursing for at least 6 months helps ensure better health throughout your baby's first year of life, reduces your little one's risk of ear infections and childhood cancers, and reduces your own risk of breast cancer. And exclusive,

338 BREASTFEEDING IN COMBAT BOOTS

frequent breastfeeding during the first 6 months, if your periods have not returned, provides 98% effective contraception.

IF YOU NURSE YOUR BABY FOR 9 MONTHS, you will have seen him through the fastest and most important brain and body development of his life on the food that was designed for him—your milk. Nursing for at least this long will help ensure better performance all through his school years. Weaning may be fairly easy at this age... but then, so is nursing! If you want to avoid weaning this early, be sure that, from the start, you nurse willingly to provide comfort, not just to provide food.

IF YOU BEGIN WEANING YOUR BABY AT A YEAR, you can avoid the expense and bother of formula. Her one-year-old body can probably handle most of the table foods your family enjoys. Many of the health benefits this year of nursing has given your child will last her whole life. She will have a stronger immune system, for instance, and will be much less likely to need orthodontia or speech therapy. The American Academy of Pediatrics recommends nursing for at least a year because it helps ensure normal nutrition and health for your baby.

IF YOU BEGIN WEANING YOUR BABY AT 18 MONTHS, you will have continued to provide the nutrition, comfort, and illness protection your baby expects, at a time when illness is common in formula-fed babies. Your baby is probably well started on table foods, too. He has had time to form a solid bond with you - a healthy starting point for his growing independence. And he is old enough that you and he can work together on the weaning process, at a pace that he can handle. A former U.S. Surgeon General said, "It is the lucky baby... that nurses to age two."

IF YOUR CHILD WEANS WHEN SHE IS READY, you can feel confident that you have met your baby's physical and emotional needs in a very normal, healthy way. In cultures where there is no pressure to wean, children tend to nurse for *at least* two years. The World Health Organization and UNICEF strongly encourage breastfeeding through toddlerhood: "Breastmilk is an important source of energy and protein, and helps to protect against disease during the child's second year of life." Our biology seems geared to a weaning age of between 2 ½ and 7 years, and it just makes sense to build our children's bones from the milk that was designed for them. Your milk provides antibodies and other protective substances as long as you continue nursing, and families of nursing toddlers often find that their medical bills are lower than their neighbors' for years to come. Research indicates that the longer a child nurses, the higher his intelligence. Mothers who nurse long term have a still lower risk of developing breast cancer. Children who were nursed long-term tend to be very secure, and are less likely to suck their thumbs or carry a blanket. Nursing can help ease both of you through the tears, tantrums, and tumbles that come with early childhood, and helps ensure that any illnesses are milder and easier to deal with. It's an all-purpose mothering tool you won't want to be without! Don't worry that your child will nurse forever. All children stop on their own, no matter what you do, and there are more nursing youngsters around than you might guess.

WHETHER YOU NURSE FOR A DAY OR FOR SEVERAL YEARS, the decision to nurse your child is one you need never regret. And whenever weaning takes place, remember that it is a big step for both of you. If you feel you must wean before your child is ready, be sure to do it gradually, and with love.

Glossary

ACU, ABU, MCCUU, NWU: Any of the various camouflage working uniforms, also known as "cammies" or "fatigues," worn by personnel in the Armed Forces. ACU-Army Combat Uniform, ABU-Airman Battle Uniform, MCCUU-Marine Corps Combat Utility Uniform, and NWU-Navy Working Uniform.

Areola: The darker part of the breast surrounding the nipple.

Alveoli: Grape-like clusters of milk producing cells within the breast.

Artificial Baby Milk: Also called breastmilk substitute or formula, it is a liquid substitute for breastmilk, often made from cow's milk or soybeans.

Baby-led Feeding: Feeding style that relies on the baby's instinctive feeding behaviors and movements.

Baby-led Weaning: Natural weaning when the baby or toddler is ready to stop breastfeeding.

Bilirubin: The natural byproduct of extra red blood cells present after birth in the baby. Levels are measured when baby is jaundiced.

Bottle Strike: When a baby refuses to take a bottle after days to weeks of formerly using one.

Breast Compression: Gentle yet firm pressure on the breast to assist with letdown and milk transfer when breastfeeding or pumping.

Breast Pump: Mechanical device that is used to remove milk from the breasts. May be battery, hand, or electrically operated.

Breast Refusal: See also Nursing Strike. When a breastfeeding baby abruptly and without warning refuses to nurse, often for unknown reasons. May last from a few hours to days or weeks, it is not to be confused with weaning.

Breastmilk Substitute: Also called artificial breastmilk or formula, it is a liquid substitute for breastmilk, often made from cow's milk or soybeans.

Colostrum: First milk produced by the breasts, appears towards the end of pregnancy and the first days after baby is born. Loaded with important and necessary antibodies and nutrients.

Commanding Officer (CO): The officer in command of a military unit, has ultimate authority over and responsibility for all personnel under her/his command. May also be known as Commander or Captain, regardless of actual rank.

Cycles: Number of times that a breast pump sucks and releases in a minute.

Ducts: Channels (or tubes) in the breast that carry milk from the alveoli to the nipple openings.

Engorgement: Very full breasts that usually feel warm, hard, heavy, and uncomfortable. The fullness and swelling result from excess milk that is not removed and increased blood flow, can cause problems with latching.

Enlisted: Personnel of any rank below commissioned officer or warrant officer. Enlisted personnel perform jobs specific to their occupational specialty.

Express: The act of removing milk from the breast either by hand or with a breast pump.

Feeding Cues: Signs given by a baby to communicate hunger, such as smacking or licking lips, rooting on fist or fingers, and episodes of light sleep.

FTX-Field Training Exercise: Days to weeks-long realistic training scenarios (mini battles) based on actual situations, conducted by military units.

Filter: Also called a membrane, milk drips through this small piece of the breast pump that attaches between the flange and bottle.

Flange, Breast Pump: Also known as a breast shield, part of the breast pump that fits directly on the breast for expressing milk.

Flange, Lips: Act of having baby's top and bottom lips roll outward to seal correctly on the breast or bottle.

Foremilk: Milk excreted by the breast at the beginning of a feeding or pumping session, generally low in calories, fat, and protein, but high in volume. Appears thin and watery.

Formula: Also called artificial baby milk or breastmilk substitute, it is a liquid substitute for breastmilk, often made from cow's milk or soybeans.

FUBAR: An acronym that means Fouled/* Up Beyond All/Any Repair/ Recognition. (* denotes a much coarser alternative word used by many in the military).

Growth Spurt: A 2-to-3-day period of time when a baby breastfeeds very frequently to increase his mother's milk supply.

Hand Expression: The act of removing milk from the breast by hand with no mechanical device.

Hindmilk: Milk excreted by the breast at the end of a feeding or pumping session, generally high in calories, fat, and protein, but low in volume. Appears thick and creamy.

Jaundice: Occurs when excess bilirubin is not excreted by the baby fast enough, causes yellowing of the eyes and skin.

Latching: The act of grasping the nipple and areola by the baby's mouth for feeding and/or sucking.

Letdown: Also known as milk-ejection reflex (MER). When the baby's sucking causes the release of oxytocin, which in turn causes the alveoli to contract and release milk.

Mastitis: An infection of the breast, with symptoms that may include fever, body aches, and sore, red, hot breast(s).

Membrane: Also called a filter, milk drips through this small piece of the breast pump that attaches between the flange and bottle.

Milk-ejection Reflex (MER): Also known as Letdown. When the baby's sucking causes the release of oxytocin, which in turn causes the alveoli to contract and release milk.

Mids: Middle of the night shift, generally 2400 to 0800 hours (12am to 8am).

Military Occupation Specialty (MOS): A nine-character code used to identify a specific job, used primarily in the Army and Marine Corps. The Air Force uses the Air Force Specialty Code (AFSC) system and the Coast Guard and Navy uses Ratings (enlisted) and Designators (officer), as well as the Navy Enlisted Classification (NEC) system to define specific job classifications.

Military Treatment Facility (MTF): The military equivalent of a civilian clinic or hospital. Active-duty personnel and family members receive medical care and medications through the local MTF.

Mother-led Feeding: Feeding style that is determined by the mother's movements, including support of her breast and helping her baby to latch and position correctly.

Mother-led Weaning: When a mother chooses to voluntarily stop breastfeeding her baby before he may be ready, should be done gradually if at all possible.

Montgomery Glands: Small, pimple-like bumps on the areola that secrete an anti-microbial substance that keeps the nipple clean and supple.

Nipple (Human): The cylindrical tissue that protrudes from the very center of the breast from which the milk flows.

Nipple Confusion: When a baby doesn't remember to change his suck from an artificial nipple to a human nipple. Often caused by poor bottle-feeding techniques that do not support breastfeeding.

Nipple Pores: 8-12 openings in the nipple where the milk ducts of the breast open to the outside of the body. Milk flows out of the nipple pores.

Non-nutritive Sucking: Also called flutter sucking. The rapid and short sucks at the beginning and during a feeding that provide the stimulation needed to trigger a letdown or MER.

Non-Commissioned Officer (NCO): An enlisted military member who holds a position of authority and responsibility over other enlisted personnel. Serve as supervisors within their area of specialty. Generally includes the ranks of Corporal, Sergeant, or Petty Officer, depending on branch of service. Personnel may be classified as Junior Non-commissioned Officer (JNCO) and Senior (Staff) Non-commissioned Officer (SNCO).

Nutritive Sucking: The long, slow sucks during a feeding that occur when the milk is flowing and are accompanied by audible swallowing.

Nursing Strike: See also Breast Refusal. When a breastfeeding baby abruptly and without warning refuses to nurse, often for unknown reasons. May last from a few hours to days or weeks, it is not to be confused with weaning.

Officer: Personnel in the ranks of commissioned officer or warrant officer. They hold a position of authority granted to them by the President of the United States, charging them with the duties and responsibilities of a specific office or position. Generally must have a university degree. Officers receive training leadership and management training in addition to job specialty (pilot, nurse, doctor, etc.).

Officer In Charge (OIC): A commissioned or warrant officer placed in charge of a unit for a temporary assignment. Has limited authority and responsibility.

OJT-On the Job Training: A form of training that takes place during normal working situations.

Oxytocin: Hormone released by the mother in response to hearing her baby cry or thinking about her baby, causes the alveoli to contract and release the milk (the let-down or MER).

Palate: The roof of the baby's mouth. Hard palate is in the front part of the mouth behind the gum ridges, while the soft palate is in the arch at the back of the mouth.

Permanent Change of Station (PCS): The official relocation of an active-duty military member (and family) to a different duty location.

Physical Fitness Assessment/Test (PFA): Also known as Physical Readiness Test. A semi-annual evaluation of every service member's muscular strength/endurance and cardiovascular fitness level. May include a Body Composition Analysis (weight, height, and body fat measurements), as well as a timed run (1.5 to 3 miles) or swim, sit-ups, push-ups, or pull-ups, depending on branch of service. It is scored based on age and gender.

Plugged Duct: When a duct in the breast is obstructed resulting in no milk flow. Usually causes a red, tender lump in the breast tissue.

Postpartum Depression: Medical diagnosis within the first year after birth of depression in the mother.

Privately Owned Vehicle (POV): Vehicle owned by the military member for personal use.

Prolactin: Hormone released by the mother that causes the alveoli to make milk.

Physical Training (PT): Mandatory exercise required of all military personnel to maintain readiness.

Pumping: To use a machine to express milk from the breasts.

Rank: System of hierarchal relationships within the military. Includes commissioned officers, warrant officers, and enlisted personnel. With increasing rank comes increasing authority and responsibility. Specific insignia on uniforms denotes rank.

Reverse Pressure Softening (RPS): Gentle pressure around the base of the nipple to move excess fluid away from the areola.

Rooting: An inborn reflex where the baby opens his mouth and searches for a nipple to grasp.

SAR-Search and Rescue: Military personnel who are specially trained to locate and retrieve persons (civilian and military) in distress on land and at sea.

Sick in Quarters (SIQ): Authorization given by a medical officer for a service member with a medical condition or injury to remain in quarters, the barracks, or at home and not report for duty.

Standard Operating Procedure (SOP): A set of procedures to perform a given operation or in response to an event. Usually based on unit experience and approved by the unit's Commanding Officer.

Stockpiling: Building a surplus (freezer stash) of frozen breastmilk for later use.

Supplement: To give additional milk, breastmilk or formula, to a baby.

Supply and Demand: How much milk a mother produces is determined by how much milk is removed from the breast by the baby or pump.

Tandem Nursing: When a mother breastfeeds two children of different ages, such as a newborn and an older toddler.

Temporary Additional Duty (TAD) or Temporary Duty (TDY): An assignment of less than a year at a location other than the service member's permanent duty station.

Thrush: A yeast infection of the baby's mouth and/or mother's nipples.

Vacuum: The suction of a breast pump.

Weaning: The gradual process of stopping breastfeeding, it begins with the introduction of solid food and ends when he no longer receives any breastmilk. Weaning also occurs with bottle-feeding, pacifier use, and pumping.

Index

P

Pacifiers 80
Physical fitness training 227
Plugged duct 91
Pneumonia 34
Positioning
  baby-led 69
  cradle 71
  cross cradle 70
  football 71
  lying down 72
  mother-led 70
Postpartum mood disorders
  postpartum psychosis 97
  posttraumatic stress disorder 98
Pregnancy/Postpartum Physical Training 230
Premature babies 87
prolactin 63
Pump
  adapters 125
  batteries 125
  carrying case 126
  clean 134
  cleaning 164
  cost 121
  cycles 125
  double 125
  double electric 129
  fit 141
  flange 141
  hand expression 137
  hand-operated 127
  hospital grade 130
  how to choose 121
  maintenance 134
  new vs used 123
  occasional-use 128
  quantities 144
  single 125
  suction 125
  suction and cycles 142
  warranty 122

Pumping
  breast compression 172
  breast massage 172
  cluster 171
  combining breastfeeding and pumping 118
  finding place 189
  how long 115
  learning how 139
  planning ahead 107
  power pump 171
  scenarios 162
  sample pumping plan 164

R

Reasons to breastfeed
  baby 33
  command 40
  family 38
  mom 36
  partner 38
  society 41
Relactation 250
Resources
  Active-Duty Mother Groups 281
  Air Force Family Support Centers 283
  Army Community Services Program 283
  Coast Guard Mutual Assistance 283
  Fleet and Family Service Centers 284
  hospital support groups 281
  La Leche League International 284
  Mom-2-Mom support groups 282
  Navy and Marine Corps Relief Society 283
  New Parent Support Program 282
  Online 286
  WIC 285
Respiratory infections 34
Reverse pressure softening 74
Rooming-in 67

AUTHOR BIO

Robyn Roche-Paull is an IBCLC in private practice with Tidewater Lactation Group, Inc. and an active La Leche League Leader. She has worked with breastfeeding mothers since 1999 and professionally since 2006. In her practice, she primarily helps military mothers balance returning to active duty while continuing to breastfeed. Robyn is not only an advocate for active-duty military mothers who wish to combine breastfeeding with military service, she is also a U.S. Navy Veteran who successfully breastfed her son for over a year while on active duty as an aircraft mechanic.

Photo courtesy of Morgan Paull.
Used with permission.

In addition to authoring *Breastfeeding in Combat Boots: A Survival Guide to Successful Breastfeeding While Serving in the Military,* Robyn is the author of "Body Modification and Breastfeeding: What You Need to Know," *New Beginnings* (2009) and "Are Tattoos Compatible with Breastfeeding," *Leaven* (2005), and she enjoys lecturing at conferences. She serves on the Board of the Military Lactation Consultant Association (MILCA) and is a member of the United States Lactation Consultant Association (USLCA), the International Lactation Consultant Association (ILCA), and the Tidewater Area Lactation Consultant Association (TALCA). Robyn earned her Bachelor of Science degree in Maternal Child Health from Union Institute and University in Cincinnati, Ohio. She currently lives in Virginia Beach, Virginia, with her husband of 16 years, a Chief Petty Officer in the U.S. Navy, and their three children.

Ordering Information

Hale Publishing, L.P.
1712 N. Forest Street
Amarillo, Texas, USA 79106

8:00 am to 5:00 pm CST

Call » 806.376.9900
Sales » 800.378.1317
Fax » 806.376.9901

Online Web Orders
www.ibreastfeeding.com